The Wideness
of
God's Mercy

THE WIDENESS OF GOD'S MERCY

Litanies To Enlarge Our Prayer
An Ecumenical Collection

Compiled and Adapted by

JEFFERY W. ROWTHORN

MOREHOUSE PUBLISHING
Harrisburg, PA

Morehouse Publishing

Editorial Office:
871 Ethan Allen Highway
Ridgefield, CT 06877

Corporate Office:
P.O. Box 1321
Harrisburg, PA 17105

Library of Congress Cataloging-in-Publication Data

The wideness of God's mercy : litanies to enlarge our prayer : an
    ecumenical collection / compiled and adapted by Jeffery W. Rowthorn.
        p.   cm.
    Originally published in 2. vols.: Minneapolis, Minn. : Seabury
Press, 1985.
    Includes bibliographical references.
    ISBN 0-8192-1606-2 (pbk.)
    1. Litanies.   I. Rowthorn, Jeffery W.
    [BV245.W47 1995]   95-2357
    264'.13—dc20   CIP

Printed in the United States of America

For Anne

Virginia, Christian and Peregrine

Their love

has enlarged my life;

their lives

have enlarged my prayer.

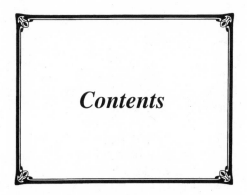

Contents

PRAYER AND TIME

Advent to Pentecost

Saints and Commemorations

Dedications and Anniversaries

PRAYER AND THE CHURCH

Its Unity

Its Sacraments

Its Ministry

Its Mission

PRAYER AND THE LOCAL COMMUNITY

Faithfulness in Daily Life

PRAYER AND THE WORLD COMMUNITY

The Nation

Confession of Social Ills

War and Peace

Acknowledgments

Notes

Bibliography

Preface

Since the Introduction that follows is meant to address the issue of how, when and where, liturgically speaking, the litanies in this collection may be used, this Preface can be devoted entirely to expressions of gratitude to those who have helped to bring this book to completion.

In the first place, I want to express my gratitude to Morehouse Publishing and to E. Allen Kelley, its President and Publisher, for encouraging me to prepare a one-volume revised edition of *The Wideness of God's Mercy*. This collection of litanies, originally published as a two-volume set in 1985, went out of print several years ago. Considerable interest was expressed in its eventual reprinting, but this has become a reality now through the generous initiative of Allen Kelley and his colleagues at Morehouse Publishing.

Since I accepted their invitation to revise the original collection, I have had ample cause to be grateful for their great patience in waiting, and their good counsel in advising, as this second edition has moved slowly to completion. During the process of revision I undertook a new sphere of work and physically relocated myself in Europe. Thus a project begun in Salem, Connecticut has been finished in Paris, France. The telephone and the fax have lessened the disruption that this move inevitably entailed, but so, too, have the understanding and support I have received from all who have seen the manuscript through the many stages leading to publication.

I am thankful for the great pains taken by my secretary, Marishka Lodigensky, who typed all the new litanies included in this revised edition, as well as all the front and back matter. If all the faults of this book are of my making, some of its virtues are surely due to care and attention to details on her part.

I would like to acknowledge with gratitude the willingness of the various owners of copyright material to allow these litanies to appear here, many of them in a form markedly different from the original, for reasons to be made plain in the Introduction. Every effort has been made to locate the copyright holders. If any errors or omissions have been made, they should be brought to the attention of the publisher and will be gladly corrected in any subsequent edition of this book.

Finally, I want to thank my wife, Anne, who has lived with this collection of litanies in its original and now in its revised form. Together with our children, she has demonstrated patience and encouragement at each step along the way. However, as the dedication of this book indicates, I have reason to value their love and their lives even more.

These litanies have been compiled and adapted in the hope that they will indeed enlarge the prayer of all who pray them, and I now offer them to the Church with the prayer that I have prayed regularly over many years:

> *Go before us, O Lord, in all our doings with thy most gracious favor, and further us now with thy continual help, that in all our works, begun, continued and ended in thee, we may glorify thy holy Name; through Christ our Lord. **Amen.***

What matters is that the Church live that prayer faithfully, for that is the best witness we can offer the world in the testing days ahead.

The American Cathedral of the Holy Trinity   December 8, 1994
Paris, France

Introduction

Liturgy is the work of the whole people of God, in praise and prayer. Christ, our High Priest and heavenly Intercessor, has made us "a kingdom, priests to his God and Father" (Revelation 1:6). The Father's family, taken as a whole, is "a holy priesthood, to offer spiritual sacrifices acceptable to God through Jesus Christ" (1 Peter 2:5). Moreover, it is a characteristics of Christian worship that all should participate effectively in the liturgy.[1]

These words from Brother Max Thurian's introduction to *Eucharist at Taizé* define the nature of all liturgical prayer undertaken by groups of Christians assembled for worship. They also provide the proper context for evaluating and using this collection of litanies.

Since its inception the Taizé community, originally Protestant and now impressively ecumenical, has sought to renew its life in the world (and the lives of those who worship with the brothers) "by means of the best possible participation in liturgical worship."[2] This book aims at much the same goal. It seeks to bring about the best possible participation in one essential element of corporate worship – prayer for others as well as for oneself, prayer for the world as well as for the Church.

Needless to say, prayer of this kind "for all sorts and conditions of men,"[3] for humanity in all its needs and aspects, will only be undertaken more faithfully, more frequently and more fervently in our day if it is inspired and filled by Christ himself. The effectiveness of these litanies depends, as all prayer must, on the Spirit of Christ who "comes to the aid of our weakness." For, as St. Paul goes on to say, "we do not even know how we ought to pray, but through our inarticulate groans the Spirit himself is pleading for us."[4] Many of these litanies may indeed appear to be not in the least inarticulate, yet they will not express the faith or fuel the witness of any Christian community unless they are one dimension of that sacrificial worship which Paul speaks of elsewhere in Romans:

> *Therefore, my brothers and sisters, I implore you by God's*
> *mercy to offer your very selves to him: a living sacrifice,*
> *dedicated and fit for God's acceptance, the worship offered by*
> *mind and heart.*[5]

However, if they are a faithful embodiment of that "worship offered by mind and heart," then they will truly become the effective prayer of the people of God.

The contemporary rediscovery of the "Prayers of the People," as they are appropriately called, is one facet of the liturgical renewal which in the past half-century has increasingly reshaped the worship of much of the Church. Intercessory prayer is once again understood and commended as a priestly ministry which God entrusts to the entire company of the faithful. By virtue of our baptism, we all enjoy this high calling to pray for the world and for people everywhere. Novel as this claim may seem to some people, it is – like many liturgical developments in this present age – simply the reappropriation of something genuinely primitive in the life of the Christian community.

In the middle years of the first century St. Paul wrote:

> *First of all, then, I urge that petitions, prayers, intercessions,*
> *and thanksgivings be offered for all people; for sovereigns and*
> *all in high office, that we may lead a tranquil and quiet life in*
> *full observance of religion and high standards of morality.*[6]

Episcopalians and others will have heard a clear echo of this apostolic injunction Sunday by Sunday in the opening phrases of Cranmer's *Prayer for the Whole State of Christ's Church:*

> *Almighty and everliving God who by thy holy Apostle hast*
> *taught us to make prayers, and supplications, and to give thanks*
> *for all men; We humbly beseech thee most mercifully . . . to*
> *receive these our prayers, which we offer unto thy Divine Majesty.*[7]

In the second century, in his brief description of Sunday worship, Justin Martyr records that the assembled company offered up prayers "for all

2

people everywhere."[8] However, the scope and content of these prayers only become known to us in the classical liturgies of the fourth century and in such innovations as the Kyrie litany of Pope Gelasius a century later. Here the range of concern is wide indeed, not least because the Church's domain had also widened until in places it was co-terminous with society at large.

Paul's desire that in every place holy hands should be lifted in prayer led in time to the emergence of litanies as the principal vehicle of the people's corporate ministry of intercession. Four things can be said of this early form of prayer:

(i)   It was broad in scope, far transcending the immediate needs or narrow interests of those who were praying;

(ii)   It was as highly regarded as the *Eighteen Benedictions,* which among Jews had come to be referred to, quite simply, as *Tefillah* – The Prayer;

(iii) It was regular, forming an integral part of the Sunday liturgy; and

(iv)   It was participatory, both in posture ("holy hands lifted in prayer") and in the repeated use of a familiar response after each petition (*Kyrie eleison* or *Amen.*)

Consequently, for a period, at least, in Christian history "intercessory prayer" and "litany" were virtually synonymous.

In the Western Church the intercessions were eventually placed within the Canon or Eucharistic Prayer. Although this was regarded as a place of honor, at the very heart of the Mass, the fact that the Canon came to be recited inaudibly meant that, to all intents and purposes, there were no longer any "Prayers of the People." In the Church's principal act of worship Sunday by Sunday an essential element was now lacking. Only the Solemn Prayers recited on Good Friday (Litany 28) and the Litany of the Saints (Litany 35), together with certain penitential litanies, survived as reminders of an earlier and universal liturgical practice.

During the later Middle Ages attempts were made to compensate for this loss. Biddings were introduced which made it possible to call on the people to pray for matters of immediate concern and local interest. Then in 1544, with the approval of King Henry VIII, Thomas Cranmer took the momentous step of issuing the *Great Litany* in English (Litany 1 in this collection). Now the whole of the people's life could be lifted up in the

3

people's prayer in the people's own language. For that reason the *Great Litany* is given the place of honor in this volume. It also has the distinction of being the very first service in English to have received official authorization for use throughout the Church of England.

In the various churches of the Reformation little provision was made for the "Prayers of the People." Generally they were usurped by a lengthy pastoral prayer recited by the minister without any interpolations or even responses on the part of the people. Even the *Prayer for the Whole State of Christ's Church* in the Anglican liturgy allowed for no variation or application to the present moment, and the people's participation was limited to the final Amen. Neither in Roman Catholic nor in Protestant congregations were the laity able to exercise the priestly ministry of intercession which was theirs by virtue of their baptism. The apostolic injunction in I Timothy languished for reasons of benign neglect. The urgency, sensitivity and sustained attention which intercessory prayer clearly calls for on the congregation's part were for centuries far more the exception than the rule in public worship.

Since the middle years of this century a process of change, startling in its cumulative effect, has been under way. One clear indication of this is the statement, *Baptism, Eucharist and Ministry,* issued a decade ago by the Faith and Order Commission of the World Council of Churches.[10] Under the auspices of the Commission more than a hundred theologians met in Lima, Peru, in January 1982. They represented "virtually all the major church traditions: Eastern Orthodox, Oriental Orthodox, Roman Catholic, Old Catholic, Lutheran, Anglican, Reformed, Methodist, United, Disciples, Baptist, Adventist and Pentecostal."[11] In their agreed statement, transmitted by unanimous vote "for the common study and official response of the churches," they made this affirmation:

> *The world, to which renewal is promised, is present in the whole eucharistic celebration. The world is present in the thanksgiving to the Father, where the Church speaks on behalf of the whole creation; in the memorial of Christ, where the Church, united with its great High Priest and Intercessor, prays for the world; in the prayer for the gift of the Holy Spirit, where the Church asks for sanctification and new creation.*[12]

Furthermore, it is the calling of every Christian community and person "to identify with the joys and sufferings of all people as they seek to witness [to Christ and to their faith in his coming kingdom] in caring love."[13]

This caring love which is spoken of here has as one of its elements, and indeed as its necessary prelude and constant companion, the willingness to pray for all people and all of life. This is in itself is a dimension of loving one's neighbor as oneself and of respecting "the dignity of every human being."[14] Consequently, the Second Vatican Council made provision for the restoration of "the common prayer" or "the prayer of the faithful," which now, as in the early Church, is to follow the Gospel reading and the homily:

> *By this prayer, in which the people are to take part, intercession will be made for holy Church, for the civil authorities, for those oppressed by various needs, for all mankind, and for the salvation of the entire world.*[15]

The General Instruction of the Roman Missal indicates that "in special celebrations, such as confirmations, marriages, funerals, etc., the list of intentions may be more closely concerned with the special occasion."[16] Thus, at every Mass celebrated with a congregation, "the people exercise their priestly function by interceding for all mankind." This is to take the form either of a common response after each intention or of silent prayer together. It is hardly surprising, therefore, that, to achieve this end, the litany has been recovered as a primary vehicle for the "Prayers of the People."

This collection of litanies is meant to contribute to the renewed recognition of the local congregation's calling to pray for the Church and the world. Both its title and its subtitle point to important aspects of that ministry of prayer and to deeply held convictions which have determined the contents of this book.

In the first place, the title is derived from the familiar hymn, *There's a Wideness in God's Mercy.*[17] Written by an Anglican priest who became a Roman Catholic, it is included in many Protestant hymnals and sung by many Protestant congregations. Its first stanza celebrates a truth about God which provides the incentive and impetus we need if we are to pray confidently for people everywhere:

> There's a wideness in God's mercy
> like the wideness of the sea;
> there's a kindness in his justice
> which is more than liberty.
> There is welcome for the sinner,
> and more graces for the good;
> there is mercy with the Savior,
> there is healing in his blood.[18]

Because God's mercy knows no limits, because "the love of God is broader than the measure of man's mind," we can cry *Kyrie eleison* in full assurance that our prayer will be heard and answered. God intends everyone to come within the reach of his saving embrace, made visible to us in Christ's arms of love outstretched on the hard wood of the cross.[19] Consequently, the range of these litanies is deliberately as broad as possible. There are some sins of omission, but it is to be hoped that leaders of prayer and planners of liturgy will find here an abundance of models and patterns which will be of use in preparing litanies for occasions and topics which are overlooked in this book. Ours must be a prayer for all needs, but no one volume can do more than begin to formulate the words of so universal a prayer.

However, such a book as this can certainly help in this regard. It can also serve the same purpose as that (legendary?) organ fashioned by St. Cecilia, the patroness of church music. In the words of W.H. Auden, "this innocent virgin constructed an organ to *enlarge her prayer.*"[20] To use a phrase beloved by the Puritans, "stinted prayer" has been a characteristic of much of our worship: stinted by clerical monopoly, by unthinking repetition, by monologue rather than dialogue, by narrow interests and limited imagination. The litanies in this collection are, on the contrary, participatory and wide-ranging, inviting congregations to stretch their praying for others beyond accustomed limits and familiar themes. As St. Paul once wrote to the Christians at Philippi,

> *Have no anxiety about anything, but in everything by prayer*
> *and supplication with thanksgiving let your requests be made*
> *known to God.*[21]

"In everything" is a challenge to our stinted praying. We are called to grow into a life of prayer for others which is expansive enough to accommodate and nourish even the most generous Christian spirit. So often that kind of spirit is being stifled at the present time. The litanies in this book are meant to lengthen the stride and strengthen the weak knees of those who walk in the company of the High Priest who "always lives to make intercession" for us.[22] In this sense they are indeed litanies to enlarge our prayer.

The use of which these litanies are put in worship will vary from tradition to tradition. Certain of them can be employed as the "Prayers of the People," serving as the climax of the Liturgy of the Word after the Gospel has been read, preached, and affirmed. In non-eucharistic settings they can be used in place of the minister's pastoral prayer or at the close of a morning or evening office. Carefully chosen, one of the litanies could be an appropriate congregational response to a sermon preached on a particular text or theme. Some are seasonal litanies, others belong in services clearly focused on such concerns as the unity of the Church, the peace of the world, the nurture of the young, or the care of the elderly. Some are meant to be sung or said in procession; no pieces of paper would be required since the same refrain is repeated throughout the litany and thus is readily learned and used (the chief reason for the popularity of litanies in the past). In the case of litanies employing more than one voice or the successive stanzas of a hymn, careful preparation is obviously called for.

In any event, each occasion of public worship should allow for an *ample* time of common prayer for others. Without doing violence to the tradition of a particular church or the structure of a given liturgical rite, it is certainly possible to make use of the litany form of prayer week by week or from time to time. As in every other aspect of liturgical planning and leadership, pastoral sensitivity and imagination are needed if these litanies are to be grafted faithfully and with integrity into the worship of a particular community of faith.

The most helpful demonstration of how this book can be used with pastoral sensitivity and imagination is to let the litanies speak for themselves. Each of the examples cited below will indicate ways in which that particular litany and others like it may serve to enlarge the Church's prayer:

Litany 1 *Adaptability and Selectivity*

These two principles are well illustrated in this first litany. The rubrics (instructions) indicate that it may be used in whole or in part. In addition, the leader is free to select some of the many petitions and omit others in order to shorten the litany. In the *Book of Common Prayer 1979,* from which it is taken, the rubrics also point out that it may be used in a variety of ways to suit a variety of needs and occasions: "To be said or sung, kneeling, standing, or in procession."[23]

Litany 4 *Silence*

The restoration of the "Prayers of the People" requires that silent prayer on the part of the whole congregation be taken with great seriousness and that ample time be allowed for it between the biddings or petitions. Instruction on the creative use of silence in corporate prayer of this kind may well be needed. What matters is that neither leader nor congregation be intimidated by sustained periods of silence. Those fearful of silence will inevitably be tempted to curtail it or to fill it needlessly with yet more words.

Times of silence can also be introduced into many of the litanies in this collection, even if no formal provision is made for them in the text. For instance, silence would be effective in Litany 133 after every contrasting versicle and response, thus allowing the sobering contents of the prayer to be more fully appropriated.

Litany 5   *Free Intercessions*

At three points in this litany the worshippers are invited to add their own petitions and thanksgivings. Ample time is again the secret of success, together with instruction, encouragement and some attention to the question of audibility, especially in a large space or a numerous company. As in the case of silence, spontaneous contributions to a litany of this kind will increase as people become familiar and comfortable with an as yet novel form of corporate prayer.

During the two periods of silence in Litany 116 the congregation could well be invited to add their own thanksgivings. During the first silence specific individuals could be mentioned, while at the end of the litany general categories could be added if they have not already been mentioned in the course of the litany. In Litany 14 the leader or the presiding minister could invite those present to add to the already extensive list of reasons for thankfulness. Since most people are reluctant to voice their gratitude to God in the context of public worship, it would be good to encourage adults and young people alike to contribute freely to the praying of this litany of thanksgiving.

Litany 6   *Particular Intentions*

As an alternative to intercessions freely interpolated into an otherwise formal litany, the leader may mention at the start various people and concerns in order that the congregation may bear them in mind during the ensuing litany. This is yet another way of ensuring that a general prayer is firmly rooted in specific lives and needs.

Litany 35   *Sung Prayer*

Traditionally, litanies were meant to be sung, and this fact draws attention to the role of the trained church musician. In many churches the minister of music is entirely capable of writing musical settings for some of the litanies in this collection. The capacities of leader, choir and congregation should be borne in mind, and some time devoted to teaching the people their response(s). Once the congregation is assured and can play a full part in the singing of this litany, it could well be sung in procession on appropriate occasions such as baptisms or ordinations.

Litany 36   *Open-ended Prayer*

This *Invocation of the Saints* would surely prompt the participants to add their own heroes and heroines of the faith to an already impressive "cloud of witnesses." Leaders of prayer are often fearful of this, lest heresy or the instant canonization of some dubious characters should result! However, if we affirm the calling of every Christian to pray in the Spirit for the world at large, it requires a willingness on our part to trust those who "share with us in [Christ's] eternal priesthood."[24]

Litany 52   *Appropriate Leadership*

This litany calls for members of the various Christian traditions to lead it. Likewise, Litany 51 would be strikingly effective if the different voices belonged to people whose spiritual home was in the particular Christian communion mentioned in each paragraph of the prayer.

The two leaders of Litany 100 should certainly be young people, just as an older member of the community or congregation should lead Litany 97. However, in view of its contents, Litany 98 *(For the Elderly)* should certainly *not* be led by an older person. Litany 146 would be strikingly effective if the different voices belonged to people whose homes were in the several continents mentioned in the course of the prayer.

Litany 70	*Adapting to a Particular Tradition*

This litany demonstrates the need for care and forethought in using material which clearly derives from and speaks to a particular tradition or denomination. New ministers are installed in churches of every tradition. As a result this litany, like others in this collection, can be imaginatively adapted to the needs of other traditions and situations. They cannot be taken over uncritically, nor need they be abandoned because at first glance they seem to belong elsewhere in the Christian household!

Litany 72	*Regular Intercession*

Writing to the Christian community in Rome, St. Paul says, "Never flag in zeal, be aglow with the Spirit . . . rejoice in your hope . . . be constant in prayer (Romans 12:11-12). Litany 72 is in fact a seven-part cycle of intercessions for the mission of the Church, and it would be most effective if used day in and day out an a regular basis. Perhaps different groups or individuals could observe different days in the cycle, or the whole congregation could share in the seven parts of the litany on seven successive Sundays. What matters is that the Church's calling to pray for the world be commended and implemented in a sustained rather than a sporadic manner.

Litany 80	*Dependence on Scripture*

The manifold references to Scripture have been deliberately reproduced in this litany in order to show the author's imaginative and faithful use of the New Testament. Indeed, Lucien Deiss originally called his book *Prières Bibliques* (Biblical Prayers). This particular litany may well inspire others to obey the Gospel injunction: "Go and do likewise."[25]

Litany 112	*Hymn Stanzas as Part of a Litany*

One effective way of helping people to sing parts of a litany is illustrated here. The tune must be familiar if congregational participation is to be strong and confident. Many such combinations are possible; for example, Litany 140, which is meant to be recited on Memorial Day, could well be matched with Rosamond Herklots' hymn, "Forgive our sins as we forgive" (set to the tune *Detroit* in the *Lutheran Book of Worship*). Similarly, Litany 114 or Litany 115 would be wonderfully enriched if used with F. Pratt Green's hymn, "O Christ, the Healer, we have come." This text may be sung to another early American tune, *Distress,* to which it is set in the *Lutheran Book of Worship.* However, more familiar tunes in the appropriate meter can readily be substituted for *Detroit* (Common Meter) or *Distress* (Long Meter).

Litany 138   *Controversial Content*

This litany should certainly be used but needs to be preceded by teaching or preaching which would indicate its thoroughly Biblical character. Without that preparation it may serve only to divide, and in that way people may be wrongly spared the "hard sayings" which are the rough edges of the Gospel proclaimed and lived by Jesus Christ.

Litany 139   *Careful Preparation*

As with Litany 138, this litany requires that great care be taken to prepare the congregation to enter into covenant together. There is a danger inherent in reading words off a page or out of a book without weighing either the content or the consequences. To make a covenant in God's name, as John Wesley certainly appreciated, is a most solemn undertaking which asks of all who participate in it both prayerful preparation and honest self-examination. That should be true of all prayer, but certainly true of a litany such as this.

Litany 143   *Long Litanies*

This is a lengthy litany which could not readily be used in a shortened form. However, there is much to be said for using it when there is ample time to ponder and pray about the as yet unfulfilled aspirations contained in the Universal Declaration of Human Rights.

The litanies mentioned above, indeed all the litanies in this collection, are meant to be models or patterns which will inspire leaders of worship to use this form of prayer imaginatively in the regular worship of their respective congregations. The book is also, of course, a resource to be drawn upon by those who take seriously the desire and hope expressed by the Second Vatican Council: "that all the faithful should be led to that full, conscious, and active participation in liturgical celebrations which is demanded by the very nature of the liturgy."[26]

One further aspects of this book calls for comment. It will quickly become obvious that no indication is given of the changes which have been made in the various litanies. Since this is not an "Oxford Book of Litanies," but an ecumenical collection intended for widespread use in worship at the end of the twentieth century, a great many alterations have proved necessary. These changes and adaptations will, in each case, have been made for one or more of the following reasons:

ecumenical applicability:	in order to extend the contents and appeal of a litany beyond the confines of a particular denomination;
inclusive language:	in order to avoid excessive use of such words as "men" or "mankind" which no longer convey the inclusive meaning they were certainly meant to convey when used in the litany in its original form;
contemporary references:	in order to broaden the categories mentioned in the various petitions of a litany and thereby to include more of life as we know it and live it in the closing years of this century;
intelligibility, brevity, and recitability;	in order to take into account the ways people pray in our day, the words they use, and the more concise forms of speech which are common to us;
inclusion of hymn stanzas:	in order to provide sung responses for use in liturgical settings where the traditional "sung litany" would not be familiar or acceptable;
division among several leaders:	in order to encourage greater diversity in the conduct and leadership of corporate prayer.

The classical form of the litany with its climax either in the Lord's Prayer or in a concluding collect said by the presiding minister has deliberately been avoided as an *invariable* model. This course has been followed for ecumenical and pastoral reasons, but those who wish to conclude a particular litany in either of these traditional ways may certainly do so.

A final word about leadership is in order. The person and presence of the leader are undoubtedly important. In an earlier and less ecumenical age, as we have seen, the Puritans denounced the lifeless reading of collects from a book (in that instance the *Book of Common Prayer*) as "stinted prayer." The reading of litanies from *this* book can certainly fall prey to the same disease of lifelessness, and merit the same unpromising diagnosis! Careful preparation, sensitive adaptation, thoughtful integration with the other parts of the service, ample provision for silence or the free interpolation of additional petitions, unhurried pacing of the prayer, clear and audible reading, specificity without unnecessary divisiveness and generality without meaningless platitudes: these are all vital to the effective use of the litany as a form of corporate prayer. No leader is meant to preempt or stifle the priestly function of the people of God as they pray for the world. In like manner, no leader is meant to inhibit or cripple their prayer by poor and unthinking leadership.

This collection of litanies calls on God's mercy in all its height and depth and length and breadth. It also calls on those who pray in the service of the Church to take St. Teresa's words to heart, remembering also that Christ has no lips now but ours with which "to ask, for ourselves and on behalf of others, those things that are necessary for our life and our salvation."[27]

Christ has
no body now on earth but yours;
no hands but yours;
no feet but yours;
yours are the eyes
through which Christ's compassion
is to look out on the world;
yours are the feet
with which he is to go about
doing good;
yours are the hands
with which he is to bless folk now.
St. Teresa of Avila[28]

Notes

1. *Eucharist at Taizé (The Eucharistic Liturgy of Taizé),* with an introductory essay by Max Thurian, Frère de Taizé; translated by John Arnold, Faith Press, London, 1962 (French original: 1959), p. 2.
2. Ibid., p. 1.
3. "A Prayer for all Conditions of Men" was first included in the *Book of Common Prayer* in 1662. It can now be found in the *Book of Common Prayer 1979* among the *Prayers and Thanksgivings* (pp. 814-5).
4. Romans 8:26 *(New English Bible).* In place of "how we ought to pray," there is a variant reading which translates "what it is right to pray for."
5. Romans 12:1 (N.E.B.).
6. I Timothy 2:1-2 (N.E.B.).
7. In a slightly revised form these are the opening words of the *Prayers of the People* in *The Holy Eucharist, Rite I* in the *Book of Common Prayer 1979,* p. 329.
8. *The First Apology,* para. 65. This early account of Christian worship in the city of Rome dates from about 155 A.D.
9. I Timothy 2:8 *(Revised Standard Version).*
10. Faith and Order Paper No. 111, World Council of Churches, Geneva, 1982.
11. This quotation appears on the back cover of *Baptism, Eucharist and Ministry.*
12. Ibid., p. 14.
13. Ibid., p. 20.
14. Part of the *Baptismal Covenant* and of the *Renewal of Baptismal Vows* (Litany 128) in the *Book of Common Prayer 1979,* p. 305 and pp. 293-4, respectively.
15. *The Constitution on the Sacred Liturgy,* para. 53. This seminal document was promulgated by Pope Paul VI on December 4, 1963, after it had been adopted almost unanimously by the bishops assembled in Rome for the Second Vatican Council.
16. Chapter II, para. 45. The *Roman Missal* appeared in its definitive English translation in 1973.
17. Frederick William Faber (1814-1863) wrote this hymn in 1862. In his original version the first stanza began with the words, "Souls of men! why will ye scatter like a crowd of frightened sheep?"
18. The hymn appears in the *Lutheran Book of Worship* (no. 290) and in the *Hymnal 1982* (nos. 469/470).
19. This sentence is a paraphrase of one of the prayers for mission in *Morning Prayer I* and *II* in the *Book of Common Prayer 1979* (pp. 58 and 101, respectively); cf. I Timothy 2:4.
20. W.H. Auden wrote his *Hymn to St. Cecilia* in 1941. It was set to music by Benjamin Britten and the first public performance was given on November 22, 1942–appropriately enough Britten's birthday and St. Cecilia's Day!
21. Philippians 4:6 (R.S.V.).

22. Hebrews 7:25 (R.S.V.).
23. The *Book of Common Prayer 1979,* p. 148.
24. Words of welcome to the newly baptized in the rite of *Holy Baptism* in the *Book of Common Prayer 1979,* p. 308.
25. Luke 10:37 (R.S.V.).
26. *The Constitution on the Sacred Liturgy,* para. 14.
27. The Call to Worship in *Morning Prayer I* and *II* in the *Book of Common Prayer 1979,* pp. 41 and 79, respectively.
28. St. Teresa of Avila (1515-1582) is one of only two women among the great doctors (teachers) of the Catholic Church. She is celebrated as a mystic, as a writer on profound spiritual matters, and as a renewer of the Church. The 400th anniversary of her death was observed on October 4, 1982.

PRAYER
AND
WORSHIP

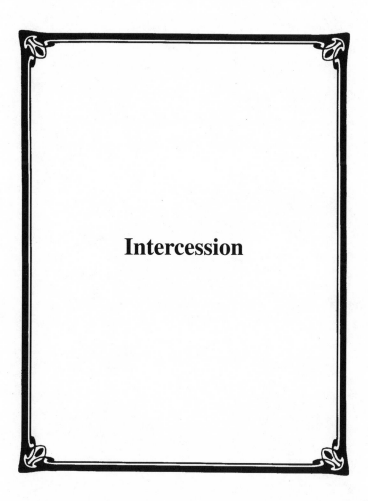

Intercession

1. The Great Litany**

This may be said in its entirety, or Sections I and VI may be used together with a selection of appropriate suffrages from Sections II, III, IV and V

I

O God the Father, Creator of heaven and earth:
Have mercy upon us.

O God the Son, Redeemer of the world:
Have mercy upon us.

O God the Holy Ghost, Sanctifier of the faithful:
Have mercy upon us.

O holy, blessed, and glorious Trinity, one God:
Have mercy upon us.

II

Remember not, Lord Christ, our offenses, nor the offenses of our forebears; neither reward us according to our sins. Spare us, good Lord, spare thy people, whom thou hast redeemed with thy most precious blood, and by thy mercy preserve us for ever.
Spare us, good Lord.

From all evil and wickedness; from sin; from the crafts and assaults of the devil; and from everlasting damnation:
Good Lord, deliver us.

From all blindness of heart; from pride, vainglory, and hypocrisy; from envy, hatred, and malice; and from all want of charity:
Good Lord, deliver us.

From all inordinate and sinful affections; and from all the deceits of the world, the flesh, and the devil:
Good Lord, deliver us.

From all false doctrine, heresy, and schism; from hardness of heart, and contempt of thy Word and commandment:
Good Lord, deliver us.

**In all the litanies in this book, the responses in italics are to be said by the whole congregation.*

From lightning and tempest; from earthquake, fire, and flood; from plague, pestilence, and famine:
Good Lord, deliver us.

From all oppression, conspiracy, and rebellion; from violence, battle, and murder; and from dying suddenly and unprepared:
Good Lord, deliver us.

By the mystery of thy holy Incarnation; by thy holy Nativity and submission to the Law; by thy Baptism, Fasting, and Temptation:
Good Lord, deliver us.

By thine Agony and Bloody Sweat; by thy Cross and Passion; by thy precious Death and Burial; by thy glorious Resurrection and Ascension; and by the Coming of the Holy Ghost:
Good Lord, deliver us.

In all time of our tribulation; in all time of our prosperity; in the hour of death, and in the day of judgment:
Good Lord, deliver us.

III

We sinners do beseech thee to hear us, O Lord God; and that it may please thee to rule and govern thy holy Church Universal in the right way:
We beseech thee to hear us, good Lord.

That it may please thee to illumine all ministers of the Gospel, with true knowledge and understanding of thy Word; and that both by their preaching and living, they may set it forth, and show it accordingly:
We beseech thee to hear us, good Lord.

That it may please thee to bless and keep all the faithful:
We beseech thee to hear us, good Lord.

That it may please thee to send forth laborers into thy harvest, and to draw all of humanity into thy kingdom:
We beseech thee to hear us, good Lord.

That it may please thee to give to all people increase of grace to hear and receive thy Word, and to bring forth the fruits of the Spirit:
We beseech thee to hear us, good Lord.

That it may please thee to bring into the way of truth all such as have erred, and are deceived:
We beseech thee to hear us, good Lord.

That it may please thee to give us a heart to love and fear thee, and diligently to live after thy commandments:
We beseech thee to hear us, good Lord.

IV

That it may please thee so to rule the hearts of thy servant, the President of the United States, and all others in authority, that they may do justice, and love mercy, and walk in the ways of truth:
We beseech thee to hear us, good Lord.

That it may please thee to make wars to cease in all the world; to give to all nations unity, peace, and concord; and to bestow freedom upon all peoples:
We beseech thee to hear us, good Lord.

That it may please thee to show thy pity upon all prisoners and captives, the homeless and the hungry, and all who are desolate and oppressed:
We beseech thee to hear us, good Lord.

That it may please thee to give and preserve to our use the bountiful fruits of the earth, so that in due time all may enjoy them:
We beseech thee to hear us, good Lord.

That it may please thee to inspire us, in our several callings, to do the work which thou givest us to do with singleness of heart as thy servants, and for the common good:
We beseech thee to hear us, good Lord.

That it may please thee to preserve all who are in danger by reason of their labor or their travel:
We beseech thee to hear us, good Lord.

That it may please thee to preserve, and provide for, all women in childbirth, young children and orphans, the widowed, and all whose homes are broken or torn by strife:
We beseech thee to hear us, good Lord.

That it may please thee to visit the lonely; to strengthen all who suffer in mind, body, and spirit; and to comfort with thy presence those who are failing and infirm:
We beseech thee to hear us, good Lord.

That it may please thee to support, help, and comfort all who are in danger, necessity, and tribulation:
We beseech thee to hear us, good Lord.

That it may please thee to have mercy upon people everywhere:
We beseech thee to hear us, good Lord.

V

That it may please thee to give us true repentance; to forgive us all our sins, negligences, and ignorances; and to endue us with the grace of thy Holy Spirit to amend our lives according to thy holy Word:
We beseech thee to hear us, good Lord.

That it may please thee to forgive our enemies, persecutors, and slanderers, and to turn their hearts:
We beseech thee to hear us, good Lord.

That it may please thee to strengthen such as do stand; to comfort and help the weak-hearted; to raise up those who fall; and finally to beat down Satan under our feet:
We beseech thee to hear us, good Lord.

That it may please thee to grant to all the faithful departed eternal life and peace:
We beseech thee to hear us, good Lord.

That it may please thee to grant that, in the fellowship of [_____ and] all the saints, we may attain to thy heavenly kingdom:
We beseech thee to hear us, good Lord.

VI

Son of God, we beseech thee to hear us.
Son of God, we beseech thee to hear us.

O Lamb of God, that takest away the sins of the world:
Have mercy upon us.

O Lamb of God, that takest away the sins of the world:
Have mercy upon us.

O Lamb of God, that takest away the sins of the world:
Grant us thy peace.

O Christ, hear us.
O Christ, hear us.

Lord, have mercy upon us.		Kyrie eleison.
Christ, have mercy upon us.	*or*	*Christe eleison.*
Lord, have mercy upon us.		Kyrie eleison.

The Officiant and People say together

Our Father, who art in heaven,
*   hallowed be thy Name,*
*   thy kingdom come,*
*   thy will be done,*
*   on earth as it is in heaven.*
Give us this day our daily bread.
And forgive us our trespasses,
*   as we forgive those who trespass against us.*
And lead us not into temptation
*   but deliver us from evil. Amen.*

O Lord, let thy mercy be shown upon us:
As we do put our trust in thee.

The Officiant concludes with the following or some other Collect.

Let us pray.

Almighty God, who hast promised to hear the petitions of those who ask in thy Son's Name: We beseech thee mercifully to incline thine ear to us who have now made our prayers and supplications unto thee; and grant that those things which we have asked faithfully according to thy will, may be obtained effectually, to the relief of our necessity, and to the setting forth of thy glory; through Jesus Christ our Lord. *Amen.*

The Officiant may add other Prayers, and end the Litany, saying

The grace of our Lord Jesus Christ, and the love of God, and the fellowship of the Holy Ghost, be with us all evermore. *Amen.*

THE BOOK OF COMMON PRAYER 1979*
*An asterisk at the end of a litany indicates that further information is to be found in the *Notes* at the end of the book.

2. Prayer of the Church †

Almighty God, giver of all things, with gladness we give thanks for all your goodness. We bless you for the love which has created and which sustains us from day to day. We praise you for the gift of your Son our Savior, through whom you have made known your will and grace. We thank you for the Holy Spirit, the comforter; for your holy Church; for the means of grace; for the lives of all faithful and good people; and for the hope of the life to come. Help us to treasure in our hearts all that our Lord has done for us, and enable us to show our thankfulness by lives that are wholly given to your service.
Hear us, good Lord.

Save and defend your whole Church, purchased with the precious blood of Christ. Give it pastors and ministers filled with your Spirit, and strengthen it through the Word and the holy sacraments. Make it perfect in love and in all good works, and establish it in the faith delivered to the saints. Sanctify and unite your people in all the world, that one holy Church may bear witness to you, the creator and redeemer of all.
Hear us, good Lord.

Give your wisdom and heavenly grace to all pastors and to those who hold office in your Church, that, by their faithful service, faith may abound and your kingdom increase.
Hear us, good Lord.

Send the light of your truth into all the earth. Raise up faithful servants of Christ to labor in the Gospel both at home and in distant lands.
Hear us, good Lord.

In your mercy strengthen the younger churches and support them in times of trial. Make them steadfast, abounding in the work of the Lord, and let their faith and zeal for the Gospel refresh and renew the witness of your people everywhere.
Hear us, good Lord.

Preserve our nation in justice and honor, that we may lead a peaceable life of integrity. Grant health and favor to all who bear office in our land, especially to the President of the United States, the Governor of this State, and all those who make, administer, and judge our laws, and help them to serve this people according to your holy will.
Hear us, good Lord.

Take from us all hatred and prejudice, give us the spirit of love, and dispose our days in your peace. Prosper the labors of those who take counsel for the nations of the world, that mutual understanding and common endeavor may be increased among all peoples.
Hear us, good Lord.

Bless the schools of the Church and all colleges, universities, and centers of research and those who teach in them. Bestow your wisdom in such measure that people may serve you in Church and state and that our common life may be conformed to the rule of your truth and justice.
Hear us, good Lord.

Sanctify our homes with your presence and joy. Keep our children in the covenant of their baptism and enable their parents to rear them in a life of faith and devotion. By the spirit of affection and service unite the members of all families, that they may show your praise in our land and in all the world.
Hear us, good Lord.

Let your blessing rest upon the seedtime and harvest, the commerce and industry, the leisure and rest, the arts and culture of our people. Take under your special protection those whose work is difficult or dangerous, and be with all who lay their hands to any useful task. Give them just rewards for their labor and the knowledge that their work is good in your sight.
Hear us, good Lord.

Special supplications, intercessions, and thanksgivings may be made here.

Comfort with the grace of your Holy Spirit all who are in sorrow or need, sickness or adversity. Remember those who suffer persecution for the faith. Have mercy on those to whom death draws near. Bring consolation to those in sorrow or mourning. And to all grant a measure of your love, taking them into your tender care.
Hear us, good Lord.

We remember with thanksgiving those who have loved and served you in your Church on earth, who now rest from their labors [especially those most dear to us, whom we name before you now_____]. Keep us in fellowship with all your saints, and bring us at last to the joy of your heavenly kingdom.
Hear us, good Lord.

All these things and whatever else you see that we need, grant us, Father, for the sake of him who died and rose again, and now lives and reigns with you in the unity of the Holy Spirit, one God forever. *Amen.*

THE LUTHERAN BOOK OF WORSHIP

3. Litany of Intercession

The Litany of Intercession may be said in its entirely or selectively. The response, "Hear our prayer, O Lord," may be used after each petition instead of the variety of responses provided.

O Lord our God: you hear our prayers before we speak, and answer before we know our need. Though we cannot pray, may your Spirit pray in us, drawing us to you and toward our neighbors on earth. *Amen.*

We pray for the whole creation: may all things work together for good, until, by your design, your children inherit the earth and order it wisely.
Let the whole creation praise you, Lord and God.

We pray for the Church of Jesus Christ; that, begun, maintained, and promoted by your Spirit, it may be true, engaging, glad, and active, doing your will.
Let the Church be always faithful, Lord and God.

We pray for men and women who serve the Church in special ways, preaching, ruling, showing charity; that they may never lose heart, but have all hope encouraged.
Let leadership be strong, Lord and God.

We pray for people who do not believe, who are shaken by doubt, or have turned against you. Open their eyes to see beyond our broken fellowship the wonders of your love displayed in Jesus of Nazareth; and to follow when he calls them.
Conquer doubt with faith, O God.

We pray for peace in the world. Disarm weapons, silence guns, and put out ancient hate that smolders still, or flames in sudden conflict. Create goodwill among every race and nation.
Bring peace to earth, O God.

We pray for all who must go to war, and for those who will not go: may they have conviction, and charity toward one another.
Guard the brave everywhere, O God.

We pray for enemies, as Christ commanded; for those who oppose us or scheme against us, who are also children of your love. May we be kept from infectious hate or sick desire for vengeance.
Make friends of enemies, O God.

We pray for those involved in world government, in agencies of control or compassion, who work for the reconciling of nations: keep them hopeful, and work with them for peace.
Unite our broken world, O God.

We pray for those who govern us, who make, administer, or judge our laws. May this country ever be a land of free and able leaders who welcome exiles and work for justice.
Govern those who govern us, O God.

We pray for poor people who are hungry, or are housed in cramped places. Increase in us, and all who prosper, concern for the disinherited.
Care for the poor, O God.

We pray for social outcasts; for those excluded by their own militance or by the harshness of others. Give us grace to accept those our world names unacceptable, and so show your mighty love.
Welcome the alienated, O God.

We pray for sick people who suffer pain, or struggle with demons of the mind, who silently cry out for healing: may they be patient, brave, and trusting.
Heal the sick and troubled, O God.

We pray for the dying, who face the final mystery: may they enjoy light and life intensely, keep dignity, and greet death unafraid, believing in your love.
Have mercy on the dying, O God.

We pray for those whose tears are not yet dry, who listen for familiar voices and look for still familiar faces: in loss, may they affirm all that you promise in Jesus, who prepares a place for us within your spacious love.
Comfort those who sorrow, O God.

We pray for people who are alone and lonely, who have no one to call in easy friendship: may they be remembered, befriended, and know your care for them.
Visit lonely people, O God.

We pray for families, for parents and children: may they enjoy each other, honor freedoms, and forgive as happily as we are all forgiven in your huge mercy.
Keep families in your love, O God.

We pray for young and old: give impatient youth true vision, and experienced age openness to new things. Let both praise your name. *Join youth and age together, O God.*

We pray for people everywhere: may they come into their own as children of God, and inherit the kingdom prepared in Jesus Christ, the Lord of all, and Savior of the world. *Hear our prayers, almighty God, in the name of Jesus Christ, who prays with us and for us, to whom be praise forever. Amen.*

THE WORSHIPBOOK

4. The Church and the World

Let us pray for the Church and for the world.

Grant, Almighty God, that all who confess your Name may be united in your truth, live together in your love, and reveal your glory in the world.

Silence

Lord, in your mercy:
Hear our prayer.

Guide the people of this land, and of all the nations, in the ways of justice and peace; that we may honor one another and serve the common good.

Silence

Lord, in your mercy:
Hear our prayer.

Give us all a reverence for the earth as your own creation, that we may use its resources rightly in the service of others and to your honor and glory.

Silence

Lord, in your mercy:
Hear our prayer.

Bless all whose lives are closely linked with ours, and grant that we may serve Christ in them, and love one another as he loves us.

Silence

Lord, in your mercy:
Hear our prayer.

Comfort and heal all those who suffer in body, mind, or spirit; give them courage and hope in their troubles, and bring them the joy of your salvation.

Silence

Lord, in your mercy:
Hear our prayer.

We commend to your mercy all who have died, that your will for them may be fulfilled; and we pray that we may share with all your saints in your eternal kingdom.

Silence

Merciful Father, accept these prayers, for the sake of your Son, our Savior Jesus Christ. Amen.

THE BOOK OF COMMON PRAYER 1979

5. A General Litany

In peace, we pray to you, Lord God.

Silence

For all people in their daily life and work:
For our families, friends, and neighbors, and for those who are alone.

For this community, the nation, and the world:
For all who work for justice, freedom, and peace.

For the just and proper use of your creation:
For the victims of hunger, fear, injustice, and oppression.

For all who are in danger, sorrow, or any kind of trouble:
For those who minister to the sick, the friendless, and the needy.

For the peace and unity of the Church of God:
For all who proclaim the Gospel, and all who seek the Truth.

For [*N*. our Presiding Bishop, and *N*. *(N.)* our Bishop(s); and for] all
bishops and other ministers:
For all who serve God in his Church.

For the special needs and concerns of this congregation.

Silence

The People may add their own petitions.

Hear us Lord:
For your mercy is great.

We thank you, Lord, for all the blessings of this life.

Silence

The People may add their own thanksgivings.

We will exalt you, O God our King:
And praise your Name for ever and ever.

We pray for all who have died, that they may have a place in your eternal kingdom.

Silence

The People may add their own petitions.

Lord, let your loving-kindness be upon them;
Who put their trust in you.

We pray to you also for the forgiveness of our sins.

Silence

Have mercy upon us, most merciful Father;
in your compassion forgive us our sins,
known and unknown,
things done and left undone;
and so uphold us by your Spirit
that we may live and serve you in newness of life,
to the honor and glory of your Name;
through Jesus Christ our Lord.
Amen.

Almighty God have mercy on us, forgive us all our sins through our Lord Jesus Christ, strengthen us in all goodness, and by the power of the Holy Spirit keep us in eternal life. *Amen.*

THE BOOK OF COMMON PRAYER 1979

6. The Prayers of God's People—
South Africa

Particular intentions may be mentioned before this prayer but it is said without interpolation.

Father, we are your children, your Spirit lives in us and we are in your Spirit: hear us, for it is your Spirit who speaks through us as we pray.
Lord, hear us.

Father, you created the heavens and the earth: bless the produce of our land and the works of our hands.
Lord, hear us.

Father, you created the human family in your own image: teach us to honor you in our brothers and sisters.
Lord, hear us.

Father, you provide for all your children: grant good rains for our crops.
Lord, hear us.

Father, you inspired the prophets of old: grant that your Church may faithfully proclaim your truth to the world.
Lord, hear us.

Father, you sent your Son into the world: reveal him to others through his life in us.
Lord, hear us.

Lord Jesus, you called the apostles to be fishers of men: bless the bishops of this Province, especially ____ our bishop and all other ministers of your Church.
Christ, hear us.

Lord Jesus, for your sake men and women forsook all and followed you: call many to serve you in Religious Communities and in the ordained ministry of your Church.
Christ, hear us.

Lord Jesus, you called men and women to be your disciples: deepen in each of us a sense of vocation.
Christ, hear us.

You prayed that your Church may be one: unite all Christians so that the world may believe you have sent us.
Christ, hear us.

You forgave the thief on the cross: bring all to penitence and reconciliation.
Christ, hear us.

You gave us your peace: bring the people of this world to live in true community and concord.
Christ, hear us.

You taught us through Paul, your apostle, to pray for all kings and rulers: bless and guide all who are in authority.
Christ, hear us.

You were rich, yet for our sake became poor: move those who have wealth to share generously with those who are poor.
Christ, hear us.

You sat among the learned, listening and asking them questions: inspire all who teach and all who learn.
Christ, hear us.

You cured by your healing touch and word: heal the sick and bless all who minister to them.
Christ, hear us.

You were unjustly condemned by Pontius Pilate: strengthen our brothers and sisters who are suffering injustice and persecution.
Christ, hear us.

You lived as an exile in Egypt: be with all migrant workers and protect their families.
Christ, hear us.

You open and none can shut: open the gates of your kingdom to those who have died without hearing your Gospel.
Christ, hear us.

You have been glorified in the lives of innumerable saints: give us strength through their prayers to follow in their footsteps.
Christ, hear us.

Father, we know that you are good and that you hear all those who call upon you: give to us and to all what is best so that we may glorify you through your Son, Jesus Christ our Lord, who is alive and reigns with you and the Holy Spirit, one God, now and for ever. *Amen.*

THE ANGLICAN CHURCH OF THE PROVINCE OF SOUTHERN AFRICA*

7. The Prayers of God's People—The United States

Father, we pray for your holy Catholic Church:
That we all may be one.

Grant that every member of the Church may truly and humbly serve you:
That your Name may be glorified by all people.

We pray for all bishops, priests, and deacons:
That they may be faithful ministers of your Word and Sacraments.

We pray for all who govern and hold authority in the nations of the world:
That there may be justice and peace on the earth.

Give us grace to do your will in all that we undertake:
That our works may find favor in your sight.

Have compassion on those who suffer from any grief or trouble:
That they may be delivered from their distress.

Give to the departed eternal rest:
Let light perpetual shine upon them.

We praise you for your saints who have entered into joy:
May we also come to share in your heavenly kingdom.

Let us pray for our own needs and those of others.

Silence

The People may add their own petitions.

The Leader concludes with one of the following Collects.

Almighty and eternal God, ruler of all things in heaven and earth: Mercifully accept the prayers of your people, and strengthen us to do your will; through Jesus Christ our Lord. *Amen.*

Heavenly Father, you have promised to hear what we ask in the Name of your Son: Accept and fulfill our petitions, we pray, not as we ask in our ignorance, nor as we deserve in our sinfulness, but as you know and love us in your Son Jesus Christ our Lord. *Amen.*

Almighty God, you have given us grace at this time with one accord to make our common supplication to you; and you have promised through your well-beloved Son that when two or three are gathered together in his Name you will be in the midst of them: Fulfill now, O Lord, our desires and petitions as may be best for us; granting us in this world knowledge of your truth, and in the age to come life everlasting. *Amen.*

Hasten, O Father, the coming of your kingdom; and grant that we your servants, who now live by faith, may with joy behold your Son at his coming in glorious majesty; even Jesus Christ, our only Mediator and Advocate. *Amen.*

THE BOOK OF COMMON PRAYER 1979

8. Our Many Communities

Father, you do not create us to live alone
    and you have not made us all alike.
We thank you for the varied societies
    into which we come,
    by which we are brought up,
    and through which we discover your purpose for our lives.
In gratitude we pray for our fellows.

This is my commandment:
Love one another, as I have loved you.

We pray for our families,
    with whom we live day by day.
May this most searching test of our character
    not find us broken and empty.
By all that we do and say
    help us to build up the faith and confidence
        of those we love,
    and when we quarrel, help us to forgive quickly.

This is my commandment:
Love one another, as I have loved you.

We pray for the places where we work,
    that there we may be workers who have no need to be ashamed.
We ask to be reliable rather than successful,
    worthy of trust rather than popular.
Whether those we work with be many or few,
    may we help to give them the sense that they are personally
        wanted and cared for.

This is my commandment:
Love one another, as I have loved you.

We pray for the communities to which we belong,
    that we may be good citizens.
Make us willing to accept responsibility
        when we are called to it;
    make us willing also to give place to others,
        that they too may have their opportunity.
Grant that our influence may be good and not evil.

This is my commandment:
Love one another, as I have loved you.

We pray for the generation to which we belong,
    those with whom we share a common fund of memory,
    common standards of behavior
    and a common attitude toward the world.
Grant that the presence of Christ may be so real to us that we may be able to
    help our generation to see him also as our contemporary.

This is my commandment:
Love one another, as I have loved you.

Father, into whose world we come
        and from whose world finally we must go:
    we thank you for all those people,
        great and humble,
        who have maintained the fabric of the world's life in the past
        and left us a great inheritance.
May we take up and encourage what is good,
    and hand it on to those who come after,
        believing that our work in your name will not be wasted or in vain.

This is my commandment:
Love one another, as I have loved you.
Amen.

CONTEMPORARY PRAYERS FOR PUBLIC WORSHIP

9. At the Start of a New Day

In the morning,
I sing your praise, O Lord.

Lord, you have always given me
tomorrow's bread:
And, although I am poor,
today I believe.

Lord, you have always mapped out
tomorrow's road:
And, although it is hidden,
today I believe.

Lord, you have always given me
tomorrow's peace:
And, in spite of my distress,
today I believe.

Lord, you have always given me
tomorrow's strength:
And, although I am weak,
today I believe.

Lord, you have always given me
tomorrow's light:
And, in spite of the darkness,
today I believe.

Lord, you have always spoken
when I was in doubt:
And, in spite of your silence,
today I believe.

Lord, you are my life;
you are my endless joy.
Even in death
forever I believe.

In the morning,
I sing your praise, O Lord. Amen.

LUCIEN DEISS*   *From Come, Lord Jesus,* ©1976, 1981 by Lucien Deiss.
                    Reprinted with permission.

10. An Evening Litany

That this evening may be holy, good, and peaceful:
We entreat you, O Lord.

That your holy angels may lead us in paths of peace and goodwill:
We entreat you, O Lord.

That we may be pardoned and forgiven for our sins and offenses:
We entreat you, O Lord.

That there may be peace to your Church and to the whole world:
We entreat you, O Lord.

That we may depart this life in your faith and fear, and not be condemned
before the great judgment seat of Christ:
We entreat you, O Lord.

That we may be bound together by your Holy Spirit in the communion of
[_____ and] all your saints, entrusting one another and all our life to Christ:
We entreat you, O Lord.

Silence

The Officiant then says one or more of the following Collects.

Lighten our darkness, we entreat you, O Lord; and in your great mercy
defend us from all perils and dangers of this night; for the love of your only
Son, our Savior, Jesus Christ. *Amen.*

O Lord God Almighty, as you have taught us to call the evening, the
morning, and the noonday one day; and have made the sun to know its
going down: Dispel the darkness of our hearts, that by your brightness we
may know you to be the true God and eternal light, living and reigning for
ever and ever. *Amen.*

Blessed are you, O Lord our God, creator of day and night, giving rest to
the weary and renewing the strength of those who are spent. As you have
protected us in the day that is past, so be with us in the coming night; keep
us from every sin, every evil, and every fear; for you are our light and
salvation, and the strength of our life. To you be glory for endless ages.
Amen.

Almighty, everlasting God, let our prayer in your sight be as incense, the lifting up of our hands as the evening sacrifice. Give us grace to behold you, present in your Word and Sacraments, and to recognize you in the lives of those around us. Stir up in us the flame of that love which burned in the heart of your Son as he bore his passion, and let it burn in us to eternal life and to the ages of ages. *Amen.*

THE BOOK OF COMMON PRAYER 1979*

Praise
and
Thanksgiving

11. Creation's Song of Praise

One or more sections of this Canticle may be used. Whatever the selection, it begins with the Invocation and concludes with the Doxology.

Invocation
Glorify the Lord, all you works of the Lord:
Praise God and highly exalt him for ever.
In the firmament of his power, glorify the Lord:
Praise God and highly exalt him for ever.

I. The Cosmic Order

Glorify the Lord, you angels and all powers of the Lord:
O heavens and all waters above the heavens.
Sun and moon and stars of the sky, glorify the Lord:
Praise God and highly exalt him for ever.

Glorify the Lord, every shower of rain and fall of dew:
All winds and fire and heat.
Winter and summer, glorify the Lord:
Praise God and highly exalt him for ever.

Glorify the Lord, O chill and cold:
Drops of dew and flakes of snow.
Frost and cold, ice and sleet, glorify the Lord:
Praise God and highly exalt him for ever.

Glorify the Lord, O nights and days:
O shining light and enfolding dark.
Storm clouds and thunderbolts, glorify the Lord:
Praise God and highly exalt him for ever.

II. The Earth and Its Creatures

Let the earth glorify the Lord:
Praise God and highly exalt him for ever.
Glorify the Lord, O mountains and hills,
and all that grows upon the earth:
Praise God and highly exalt him for ever.

Glorify the Lord, O springs of water, seas, and streams:
O whales and all that move in the waters.
All the birds of the air, glorify the Lord:
Praise God and highly exalt him for ever.

Glorify the Lord, O beasts of the wild:
And all you flocks and herds.
O men and women everywhere, glorify the Lord:
Praise God and highly exalt him for ever.

III. The People of God

Let the people of God glorify the Lord:
Praise God and highly exalt him for ever.
Glorify the Lord, O priests and servants of the Lord:
Praise God and highly exalt him for ever.

Glorify the Lord, O spirits and souls of the righteous:
Praise God and highly exalt him for ever.
You that are holy and humble of heart, glorify the Lord:
Praise God and highly exalt him for ever.

Doxology

Let us glorify the Lord: Father, Son, and Holy Spirit:
Praise God and highly exalt him for ever.
In the firmament of his power, glorify the Lord:
Praise God and highly exalt him for ever.

THE BOOK OF COMMON PRAYER 1979*

12. Litany of Thanksgiving

Give thanks to the Lord, for God is good.
God's love is everlasting.

Come, let us praise God joyfully.
Let us come to God with thanksgiving.

For the good world; for things great and small, beautiful and awesome;
for seen and unseen splendors:
Thank you, God.

For human life; for talking and moving and thinking together;
for common hopes and hardships shared from birth until our dying:
Thank you, God.

For work to do and strength to work; for the comradeship of labor;
for exchanges of good humor and encouragement:
Thank you, God.

For marriage; for the mystery and joy of flesh made one; for mutual
forgiveness and burdens shared; for secrets kept in love:
Thank you, God.

For family; for living together and eating together; for family amusements
and family pleasures:
Thank you, God.

For children; for their energy and curiosity; for their brave play and their
startling frankness; for their sudden sympathies:
Thank you, God.

For the young; for their high hopes; for their irreverence toward worn-out
values; their search for freedom; their solemn vows:
Thank you, God.

For growing up and growing old; for wisdom deepened by experience;
for rest in leisure; and for time made precious by its passing:
Thank you, God.

For your help in times of doubt and sorrow; for healing our diseases; for
preserving us in temptation and danger:
Thank you, God.

For the Church into which we have been called; for the good news we receive by Word and Sacrament; for our life together in the Lord:
We praise you, God.

For your Holy Spirit, who guides our steps and brings us gifts of faith and love; who prays in us and prompts our grateful worship:
We praise you, God.

Above all, O God, for your Son Jesus Christ, who lived and died and lives again for our salvation; for our hope in him; and for the joy of serving him:
We thank and praise you, God our Father, for all your goodness to us.

Give thanks to the Lord, for God is good.
God's love is everlasting. Amen.

THE WORSHIPBOOK

13. Thanksgiving for All God's Gifts

Let us give thanks to God our Father for all God's gifts so freely bestowed upon us.

For the beauty and wonder of your creation, in earth and sky and sea,
We thank you, Lord.

For all that is gracious in the lives of men and women, revealing the image of Christ,
We thank you, Lord.

For our daily food and drink, our homes and families, and our friends,
We thank you, Lord.

For minds to think, and hearts to love, and hands to serve,
We thank you, Lord.

For health and strength to work, and leisure to rest and play,
We thank you, Lord.

For the brave and courageous, who are patient in suffering and faithful in adversity,
We thank you, Lord.

For all valiant seekers after truth, liberty, and justice,
We thank you, Lord.

For the communion of saints, in all times and places,
We thank you, Lord.

Above all, we give you thanks for the great mercies and promises given to us in Christ Jesus our Lord;
To him be praise and glory, with you, O Father, and the Holy Spirit, now and for ever. Amen.

THE BOOK OF COMMON PRAYER 1979

14. A General Thanksgiving

Accept, O Lord, our thanks and praise for all that you have done for us.

Silence

For the splendor of the whole creation, for the beauty of this world, for the wonder of life, and for the mystery of love,
We thank you, Lord.

For the blessing of family and friends, and for the loving care which surrounds us on every side,
We thank you, Lord.

For setting us at tasks which demand our best efforts, and for leading us to accomplishments which satisfy and delight us,
We thank you, Lord.

For those disappointments and failures that lead us to acknowledge our dependence on you alone,
We thank you, Lord.

Above all, for your Son Jesus Christ, for the truth of his Word and the example of his life; for his steadfast obedience, by which he overcame temptation; for his dying through which he overcame death, and for his rising to life again, in which we are raised to the life of your kingdom,
We thank you, Lord.

Grant us the gift of your Spirit, that we may know him and make him known; and through him, at all times and in all places, may give thanks to you in all things. *Amen.*

THE BOOK OF COMMON PRAYER 1979

15. Prayers of Adoration, Confession, and Thanksgiving

These prayers may be used separately or as one continuous litany. The hymn stanzas may be sung or said, as desired.

Stand

Adoration

Let us give glory to God: Father, Son, and Holy Spirit.
Let us pray.

Let us adore the God of love who created us;
who every moment preserves and sustains us;
who has loved us with an everlasting love, and given us the light of the
    knowledge of God's glory in the face of Jesus Christ.
We praise you, O God, we acknowledge you to be the Lord.

Let us glory in the grace of our Lord Jesus Christ;
who, though he was rich, yet for our sakes became poor;
who went about doing good and preaching the Gospel of the Kingdom;
who was tempted in all points like as we are, yet without sin;
who became obedient unto death, even the death of the Cross;
who was dead, and now lives for evermore;
who opened the Kingdom of Heaven to all believers;
who is seated at the right hand of God in the glory of the Father.
You are the King of Glory, O Christ.

Let us rejoice in the fellowship of the Holy Spirit, the Lord and Giver of
life, by whom we are born into the family of God, and made members of
the Body of Christ;
    whose witness confirms us;
    whose wisdom teaches us;
    whose power enables us;
    who waits to do for us exceeding abundantly
        above all that we ask or think.
All praise to you, O Holy Spirit.

Silence

The following hymn is sung or said.

You servants of God, your master proclaim,
and publish abroad his wonderful name;
the name, all-victorious, of Jesus extol;
his Kingdom is glorious and rules over all!

Then let us adore and give him his right,
all glory and power and wisdom and might,
all honor and blessing, with angels above,
and thanks never ceasing, and infinite love!

Sit or kneel

Confession

Let us examine ourselves and humbly confess our sins before God.
Let us pray.

O God, you have set forth the way of life for us in your beloved Son: we
confess with shame our slowness to learn of him, our reluctance to follow
him. You have spoken and called, and we have not given heed; your
beauty has shone forth and we have been blind; you have stretched out
your hands to us through our fellows and we have passed by. We have
taken great benefits with little thanks; we have been unworthy of your
changeless love.
Have mercy upon us and forgive us, O Lord.

Forgive us, we pray, the poverty of our worship, the formality and
selfishness of our prayers, our inconstancy and unbelief, our neglect of
fellowship and of the means of grace, our hesitating witness for Christ, our
false pretenses and our willful ignorance of your ways.
Have mercy upon us and forgive us, O Lord.

Forgive us wherein we have wasted our time or misused our gifts. Forgive
us wherein we have excused our own wrong-doing or evaded our
responsibilities. Forgive us that we have been unwilling to overcome evil
with good, that we have drawn back from the Cross.
Have mercy upon us and forgive us, O Lord.

Forgive us that so little of your love has reached others through us, and that
we have borne so lightly wrongs and sufferings that were not our own.
Forgive us wherein we have cherished the things that divide us from others,
and wherein we have made it hard for them to live with us. Forgive us
wherein we have been thoughtless in judgment, hasty in condemnation,
grudging in forgiveness.
Have mercy upon us and forgive us, O Lord.

If we have made no ventures in fellowship; if we have kept in our heart a grievance against another; if we have not sought reconciliation; if we have been eager for the punishment of wrong-doers, and slow to seek their redemption:
Have mercy upon us and forgive us, O Lord.

Silence

The following hymn is sung or said.

Come, O thou all-victorious Lord,
thy power to us make known;
strike with the hammer of thy Word,
and break these hearts of stone.

Give us ourselves and thee to know,
in this our gracious day;
repentance unto life bestow,
and take our sins away.

Stand

Thanksgiving

Let us give thanks to God for all the blessings of our life in Christ.
Let us pray.

O God, the fountain of all goodness, you have been gracious to us through all the years of our life: we give you thanks for your loving-kindness which has filled our days and brought us to this time and place.
We praise your holy Name, O Lord.

You have given us life and reason and set us in a world which is full of your glory. You have comforted us with family and friends, and ministered to us through the hands and minds of our fellows.
We praise your holy Name, O Lord.

You have set in our hearts a hunger for you, and given us your peace. You have redeemed us and called us to a high calling in Christ Jesus. You have given us a place in the fellowship of your Spirit and the witness of your Church.
We praise your holy Name, O Lord.

In darkness you have been our light; in adversity and temptation a rock of strength; in our joys the very spirit of joy; in our labors the all-sufficient reward.
We praise your holy Name, O Lord.

You have remembered us when we have forgotten you, followed us even when we fled from you, met us with forgiveness when we turned back to you. For all your long-suffering and the abundance of your grace:
We praise your holy Name, O Lord.

Silence

The following hymn is sung or said.

O, for a thousand tongues to sing
my great Redeemer's praise,
the glories of my God and King,
the triumphs of his grace!

My gracious Master and my God,
assist me to proclaim,
to spread through all the earth abroad
the honors of thy name.

JOHN WESLEY'S COVENANT SERVICE
- HYMN STANZAS BY CHARLES WESLEY*

Confession

16.   The Ten Commandments and Our Lord's Summary of the Law

Our Lord Jesus Christ said, If you love me, keep my commandments;
happy are those who hear the word of God and keep it. Hear then these
commandments which God has given to his people, and take them to heart.

I am the Lord your God: you shall have no other gods but me.
You shall love the Lord your God with all your heart, with all your soul,
with all your mind, and with all your strength.
Amen. Lord, have mercy.

You shall not make for yourself any idol.
God is spirit, and those who worship God must worship in spirit and in
truth.
Amen. Lord, have mercy.

You shall not dishonor the name of the Lord your God.
You shall worship God with awe and reverence.
Amen. Lord, have mercy.

Remember the Lord's day and keep it holy.
Christ is risen from the dead: set your minds on things that are above,
not on things that are on the earth.
Amen. Lord, have mercy.

Honor your father and mother.
Live as servants of God; honor all people; love your brothers and sisters in
Christ.
Amen. Lord, have mercy.

You shall not commit murder.
Be reconciled to each other; overcome evil with good.
Amen. Lord, have mercy.

You shall not commit adultery.
Know that your body is a temple of the Holy Spirit.
Amen. Lord, have mercy.

You shall not steal.
Be honest in all that you do and care for those in need.
Amen. Lord, have mercy.

You shall not be a false witness.
Let everyone speak the truth.
Amen. Lord, have mercy.

You shall not covet anything which belongs to your neighbor.
Remember the words of the Lord Jesus: It is more blessed to give than to receive. Love your neighbor as yourself, for love is the fulfilling of the law.
Amen. Lord, have mercy.

Our Lord Jesus Christ said: The first commandment is this: "Hear, O Israel, the Lord our God is the only Lord. You shall love the Lord your God with all your heart, with all your soul, with all your mind, and with all your strength." The second is this: "Love your neighbor as yourself." There is no other commandment greater than these.
Amen. Lord, have mercy.

THE ALTERNATIVE SERVICE BOOK 1980*

17. Litany of the Commandments

The Law was given through Moses.
Grace and truth came through Jesus Christ.

I am the Lord your God, who brought you out of the land of Egypt, out of the house of bondage: you shall have no other gods before me.
No one can serve two masters: you cannot serve God and mammon.

You shall not make yourself any graven images: for I, the Lord, am a jealous God.
Render therefore to Caesar the things that are Caesar's, and to God the things that are God's.

You shall not take the name of the Lord your God in vain.
Let what you say be simply "Yes" or "No"; anything more than this comes from the Evil One.

Remember the Sabbath day to keep it holy.
The Sabbath was made for man, not man for the Sabbath: and the Son of man is Lord even of the Sabbath.

Honor your father and your mother, that your days be long in the land which the Lord your God gives you.
Who is my mother? Who are my brothers? Whoever does the will of my Father in heaven is my brother, and sister, and mother.

You shall not kill.
Love your enemies. Pray for those who persecute you. For if you love those who love you, what reward have you?

You shall not commit adultery.
Woman, has no one condemned you? Neither do I condemn you. Go, and sin no more.

You shall not steal.
Go, sell what you possess, and give to the poor, and you will have treasure in heaven.

You shall not bear false witness against your neighbor.
When it was evening, Jesus sat at table with the twelve disciples, and as they were eating, he said, "Truly, I say to you, one of you will betray me."

You shall not covet.
This is my body broken for you. This is my blood of the new covenant,
which is poured out for many, for the forgiveness of sins.

The Law was given through Moses.
Grace and truth came through Jesus Christ.
Amen.

MODELS FOR MINISTERS I*

18. Confession of the Community

O Lord, you open your hand, and all the earth is filled with good things, but we have cried out against you, saying, "What shall we eat and what shall we drink?"

Men: Lord, have mercy upon us.
Women: Christ, have mercy upon us.
All: Lord, have mercy upon us.

O Lord, you have said, "In returning and rest you shall be saved; in quietness and trust shall be your strength," but we have shouted, "No! We will speed upon horses, we will ride upon swift steeds."

Men: Lord, have mercy upon us.
Women: Christ, have mercy upon us.
All: Lord, have mercy upon us.

O Lord, you have said, "Let justice roll down like waters, and righteousness like an everflowing stream," but we have said, "When will the Sabbath be over that we may buy the poor for silver and the needy for a pair of sandals?"

Men: Lord, have mercy upon us.
Women: Christ, have mercy upon us.
All: Lord, have mercy upon us.

O Lord, we have come before you with thousands of rams and ten thousand rivers of oil, and we have caused you to cry out, "Oh my people, what have I done to you? In what have I wearied you? Answer me!"

Men: Lord, have mercy upon us.
Women: Christ, have mercy upon us.
All: Lord, have mercy upon us.

O Lord, you have said, "How can I give you up, O Ephraim? How can I hand you over, O Israel?" but we have cried out, "Away with him, away with him! We have no king but Caesar!"

Men: Lord, have mercy upon us.
Women: Christ, have mercy upon us.
All: Lord, have mercy upon us.

KATHERINE P. MEYER*

19. We're Sorry, God

That we don't think much about you:
We're sorry, God.

That we use your name cheaply:
We're sorry, God.

That we make believe we don't care about you:
We're sorry, God.

That we think it's big to be like that:
We're sorry, God.

That we poke fun at people who go to church:
We're sorry, God.

That we've waited so long to say we're sorry:
We're sorry, God.

That we've caused you pain:
We're sorry, God.

That we forget your love:
We're sorry, God.

For showing off and making fools of ourselves:
We're sorry, God.

For not finding out about you:
We're sorry, God.

For fighting you:
We're sorry, God.

For not trusting you:
We're sorry, God.

For thinking we are all alone:
We're sorry, God.

For the times we've said, "Who needs God?"
We're sorry, God.

For all that sort of thing:
We're sorry, God.
Amen.

CARL F. BURKE

20. A Cry from the Heart

With the tax-collector in St. Luke's Gospel, let us say:
O God, be merciful to me, a sinner.

You come to look for the lost sheep;
joyfully you carry it on your shoulders-
    we beg you:
O God, be merciful to me, a sinner.

You go to meet the prodigal son;
you clasp him in your arms and kiss him-
    we beg you:
O God, be merciful to me, a sinner.

You choose, as your apostle, Matthew the tax-collector;
you have not come to call the righteous, but sinners-
    we beg you:
O God, be merciful to me, a sinner.

You enter the house of Zachaeus the tax-gatherer
in order to seek out and save what was lost-
    we beg you:
O God, be merciful to me, a sinner.

You accept the ointment of the sinful woman;
because of her tears you pardon and defend her-
    we beg you:
O God, be merciful to me, a sinner.

To the good thief who implores you,
you open the gate of Paradise-
    we beg you:
O God, be merciful to me, a sinner.
Amen.

LUCIEN DEISS

From *Come, Lord Jesus*, ©1976, 1981 by Lucien Deiss. Reprinted with permission.

PRAYER
AND
TIME

Advent
to
Pentecost

21. The Advent Antiphons

O Wisdom, Breath of the Most High, pervading and permeating all creation:
Come and make us friends of God.

O Lord of lords and Leader of the house of Israel, who appeared to Moses in the burning bush and gave him your law on Sinai:
Come and save us with outstretched arm.

O Root of Jesse, standing as a signal to the nations, before whom all kings are mute, to whom the nations will do homage:
Come and save us, delay no longer.

O Key of David and Ruler of the house of Israel, when you open nobody can close, when you close nobody can open:
Come and proclaim liberty to captives and set the down-trodden free.

O radiant Dawn, Splendor of eternal light and Sun of justice:
Come and give light to those who live in darkness and the shadow of death.

O King of the nations, the Ruler they long for, the Cornerstone binding all together:
Come and save the people you fashioned from the dust of the earth.

O Emmanuel, our King and our Lawgiver, the Anointed of the nations and their Savior:
Come and save us, O Lord our God.

The Spirit and the Bride say, Come!
Amen! Lord Jesus, come soon!

PRAY LIKE THIS*

22. Litany of the Incarnation

O God, the ruler of ages eternal,
you are without beginning or end:
Yet you choose to be born an infant in time.
> *Praise to you, O Lord.*

O God, the invisible,
you are the One whom nobody has seen or can see:
Yet you assume the face of the Son of Mary.
> *Praise to you, O Lord.*

O God, the all-powerful,
you hold the mountains in the palm of your hand:
Yet you let yourself be wrapped in swaddling clothes.
> *Praise to you, O Lord.*

O God, the eternal glory,
innumerable angels acclaim you endlessly:
Yet you choose to be rocked to sleep by the songs of the daughter of David.
> *Praise to you, O Lord.*

O God, the universal provider, you feed every creature:
Yet you choose to hunger for the milk of your mother.
> *Praise to you, O Lord.*

O God, the infinite,
heaven and earth cannot contain you:
Yet you rest in the arms of Mary.
> *Praise to you, O Lord.*

O God, the perfect joy,
you are the source of the happiness of heaven and earth:
Yet you cry like a little child.
> *Praise to you, O Lord.*

O God, the eternal Word,
you are the light of all created intelligence:
Yet you are laid in a manger and cannot even speak.
> *Praise to you, O Lord. Amen.*

LUCIEN DEISS
From *Come, Lord Jesus,* ©1976, 1981 by Lucien Deiss. Reprinted with permission.

23. Christmas Present

Two voices may lead this.

1:      For all who give you a face, Lord Jesus,
2:      by spreading your love in the world:
          We praise you.

1:      For all who give you hands, Lord Jesus,
2:      by doing their best toward their brothers and sisters:
          We praise you.

1:      For all who give you a mouth, Lord Jesus,
2:      by defending the weak and the oppressed:
          We praise you.

1:      For all who give you eyes, Lord Jesus,
2:      by seeing every bit of love in the heart of man and woman:
          We praise you.

1:      For all who give you a heart, Lord Jesus,
2:      by preferring the poor to the rich, the weak to the strong:
          We praise you.

1:      For all who give to your poverty, Lord Jesus,
2:      the look of hope for the Kingdom:
          We praise you.

1:      For all who reveal you simply by what they are, Lord Jesus,
2:      because they reflect your beauty in their lives:
          We praise you.

1:      God our Father, you are the God of a thousand faces,
2:      yet nothing can reveal you completely except the face of the child
          of Bethlehem:
          We pray to you:
          Continue in our lives the mystery of Christmas.
          Let your Son become flesh in us
          so that we may be for all our brothers and sisters
          the revelation of your ever-present love. Amen.

LUCIEN DEISS

From *Come, Lord Jesus,* ©1976, 1981 by Lucien Deiss. Reprinted with permission.

24. Litany of the Magi

As the Wise Men of old followed the star:
Help us, O God, to follow the leading of your Spirit.

As they were led to the Savior:
Lead us, O God, to him who is the Way, the Truth and the Life.

As they brought treasures to the King:
Empower us, O God, to bring his gifts of faith and hope and love to the world.

As they fell down and worshiped the Child:
Inspire us, O God, to serve him every moment of our lives.

As Herod was kept from doing him harm:
Keep us, O God, from doing violence to his Name by thought or word or deed.

As Mary kept all things and pondered them in her heart:
Enable us, O God, to remember and to love.

As your Son shines forever as the Light of the world:
Shine forth in us, O God, that we may be lights of the world in our generation.

Holy Jesus, come from God:
Fill us now and always with your light. Amen.

ELMER N. WITT
-HELP IT ALL MAKE SENSE, LORD

25. The Acceptable Fast

"The fast that I like," says the Lord,
"is the breaking of the chains of evil,
the untying of the bonds of slavery."
Help us to fast, O Lord,
by loving our brothers and sisters.

"It is freeing the oppressed,
and welcoming the poor into your home."
Help us to fast, O Lord,
by loving our brothers and sisters.

"It is clothing the person you find naked,
and not despising your neighbor."
Help us to fast, O Lord,
by loving our brothers and sisters.

"Then will your light shine like the dawn,
and your wound be quickly healed over."
Help us to fast, O Lord,
by loving our brothers and sisters.

"Then, if you cry, God will answer;
if you call, God will say: I am here."
Help us to fast, O Lord,
by loving our brothers and sisters. Amen.

LUCIEN DEISS

From *Come, Lord Jesus,* ©1976, 1981 by Lucien Deiss.
Reprinted with permission.

26. A Litany for Lent

Most holy and merciful Father:
We confess to you and to one another,
and to the whole communion of saints
in heaven and on earth,
that we have sinned by our own fault
in thought, word, and deed;
by what we have done, and by what we have left undone.

We have not loved you with our whole heart, and mind, and strength. We have not loved our neighbors as ourselves. We have not forgiven others, as we have been forgiven.
Have mercy on us, Lord.

We have been deaf to your call to serve, as Christ served us. We have not been true to the mind of Christ. We have grieved your Holy Spirit.
Have mercy on us, Lord.

We confess to you, Lord, all our past unfaithfulness: the pride, hypocrisy, and impatience of our lives:
We confess to you, Lord.

Our self-indulgent appetites and ways, and our exploitation of other people:
We confess to you, Lord.

Our anger at our own frustration, and our envy of those more fortunate than ourselves:
We confess to you, Lord.

Our intemperate love of worldly goods and comforts, and our dishonesty in daily life and work:
We confess to you, Lord.

Our negligence in prayer and worship, and our failure to commend the faith that is in us:
We confess to you, Lord.

Accept our repentance, Lord, for the wrongs we have done: for our blindness to human need and suffering, and our indifference to injustice and cruelty:
Accept our repentance, Lord.

For all false judgments, for uncharitable thoughts toward our neighbors, and for our prejudice and contempt toward those who differ from us:
Accept our repentance, Lord.

For our waste and pollution of your creation, and our lack of concern for those who come after us:
Accept our repentance, Lord.

Restore us, good Lord, and let your anger depart from us:
Favorably hear us, for your mercy is great.

Accomplish in us the work of your salvation:
That we may show forth your glory in the world.

By the Cross and Passion of your Son our Lord:
Bring us with all your saints to the joy of his resurrection.

The Presiding Minister, facing the people, says:

Almighty God, the Father of our Lord Jesus Christ, who desires not the death of sinners, but rather that they may turn from their wickedness and live, has given power and commandment to his ministers to declare and pronounce to his people, being penitent, the absolution and remission of their sins. God pardons and absolves all those who truly repent, and with sincere hearts believe his holy Gospel.

Therefore we beseech God to grant us true repentance and his Holy Spirit, that those things may please God which we do on this day, and that the rest of our life hereafter may be pure and holy, so that at the last we may come to his eternal joy; through Jesus Christ our Lord. *Amen.*

THE BOOK OF COMMON PRAYER 1979

27. Dayyenu: It Would Have Been Enough

The original Hebrew response used at the Passover Seder may be said after each reason for celebration and thanksgiving, or otherwise the English equivalent.

If God had created us and not revealed himself in all his marvelous works:
Dayyenu. (It would have been enough.)

If God had revealed himself and not made a covenant with his people:
Dayyenu.

If God had made a covenant with his people and not breathed his Spirit into us:
Dayyenu.

If God had breathed his Spirit into us and not shared with us his love:
Dayyenu.

If God had shared his love with us and not watched over us when we strayed from him:
Dayyenu.

If God had watched over us when we strayed from him and not delivered us from the bonds of slavery:
Dayyenu.

If God had delivered us from the bonds of slavery and not led us into a land of freedom:
Dayyenu.

If God had led us into a land of freedom and not sent us holy men and women to speak to us of his love:
Dayyenu.

If God had sent us holy men and women to speak to us of his love and not promised us a Savior:
Dayyenu.

If God had promised us a Savior and not sent us his own beloved Son:
Dayyenu.

If God had sent us Jesus, his own beloved Son, and had he not become our very brother:
Dayyenu.

If Jesus had become our very brother and not shared our joy and sorrows, our laughter and tears:
Dayyenu.

If Jesus had shared our life and not taught us how to forgive each other:
Dayyenu.

If Jesus had taught us how to forgive each other and had not shown us how to love:
Dayyenu.

If Jesus had taught us how to love and had not taught us how to serve each other:
Dayyenu.

If Jesus had shown us how to serve each other and had not left us this supper *(eucharist)* as a reminder of his love:
Dayyenu.

If Jesus had left us this supper *(eucharist)* as a reminder of his love and not called us to carry on his work in the world:
Dayyenu.

But as it is, Father, your Son Jesus has revealed your love for us. His whole life, his death and his resurrection from the dead testify to your deep mercy and compassion. Therefore, Father, we bless and thank you, we praise and worship you with all creation, for you are worthy of our worship, and beyond all the praises of our hearts. To you and to your Son, Jesus, and to the Holy Spirit belong all glory, now and for ever. *Amen.*

MICHAEL E. MOYNAHAN, S.J.
-MODERN LITURGY*

28. The Solemn Prayers of Good Friday

These prayers may be used either in part or in their entirety.

1. For the Church:

Let us pray, dear friends,
for the holy Church of God throughout the world,
that God the almighty Father
may guide it and gather it together
so that we may worship God
in peace and tranquility.

Silence

Almighty and eternal God,
you have shown your glory to all nations
in Christ, your Son.
Guide the work of your Church.
Help it to persevere in faith,
proclaim your name,
and bring your salvation to people everywhere.

We ask this through Christ our Lord. Amen.

2. For the Pope:

Let us pray
for our Holy Father, Pope _____,
that God who chose him to be bishop
may give him health and strength
to guide and govern God's holy people.

Silence

Almighty and eternal God,
you guide all things by your word,
you govern all Christian people.
In your love protect the Pope you have chosen for us.
Under his leadership deepen our faith
and make us better Christians.

We ask this through Christ our Lord. Amen.

3. For the People of God:

Let us pray
for _____, our bishop,
for all bishops, priests, and deacons;
for all who have a special ministry in the Church,
and for all God's people.

Silence

Almighty and eternal God,
your Spirit guides the Church
and makes it holy.
Listen to our prayers
and help each of us
in our own vocation
to do your work more faithfully.

We ask this through Christ our Lord. Amen.

4. For those preparing for Baptism:

Let us pray for those [*among us*] preparing for baptism,
that God in his mercy
may make them responsive to his love,
forgive their sins through the waters of new birth,
and give them life in Jesus Christ our Lord.

Silence

Almighty and eternal God,
you continually bless your Church with new members.
Increase the faith and understanding
of those [among us] preparing for baptism.
Give them a new birth in the[se] living waters
and make them members of your chosen family.

We ask this through Christ our Lord. Amen.

5. For the unity of Christians:

Let us pray
for all our brothers and sisters
who share our faith in Jesus Christ,
that God may gather and keep together in one Church
all those who seek the truth with sincerity.

Silence

Almighty and eternal God,
you keep together those you have united.
Look kindly on all who follow Jesus your Son.
We are all consecrated to you by our common baptism.
Make us one in the fullness of faith,
and keep us one in the fellowship of love.

We ask this through Christ our Lord. Amen.

6. For the Jewish People:

Let us pray
for the Jewish people,
the first to hear the word of God,
that they may continue to grow in the love of his Name
and in faithfulness to his covenant.

Silence

Almighty and eternal God,
long ago you gave your promise to Abraham and his posterity.
Listen to your Church as we pray
that the people you first made your own
may arrive at the fullness of redemption.

We ask this through Christ our Lord. Amen.

7. For those who do not believe in Christ:

Let us pray for those who do not believe in Christ,
that the light of the Holy Spirit
may show them the way to salvation.

Silence

Almighty and eternal God,
enable those who do not acknowledge Christ
to find the truth
as they walk before you in sincerity of heart.
Help us to grow in love for one another,
to grasp more fully the mystery of your godhead,
and to become more perfect witnesses of your love
in the sight of all.

We ask this through Christ our Lord. Amen.

8. For those who do not believe in God:

Let us pray
for those who do not believe in God,
that they may find God
by sincerely following all that is right.

Silence

Almighty and eternal God,
you created the human race
so that all might long to find you
and have peace when you are found.
Grant that, in spite of the hurtful things
that stand in their way,
they may all recognize in the lives of Christians
the tokens of your love and mercy,
and gladly acknowledge you
as the one true God and Father of us all.

We ask this through Christ our Lord. Amen.

9. For all in public office:

Let us pray for those who serve us in public office,
that God may guide their minds and hearts,
so that all people everywhere may live in true peace and freedom.

Silence

Almighty and eternal God,
you know the longings of human hearts
and you protect our human rights.
In your goodness watch over those in authority,
so that people everywhere may enjoy
religious freedom, security, and peace.

We ask this through Christ our Lord. Amen.

10. For all in special need:

Let us pray, dear friends,
that God the almighty Father

may heal the sick,
comfort the dying,
give safety to travelers,
free those unjustly deprived of liberty,
and rid the world of falsehood,
hunger, and disease.

Silence

Almighty, ever-living God,
you give strength to the weary
and new courage to those who have lost heart.
Hear the prayers of all who call on you in any trouble
that they may have the joy of receiving your help in their need.

We ask this through Christ our Lord. Amen.

THE ENGLISH TRANSLATION OF THE ROMAN MISSAL, 1973*

29. . . . They Crucified Him

O God, the lover of humankind,
we remember before you
all who took part in Christ's passion
from evil or from good:

The priests and Pharisees and elders
     who conspired to arrest him;
Judas, his disciple,
     who betrayed him with a kiss;
the apostles who deserted him,
     yet bore witness to his glory on the Cross:
Have mercy on them and us.

Malchus, struck by Peter's sword,
     whom Jesus touched and healed;
the young man who followed Jesus,
     yet fled naked from the crowd;
the high priest's maids and servants
     before whom Peter denied the Lord:
Have mercy on them and us.

Annas, the high priest's father-in-law,
     who handed Jesus to Caiaphas;
Caiaphas, the high priest,
     who convicted him of blasphemy;
the chief priests, scribes, and officers
     who mocked and beat him
     and condemned him as worthy of death:
Have mercy on them and us.

Herod the king
     who arrayed him in gorgeous apparel
     and treated him with contempt;
The Roman soldiers
     who clothed him in purple
     and put a crown of thorns on his head
     and pretended to worship him;
the people who once had welcomed him
     but now taunted him and required his death:
Have mercy on them and us.

Pilate's wife who begged her husband
  to be innocent of the blood of this righteous man;
Barabbas, the robber and murderer,
  whose condemnation was exchanged for Christ's;
Pontius Pilate, who delivered Jesus to be crucified,
  yet confessed him the Man and our King:
Have mercy on them and us.

Simon of Cyrene, a passerby,
  who was compelled to follow Jesus
  and bear his Cross;
the women of Jerusalem,
  bewailing and lamenting him,
  whom Jesus told to weep for themselves and their children;
the soldiers who nailed him to the Cross
  and whom Jesus prayed his Father to forgive:
Have mercy on them and us.

The crowd that scoffed at him
  as one who saved others
  but could not save himself;
the thieves crucified with him,
  the one who reviled him,
  the other who asked to be remembered in his Kingdom;
the unknown man
  who heard his cry of desolation
  and ran to quench his thirst:
Have mercy on them and us.

Mary, his mother,
  who stood by the Cross of her dying son,
  and was made the mother of the disciple whom he loved;
the centurion
  who watched when he gave up the spirit
  and proclaimed him the Son of God;
the women who had followed him and ministered to him
  and stood either near or afar, among them
Mary Magdalene, Mary the mother of James and Joseph, his mother's
  sister, Mary the wife of Cleopas, and Salome, the mother of James
  and John:
Have mercy on them and us.

Almighty and eternal God,
     by the Cross of your beloved Son
     joy has come into the world:
     grant that all who were with him when he suffered
     may share the victory he accomplished by his death.
Have mercy on them and us.

Silence

Eternal God,
     you have called people everywhere not to certainty
     but to trust in your faithfulness:
     give your grace to those who are tempted
     to deny the holy insecurity of faith,
     that they may take the risk of self-abandonment
     to him who abandoned himself on the Cross for us,
     even Jesus Christ our Lord. *Amen.*

Holy Father,
     whose only Son gave himself to us
     without limit and without reserve,
     and who fills us with the love
     by which to love others:
     enable us to give ourselves to our enemies and friends
     so that they may know the immeasurable love
     which is in Christ Jesus our Lord;
     who is alive and reigns with you and the Holy Spirit,
     one God, now and for ever. Amen.

RAYMOND HOCKLEY*

30. The Cross of Christ

Lord, when we pity ourselves and think we make great sacrifices for others:
Remind us of your life-giving sacrifice on the Cross.

Lord, when our patience wears thin and we are ready to give up:
Speak to us through the example of your endurance on the Cross.

Lord, when we get angry and wish to retaliate against our enemies:
Bring to our remembrance your words to your enemies from the Cross.

Lord, when we feel rejected or persecuted for doing what is right and good:
Sustain us by the knowledge of how you were reviled and rejected on the Cross.

Lord, when we suffer pain of body or anguish of mind in this life:
Keep us near the Cross.

Lord, when we are afraid to stand for that which is true and honorable:
Strengthen us with the courage with which you went to the Cross.

Lord, when we feel alone in the world, forsaken and forgotten:
Comfort us with your love made known on the Cross.

Lord, when we come to the time of our own death:
Uphold us with the assurance that life did not end for you on the Cross.

Lord, when we are tempted by despair or fear of what lies ahead:
Fill us with the hope of resurrection and new life which are the fruits of your Cross. Amen.

LARRY HARD

31. The Easter Victory

Let us pray, thanking God for the victory that Jesus, God's Son and our Brother, has won by his death and resurrection. It is for us that he has triumphed.

Silence

Christ died for all, in order that they who are alive may live no longer for themselves, but for him who died for them and rose again.
Thanks be to God who has given us the victory through our Lord Jesus Christ.

If then any are in Christ, they are a new creation; the former things have passed away: behold, they are made new.
Thanks be to God who has given us the victory through our Lord Jesus Christ.

For God, who commanded light to shine out of darkness, has shone in our hearts, to give enlightenment concerning the knowledge of the glory of God, shining on the face of Christ Jesus.
Thanks be to God who has given us the victory through our Lord Jesus Christ.

For you were once darkness, but now you are light in the Lord.
Thanks be to God who has given us the victory through our Lord Jesus Christ.

Walk, then, as children of light, for the fruit of the light is in all goodness and justice and truth, and test what is well pleasing to God.
Thanks be to God who has given us the victory through our Lord Jesus Christ.

For if we live, we live to the Lord, or if we die, we die to the Lord.
Whether we live or die, we are the Lord's.

You were buried together with Christ in Baptism, and in him also you rose again through faith in the working of God who raised him from the dead.
Whether we live or die, we are the Lord's.

"Death is swallowed up in victory! O death, where is thy victory? O death, where is thy sting?"
Thanks be to God who has given us the victory through our Lord Jesus Christ.
Amen.

SCRIPTURE SERVICES

32. A Litany for Pentecost

When the day of Pentecost had come, they were all together in one place and all of the many foreigners heard the witnesses speaking in their own tongue.
Come, Holy Spirit, witness to us also in our several languages.

Speak in the language of our need.
Let us hear how our deepest hungers, desires, and aspirations can be fulfilled by your goodness and in your service.
Come, Holy Spirit, give us that good news again.

Speak in the language of our fear.
Let us hear how our worries about the future, and about each other, and about ourselves, can find rest in your providential care.
Come, Holy Spirit, give us that encouraging news again.

Speak in the language of our guilt.
Let us hear how our confessed shame for wrong things done and for good things undone is covered by your forgiveness.
Come, Holy Spirit, give us that liberating news again.

Speak in the language of our gratitude.
Let us hear how our honest thanks relate us, not only to those with whom we live, but also to you, the Lord and Giver of life.
Come, Holy Spirit, give us that enlarging news again.

Speak to us in the language of our joy.
Let us hear how our gladness and our delight not only brighten this world, but honor you who made the world.
Come, Holy Spirit, give us that enlivening news again.

Speak to us in the language of our hope.
Let us hear how our yearning and our expectations are not just wishful thinking, but responses to your promise.
Come, Holy Spirit, give us that good news again.

For all your Spirit's illuminations,
and all your Spirit's quickening powers,
we praise you, Father, on this Pentecost,
in the name of your Son. Amen.

MODELS FOR MINISTERS I*

33. Litany of the Holy Spirit

O Holy Spirit, who at the beginning moved upon the face of the waters:
Have mercy upon us.

O Holy Spirit, by whose inspiration holy men and women spoke of old as they were moved:
Have mercy upon us.

O Holy Spirit, power of the highest, who overshadowed Mary:
Have mercy upon us.

O Holy Spirit, through whom the holy Child Jesus grew strong in faith, and was filled with wisdom:
Have mercy upon us.

O Holy Spirit, who descended like a dove, and alighted upon Christ our Lord at his baptism:
Have mercy upon us.

O Holy Spirit, by whom Jesus was led up into the wilderness to be tempted of the devil:
Have mercy upon us.

O Holy Spirit, through whom Christ offered himself without spot to God:
Have mercy upon us.

O Holy Spirit, who on the Day of Pentecost descended upon the apostles in the likeness of fiery tongues:
Have mercy upon us.

O Holy Spirit, by whom we have been brought out of darkness and error into the clear light and true knowledge of God, and of his Son Jesus Christ:
Have mercy upon us.

O Holy Spirit, by whom the whole body of the Church is governed and sanctified:
Have mercy upon us.

O Holy Spirit, by whom we were born to new life in Baptism:
Have mercy upon us.

O Holy Spirit, interceding for us with groanings that cannot be uttered:
Have mercy upon us.

O Holy Spirit, by whom the love of God is shed abroad in our hearts:
Have mercy upon us.

By your life-giving power and might:
Deliver us, O Holy Spirit.

By your all-powerful intercession:
Deliver us, O Holy Spirit.

By your continual abiding in the Church:
Deliver us, O Holy Spirit.

We beseech you to hear us, O Holy Spirit, that it may please you to guide
your holy Church universal into all truth, and to fill it with your love:
Hear us, O Holy Spirit.

That we may strive to keep the unity of the Spirit in the bond of peace:
Hear us, O Holy Spirit.

That, as we live in the Spirit, we may also walk in the Spirit:
Hear us, O Holy Spirit.

That we may grow in grace, and in the knowledge of our Lord and Savior
Jesus Christ:
Hear us, O Holy Spirit.

That with sincerity of purpose we may seek in all things God's greater glory:
Hear us, O Holy Spirit.

That, in all our thoughts, words, and works, we may be conformed more
and more to the life and passion of the Lord Jesus:
Hear us, O Holy Spirit.

That we may be filled with your sevenfold gift: the spirit of wisdom and
understanding, the spirit of counsel and inner strength, the spirit of
knowledge and true godliness, and the spirit of your most holy fear:
Hear us, O Holy Spirit.

That we may ever be mindful of that solemn account, which, for ourselves
and others, we must one day give at the judgment-seat of Christ:
Hear us, O Holy Spirit.

That we may have grace to persevere unto the end:
Hear us, O Holy Spirit.

Holy Spirit:
We beseech you to hear us.

Lord and Giver of life:
We beseech you to hear us.

Lord, have mercy upon us.
Christ, have mercy upon us.
Lord, have mercy upon us.

Let us pray.

O God, who *(on this day)* taught the hearts of your faithful people by sending to them the light of your Holy Spirit: Grant us by the same Spirit to have a right judgment in all things, and evermore to rejoice in his holy comfort; through Jesus Christ your Son our Lord, who lives and reigns with you, in the unity of the Holy Spirit, one God, for ever and ever. *Amen.*

Almighty God, to you all hearts are open, all desires known, and from you no secrets are hid: Cleanse the thoughts of our hearts by the inspiration of your Holy Spirit, that we may perfectly love you, and worthily magnify your holy Name; through Christ our Lord. *Amen.*

Almighty and everlasting God, by whose Spirit the whole body of your faithful people is governed and sanctified: Receive our supplications and prayers, which we offer before you for all members of your holy Church, that in their vocation and ministry they may truly and devoutly serve you; through our Lord and Savior Jesus Christ, who lives and reigns with you, in the unity of the Holy Spirit, one God, now and for ever. *Amen.*

THE CUDDESDON COLLEGE OFFICE BOOK
AND THE BOOK OF COMMON PRAYER 1979

34. A Litany for Sunday

Jesus, who on this day of the week rose from the dead:
Have mercy on us.

Jesus, who on this same day put on life immortal:
Have mercy on us.

Jesus, who on this same day appeared to Mary Magdalene and to the
   apostles:
Have mercy on us.

Jesus, who on this same day opened the eyes of the two disciples going to
   Emmaus:
Have mercy on us.

Jesus, who on this same day comforted your apostles and gave them peace:
Have mercy on us.

Jesus, who on this same day confirmed your apostles in the faith of the
   Resurrection by showing them your hands and your feet:
Have mercy on us.

Jesus, who on this same day breathed on the apostles and gave them the
   Holy Spirit:
Have mercy on us.

Jesus, who on this same day opened their understanding to know the
   Scriptures:
Have mercy on us.

Jesus, who on this same day gave them power to remit sins:
Have mercy on us.

Jesus, who on this same day sent the apostles on their mission, and
   commanded them to go and teach all nations:
Have mercy on us.

Jesus, who on a Sunday condescended to the weakness of St. Thomas, and
   by the evidence of your sacred wounds healed his unbelief:
Have mercy on us.

Jesus, who on a Sunday sent down the Holy Spirit on the apostles, and thus
    prepared them for laying the foundation of your Church:
Have mercy on us.

Jesus, who on a Sunday moved your apostle Peter to preach the first
    Christian sermon to his fellow Jews:
Have mercy on us.

Jesus, who on this Sunday is present among us now in Word and Sacrament
    to heal and forgive and empower:
Have mercy on us.

Jesus, who on this Sunday gives us a vision of heaven and a foretaste of
    everlasting life:
Have mercy on us, now and always. Amen.

KYRIE ELEISON

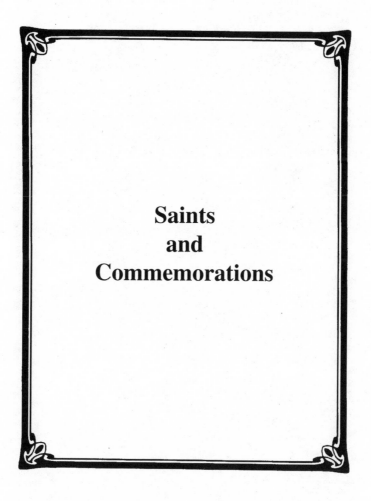

Saints
and
Commemorations

35. Litany of the Saints

God the Father in heaven: *Have mercy on us.*
God the Son, Redeemer of the world: *Have mercy on us.*
God the Holy Spirit: *Have mercy on us.*
Holy Trinity, one God: *Have mercy on us.*

After each of the following, the response is "Pray for us."

> Mary and Joseph: *Pray for us.*
> Peter and Paul:
> Thomas and Andrew:
> James and John:
> Matthew, Mark and Luke:
> Mary and Martha and Mary Magdalene:
> Barnabas and Timothy:
>
> Stephen, the first of the martyrs: *Pray for us.*
> Polycarp and Ignatius:
> Justin and Hippolytus:
> Agnes, Perpetua and Felicity:
> Lawrence and Cyprian:
> Thomas Becket and Thomas More:
> Jan Hus and William Tyndale:
> Dietrich Bonhoeffer and Martin Luther King:
> Camillo Torres and Janani Luwum:
>
> Ambrose and Jerome: *Pray for us.*
> Leo and Gregory:
> Athanasius and Augustine of Hippo:
> Basil of Caesarea and John Chrysostom:
> Martin of Tours and Nicholas of Myra:
> Catherine, Monica and Elizabeth of Hungary:
> Columba and David:
> Patrick and Brigid:
> Cyril and Methodius:
> Augustine of Canterbury and Boniface:
> Ignatius Loyola and Francis Xavier:
> John Carroll and Samuel Seabury:
> Thomas Coke and Francis Asbury:
> Roger Williams and Alexander Campbell:
> William Carey and Adoniram Judson:
> David Livingstone and Albert Schweitzer:

Antony, Benedict and Scholastica: *Pray for us.*
Francis, Clare and Dominic:
Bernard of Clairvaux and Thomas Aquinas:
Theresa of Avila and John of the Cross:
Martin de Porres and Jean-Baptiste Vianney:
Martin Luther and John Calvin:
Cranmer, Latimer and Ridley:
George Fox and John Bunyan:
John and Charles Wesley:
George Whitefield and Jonathan Edwards:
Nathan Söderblom and John XXIII:

Dürer, Michelangelo and Palestrina: *Pray for us.*
John Donne and George Herbert:
Isaac Watts and T.S. Eliot:
Philip Nicolai and Paul Gerhardt:
Catherine Winkworth and John Mason Neale:
Bach, Schütz and Handel:
Florence Nightingale and Elizabeth Seton:
Dag Hammarskjöld and C.S. Lewis:
All holy men and women:
All our brothers and sisters who now rest in the Lord:

We remember with thanksgiving and praise, O Lord, all of your faithful
servants who throughout the long centuries have witnessed to your Name: the
mighty and the lowly, great leaders and humble men and women, those who
have served you amid prosperity and those who in the day of trouble have
not failed, those in foreign places and those in this land.
Father of us all,
make us ever aware of the presence of this great company.
Grant that we may find,
in the reality of your nearness,
the nearness of those countless other servants
who are separated from us by years and distance.
As we join our worship and labor to theirs,
may we know ourselves to be part of that great cloud of witnesses.
And so may all your people be united in faith,
that your Church may live to serve and praise you
in the one unbroken fellowship of your love,
through our Lord and Savior, Jesus Christ. Amen.

ADAPTED BY JEFFERY W. ROWTHORN*

36. Invocation of the Saints

This may be led by two voices.

1:       Bridegroom of poverty, our brother Francis, follower of Jesus and
friend of creation:
Stand here beside us.

2:       Apostle of nonviolence, Gandhi the Mahatma, reproach to the churches:
Stand here beside us.

1:       John XXIII, Pope and friend of the poor, who longed for the unity of
all people:
Stand here beside us.

2:       Peacemakers in the world, Dag Hammarskjöld and Desmond Tutu,
called children of God:
Stand here beside us.

1:       Mask of the Christ, Gautama the Buddha, and Mother Teresa,
fountains of compassion:
Stand here beside us.

2:       Harriet Tubman and Frederick Douglass, and all fighters for freedom:
Stand here beside us.

1:       Madman in America, Johnny Appleseed, planter of Eden:
Stand here beside us.

2:       Visionary and apostle, John of Patmos, resisting the Beast:
Stand here beside us.

1:       Visionaries and poets, Caedmon, Dante, William Blake, John
Bunyan and Isaac Watts, pilgrims of the inner light:
Stand here beside us.

2:       Faithful harlot, Mary Magdalene, first witness of the new life:
Stand here beside us.

1:       Johann Sebastian Bach, Wolfgang Amadeus Mozart, Ludwig van
Beethoven, and all who speak the soul's language:
Stand here beside us.

2:       Students of the earth, Charles Darwin, Pierre Teilhard de Chardin
and Margaret Mead, voyagers in the past and in the future:

Stand here beside us.

1:     Children of the synagogue, Albert Einstein, Karl Marx, and Sigmund Freud, divers in the sea of humanity:
Stand here beside us.

2:     Witnesses in England, John and Charles Wesley, street ministers:
Stand here beside us.

1:     Reformers and leaders of protest, Amos of Tekoa, Paul of Tarsus, Jan Hus, Martin Luther, and all your companions:
Stand here beside us.

2:     Menno Simons and George Fox, explorers in the Gospel:
Stand here beside us.

1:     Confessors in chains, Dietrich Bonhoeffer and the Berrigan brothers, war resisters:
Stand here beside us.

2:     Confessor in Africa, Augustine of Hippo, city-planner for God's people:
Stand here beside us.

1:     Confessor in Russia, Boris Pasternak, poet of reconciliation:
Stand here beside us.

2:     Confessors in America, Henry David Thoreau, Robert Frost and Thomas Merton, hermits and free thinkers:
Stand here beside us.

1:     Innocents of Guernica, Sharpeville, and Birmingham, and all victims of lynching, in your undeserved deaths:
Stand here beside us.

2:     Innocents of Coventry, Dresden, Tokyo, and all victims of bombing, caught up in a sea of fire:
Stand here beside us.

1:     Innocents of Hiroshima and Nagasaki, pierced by needles of flame:
Stand here beside us.

2:     Innocents of Auschwitz, Dachau, and all concentration camps, in your despair and dying:
Stand here beside us.

1:     Innocents of Biafra and Armenia, objects of genocide:
Stand here beside us.

2:     Innocents of Wounded Knee and Mylai, God's wheat ground in the mill of war:
Stand here beside us.

1:     Martyrs of Africa: Perpetua, mother; Felicity, slave; and all your companions:
Stand here beside us.

2:     Martyrs and confessors, Polycarp, Ignatius, and Justin, who refused to offer incense to Caesar:
Stand here beside us.

1:     Martyr in England, Thomas Cranmer, and all who died to renew the Church:
Stand here beside us.

2:     Martyr in Columbia, Camillo Torres, priest and revolutionary:
Stand here beside us.

1:     Martyrs of Kent State, witnesses to the hopes of the young:
Stand here beside us.

2:     Martyr for America, Martin Luther King, organizer for peace and justice:
Stand here beside us.

1:     Unwed mother, blessed Mary, fair wellspring of our liberation:
Stand here beside us.

2:     Our leader and Lord, Jesus the Son of God, bright cornerstone of our unity in a new Spirit:
Stand here beside us.

1:     Almighty God, you have surrounded us with a great cloud of witnesses: Grant that we, encouraged by the good example of these your servants, may persevere in running the race that is set before us, until at last, with all your saints, we attain to your eternal joy; through Jesus Christ, the pioneer and perfecter of our faith, who lives and reigns with you and the Holy Spirit, one God, for ever and ever. *Amen.*

THE COVENANT OF PEACE
-A LIBERATION PRAYER BOOK*

37. A Great Cloud of Witnesses

We give thanks to you, O Lord our God, for all your servants and witnesses of time past.

For Abraham, the father of believers, and Sarah his wife:
We give you thanks, O Lord.

For Moses, the lawgiver, and Aaron, the priest:
We give you thanks, O Lord.

For Miriam and Joshua, Deborah and Gideon:
We give you thanks, O Lord.

For Samuel with Hannah his mother:
We give you thanks, O Lord.

For Isaiah and all the prophets:
We give you thanks, O Lord.

For Mary, the mother of our Lord:
We give you thanks, O Lord.

For Peter and Paul and all the apostles:
We give you thanks, O Lord.

For Mary and Martha, and Mary Magdalene:
We give you thanks, O Lord.

For Stephen, the first martyr:
We give you thanks, O Lord.

For all the martyrs and saints in every age and in every land:
We give you thanks, O Lord.

In your mercy, O Lord our God, give us, as you gave to them, the hope of salvation and the promise of eternal life; through Jesus Christ our Lord, the first-born of many from the dead. *Amen.*

THE BOOK OF COMMON PRAYER 1979

38. Reformation Sunday

Let us celebrate the lives and legacy of our spiritual forebears, the Protestant Reformers.
They lived and died long ago, but are alive with God and in the Church.

We thank you, Lord, for the forerunners: for Peter Waldo, John Wycliffe, and John Hus.
They fought lonely fights and died lonely deaths, but their sacrifice was not in vain.

We thank you for your servant Martin Luther:
For his experience of your grace, his love of music and family, his glorious stubbornness.

We thank you for your servant John Calvin:
For his giant intellect, his pastoral faithfulness, his insistence upon the social dimension of the Gospel.

We thank you for your servant John Knox:
For his rough-hewn courage, his tireless striving, his eventual success in bringing an entire nation under the sway of your Word.

We thank you for your servant Thomas Cranmer:
For his way with words, his legacy of common prayer, and his gift to us of worship in our mother tongue.

We reaffirm, O Lord, the Reformers' commitment to the supremacy of the Scriptures.
Help us to spend more time in the study of your Word.

We reaffirm their commitment to the weekly celebration of the Lord's Supper.
Help us to gather with regularity around your Table.

We reaffirm their commitment to one, and only one, Mediator between you and us.
Help us to engage in prayer to you more frequently and more honestly.

We reaffirm the Reformers' commitment to justification by faith.
Help us to find new ways to serve you in our relations with others.

We reaffirm their commitment to liberty of conscience.
Help us to be more responsible in using our civil and religious freedoms.

We pray, Lord, that we may be positive Protestants:
Not just protesting against wrongs, but witnessing for the Good News of your love.

We pray that ancient grudges may be buried and forgotten:
And that, in this new day, we may unite with all our fellow-Christians in common, ongoing reformation.

This is our deepest plea, Lord:
That the reforming of your Church may continue, beginning with us, with each of us, with all of us. Amen.

MODELS FOR MINISTERS I*

39. A New Year's Litany †

O God, who inhabits eternity, whose name is holy, with hushed spirits in the quiet of thy sanctuary we wait the closing moment of another year.
We lift up our hearts to thee, O Lord.

From the failures of the past, from broken hopes and disappointed ambitions, from our sins against ourselves and against others, and from the transiency and vicissitude of our lives:
We lift up our hearts to thee, O Lord.

We confess the unworthy living that has stained the record of the year that now is dying. For pardon, for grace to make restitution, for a clean heart and a right spirit with which to enter the new year:
We lift up our hearts to thee, O Lord.

Grant us honesty to face ourselves before we confront another year. Save us from self-deceit, mean excuses, unworthy evasions, and prepare us with inner integrity and spiritual resource, that we may be adequate for all that lies before us.
Lord, have mercy upon us and grant us this blessing.

From loss of faith and hope and courage, from anxiety that harasses us, fear that affrights us, cowardice that defeats us, and from the loss of thy companionship, without which no life is good, no soul is strong:
Good Lord, deliver us.

From cherishing ill will in a world that perishes for want of good will, from selfishness in a world whose need of generosity and magnanimity is deep and desperate, from so living that Christ shall be crucified again and the Kingdom of God delay its coming:
Good Lord, deliver us.

Confirm now in each of us some worthy decision. Bring us to the new year's beginning with such vision of our duty, such resolution to perform it, and such resources for its consummation that, whether in the year ahead we live or fall asleep, we shall be neither dishonored nor ashamed before thee.
Lord, have mercy upon us and grant us this blessing. Amen.

HARRY EMERSON FOSDICK

Dedications
and
Anniversaries

40. In Thanksgiving for a Church

This Litany may also be used on the anniversary of the dedication or consecration of a church, or on other suitable occasions.

Let us thank God whom we worship here in the beauty of holiness.

Eternal God, the heaven of heavens cannot contain you, much less the walls of temples made with hands. Graciously receive our thanks for this place, and accept the work of our hands, offered to your honor and glory.

For the Church universal, of which these visible buildings are the symbol:
We thank you, Lord.

For your presence whenever two or three have gathered together in your Name:
We thank you, Lord.

For this place where we may be still and know that you are God:
We thank you, Lord.

For making us your children by adoption and grace, and refreshing us day by day with the bread of life:
We thank you, Lord.

For the knowledge of your will and the grace to perform it:
We thank you, Lord.

For the fulfilling of our desires and petitions as you see best for us:
We thank you, Lord.

For the pardon of our sins, which restores us to the company of your faithful people:
We thank you, Lord.

For the blessing of our vows and the crowning of our years with your goodness:
We thank you, Lord.

For the faith of those who have gone before us and for our encouragement by their perseverance:
We thank you, Lord.

For the fellowship of [_____, our patron, and of] all your saints:
We thank you, Lord.

Silence.
The Litany concludes with the following Doxology.

Yours, O Lord, is the greatness, the power, the glory, the victory, and the majesty:
For everything in heaven and on earth is yours.
Yours, O Lord, is the kingdom:
And you are exalted as head over all. Amen.

THE BOOK OF COMMON PRAYER 1979

41. On the Anniversary of a Church

For those whose faith, courage, and Christian conviction and whose
diligent effort and financial sacrifice resulted in the building of this house
of worship:
We thank you, O God.

For those who labored with mind and hand to design and construct this
sanctuary that Christian people might worship the Lord in the beauty of
holiness:
We thank you, O God.

For all those servants of God who have led your people in worship here,
who have preached your word from this pulpit, and who have administered
the sacraments to waiting and believing hearts:
We thank you, O God.

For all those who have come to this place seeking you, and who, in
worshiping you in spirit and in truth, have found you:
We thank you, O God.

For those who have brought their children here for Christian baptism, for
those who have pledged their love to one another at this holy altar, and for
those who in Christian faith and trust have here parted with loved ones and
committed them to your love and care:
We thank you, O God.

For all those who have here confessed their faith in Jesus Christ, have
shared in the life and witness of the Church, and committed themselves to
the Christian life:
We thank you, O God.

For sins that have been confessed and forgiven here, for burdens that have
been made easier to carry, for distressed and troubled hearts that have
known the peace that passes all understanding, and for lives that have been
inspired to new heights of love and of service:
We thank you, O God.

*For all your goodness and love revealed to us in this house of worship, we
praise you and we thank you, O God. Amen.*

ERNEST O. GEIGIS
-WORSHIP SERVICES FOR SPECIAL OCCASIONS

42. The Dedication of a New Church

The Leaders of the Congregation say:

We present this building to be dedicated to the glory of God and the service of humanity.

The Minister asks:

By what name shall this church henceforth be known?

Answer:

It shall be called _____.

The Minister says:

Beloved in the Lord, we rejoice that God put it into the hearts of his people to build this house to the glory of his name. Let us now dedicate it and set it apart for the worship of Almighty God and the service of all his people.

To the glory of God the Father, who has called us by his grace:
We dedicate this house.

To the honor of his Son, who loved us and gave himself for us:
We dedicate this house.

To the praise of the Holy Spirit, who illumines and sanctifies us:
We dedicate this house.

For the worship of God in prayer and praise,
For the preaching of the everlasting Gospel,
For the celebration of the holy Sacraments:
We dedicate this house.

For comfort to all who mourn,
For strength to those who are tempted,
For light to those who seek the way:
We dedicate this house.

For the hallowing of family life,
For the teaching and guiding of the young,
For the perfecting of the saints:
We dedicate this house.

For the conversion of sinners,
For the promotion of righteousness,
For the extension of the Kingdom of God:
We dedicate this house.

In the unity of the faith,
In the bond of Christian fellowship,
In charity and good will to all:
We dedicate this house.

In gratitude for the labors of all who love and serve this church,
In loving remembrance of those who have finished their course,
In the hope of everlasting life through Jesus Christ, our Lord:
We dedicate this house.

We, the people of this church,
being compassed about with so great a cloud of witnesses,
grateful for our heritage,
sensible of the sacrifice of our forebears in the faith,
and confessing that apart from us their work cannot be made perfect,
now dedicate ourselves anew to the worship and service of Almighty God;
through Jesus Christ our Lord. Amen.

Minister:

Accept, O God our Father, this service at our hands, and bless it to the end that this congregation of faithful people may show forth in their lives your love and your truth; and grant that this house may be the place where your honor dwells and the whole earth be filled with your glory;
through Jesus Christ our Lord. *Amen.*

EARL S. WALKER
-WORSHIP SERVICES FOR SPECIAL OCCASIONS

43. The Dedication of a Bible

In honor of God our Heavenly Father who created us and gave us the priceless gift of speech:
We dedicate this Bible.

In praise of Jesus Christ, the Incarnate Word, who spoke with matchless power and grace:
We dedicate this Bible.

In remembrance of the Holy Spirit, who speaks to the hidden things in our hearts:
We dedicate this Bible.

In celebration of all those who were inspired to write and to translate the sacred scriptures:
We dedicate this Bible.

So that we may continue to hear the story of God's love and Christ's redemptive sacrifice:
We dedicate this Bible.

So that our children may come to know the life of Christ and understand his message:
We dedicate this Bible.

So that our young people may receive direction, comfort, and counsel from the treasure-store of our faith:
We dedicate this Bible.

So that we may all have the comforting assurance of pardon and forgiveness, and be encouraged to walk in newness of life:
We dedicate this Bible.

To the glory of God, the enlightening of this congregation, and the strengthening of the ties which bind us to people everywhere, this Bible is now dedicated. May humble tongues proclaim its undying truths and receptive hearts receive the message it imparts. *Amen.*

Almighty God, you have spoken to us through your Holy Word; we thank you for this Bible and ask you to bless and sanctify its use.
May all who read from it in the appointed services of our church, and all who hear it, receive the fullest blessing of your love.

May its eternal message serve as a lamp to our feet as we travel through darkened places.
May its inspiration lift us when we feel discouraged and downtrodden.
May it illumine our lives with the light of the life of our Lord Jesus Christ.
In his Name we pray. Amen.

WILLIAM T. GRIFFITHS
-WORSHIP SERVICES FOR SPECIAL OCCASIONS

44. The Dedication of a New Organ

Men:	Alleluia! Praise God in his holy temple;
Women:	Praise God in the firmament of his power.
Men:	Praise God for his mighty acts;
Women:	Praise God for his excellent greatness.
Men:	Praise God with the blast of the ram's horn;
Women:	Praise God with lyre and harp.
Men:	Praise God with timbrel and dance;
Women:	Praise God with strings and pipe.
Men:	Praise God with resounding cymbals;
Women:	Praise God with loud-clanging cymbals.
All:	*Let everything that has breath praise the Lord. Alleluia!*

The Leader continues

To the honor and glory of God, author of all beauty and goodness, giver of all talents and appreciation for music:
We dedicate this organ.

With faith in Jesus Christ, that he will continue to inspire men and women to offer God their best in music and song:
We dedicate this organ.

Moved by the Holy Spirit, who gives life to our worship and service of God, and guides us in the understanding of truth and beauty:
We dedicate this organ.

To aid in the healing of discord, in the uplifting of the depressed, and in the comforting of the sorrowful:
We dedicate this organ.

To support the singing of psalms and hymns and spiritual songs in such ways that men and women may go forth from this house of God joyfully renewed and determined to do God's holy will:
We dedicate this organ.

Holy and eternal God, Father, Son, and Holy Ghost, to whom all the joyful companies of heaven give adoration and glory: Graciously grant that this organ may minister to the excellency of praise in your holy temple; and so bless us as we magnify you upon earth with music and the voice of melody, that hereafter we may sing the new song in the heavenly city, where you reign, almighty, all-glorious, world without end. *Amen.*

A hymn of praise, accompanied on the organ, is now sung by all.

ADAPTED BY JEFFERY W. ROWTHORN

45. The Dedication of New Hymnals

The congregation holds the old hymnal in their hands as they make their response.

For all people of wisdom and understanding, of vision and poetry, who have given us memorable words wherein our hearts may rejoice and our minds be lifted up to thee:
We thank thee, O Lord.

For peal of organ and lilt of song, and for consecrated men and women who through the ages have brought forth melodies that have made our hearts rejoice and our souls stir within us:
We thank thee, O Lord.

For printers and engravers, binders and publishers, through whose labors we share in the inspiration of others:
We thank thee, O Lord.

For builders of organs and those who create music to make worship our delight:
We thank thee, O Lord.

That thou didst endow thy children with gifts of music and song; for noble themes and glorious voices:
We thank thee, O Lord.

For hearts and minds that thrill to praise thee; for moments that are precious, when, for an instant, thou reveatest thyself in the span of a tune; for spirits awakened and deep calling unto deep; for the sound of thy still small voice calling us to follow thee:
We thank thee, O Lord.

O Lord, how manifold are thy works. In wisdom hast thou made them all; the whole earth is full of thy riches. *Amen.*

Hymn: A hymn is now sung, which is to be found only in the hymnal which is being replaced.

We are mindful, O Lord, of the blessings these books have brought to those who through the years have sought thee in this house of prayer. We thank thee for dead hearts quickened, for courage renewed, for comfort found, for sin redeemed and grace bestowed through thy truth declared in these hymns. Through them we have entered into the labors of others and have been inspired to set forth thy love not only with our lips but in our lives, by giving up ourselves to thy service all the days of our lives. *Amen.*

Organ Voluntary: During this voluntary the copies of the hymnal to be replaced are collected, and copies of the new hymnal are distributed throughout the congregation.

The congregation, holding the new hymnal in their hands, stresses the word in bold face type in each indicated response.

We come together as thy Church, our Father, to worship thee and to sing thy praise. We dedicate these hymnals that by their use our worship may be enriched through the glory of song:
O God, **we** *dedicate these hymnals.*

These are no ordinary books, our Father. Within these pages are living words of trust and assurance, commitment and faith. These hymnals are a part of thy living Church; they are the vessels of thy love. We cannot use them except as they are truly placed before thee and consecrated in thy service:
O God, we **dedicate** *these hymnals.*

We have chosen these particular hymnals, our Father, because they remind us of our heritage of faith, the traditions of the Church of which we are a part, and open up for us new avenues of meaning and understanding in our continuing search for thy truth:
O God, we dedicate **these** *hymnals.*

In the months and years to come, our Father, we will again and again open these pages. These books will serve as a means of grace in our corporate worship together as the Church of Jesus Christ. May their special ministry be to lift our voices in song and bind our hearts in Christian love:
O God, we dedicate these **hymnals.**

O God, we dedicate these hymnals this day and rededicate ourselves to the following of thy way for all humanity as we have come to know it in Jesus Christ. May we truly persevere in that way in our lives and may the words of our mouths and the meditations of our hearts be ever acceptable in thy sight, O Lord, our strength and our redeemer. *Amen.*

Hymn: A hymn, chosen from the newly dedicated hymnal, is now sung.

WORSHIP SERVICES FOR SPECIAL OCCASIONS

46. The Dedication of a Carillon of Bells

By the generosity of _____ these new bells have been provided to assist us in our worship of God, and to invite all who hear them to come and worship with us. It is right that we should now dedicate these bells and set them apart to the holy use for which they are designed.

To the glory of God, Author of all beauty and goodness, Giver of all skill of mind and hand:
We dedicate these bells.

In faith in our Lord Jesus Christ, who has inspired each generation to offer in his presence the best of music:
We dedicate these bells.

Moved by the Holy Spirit, our Guide in the worship of God, our Inspiration in praise, our Helper in the understanding of truth and beauty, love and service:
We dedicate these bells.

To kindle the flame of devotion and to call by their ringing voices all who hear, to worship the Father in spirit and in truth:
We dedicate these bells.

To ring in joyous affirmation when before the altar of this church a man and woman stand to pledge to each other their lifelong affection and to establish a new home where God may be glorified and his name honored:
We dedicate these bells.

To comfort the sorrowful, to cheer the faint-hearted, to bring peace and love to human hearts, and to lead all who hear in the way of eternal life:
We dedicate these bells.

To the glory of God *(and in loving memory of _____).*
We dedicate these bells.

O God, our Father, most holy and most high, to whom we have access by the one Spirit through our Lord Jesus Christ, we give you praise and honor and worship. We thank you that you have so made us that music can lift our hearts and minds to you. Grant that we and all who will hear the music of these bells may be moved to love you more, serve you better, worship, praise and pray to you more regularly, led and inspired by your Holy Spirit. This we ask in the Name of our Lord Jesus Christ. *Amen.*

Blessing and glory,
wisdom and thanksgiving,
honor and power and might
be to our God
for ever and ever Amen.

(The newly dedicated bells are now rung.)

GRANVILLE T. WALKER
-WORSHIP SERVICES FOR SPECIAL OCCASIONS

47. The Dedication of Annual Pledges

> *We give thee but thine own*
> *whate'er the gift may be;*
> *all that we have is thine alone,*
> *a trust, O Lord, from thee.*

As you have chosen us, O God, and enriched our lives:
We offer you ourselves, our time and talents and income.

For the ministry of the Christian Gospel, the inspiration of sacred music, and the singing of hymns from every age:
We offer you ourselves, our time and talents and income.

For the Christian education of children, for the guidance of youth, and for the spiritual well-being of adults:
We offer you ourselves, our time and talents and income.

For the Christian character of our city, and for a spirit of tolerance and good will:
We offer you ourselves, our time and talents and income.

For the calling of the world to Christ, and for the economic and spiritual elevation of untold millions:
We offer you ourselves, our time and talents and income.

For the sake of that day when the spirit of Christ shall clothe itself in the hearts of our age, and swords shall be beaten into plowshares, and peace shall embrace the world:
We offer you ourselves, our time and talents and income.

Let us pray.

Silence

Almighty and everlasting God, you have given us new life in Christ, and Christian homes, and a Christian land: accept the gifts which symbolize the giving of our lives to you. Transform the money we give into programs which enlarge our vision and strengthen your Church. In Jesus' name we pray. *Amen.*

Leader and People

> *We give thee but thine own*
> > *whate'er the gift may be;*
> *all that we have is thine alone,*
> > *a trust, O Lord, from thee. Amen.*

CHARLES F. JACOBS
-WORSHIP SERVICES FOR SPECIAL OCCASIONS

PRAYER
AND
THE CHURCH

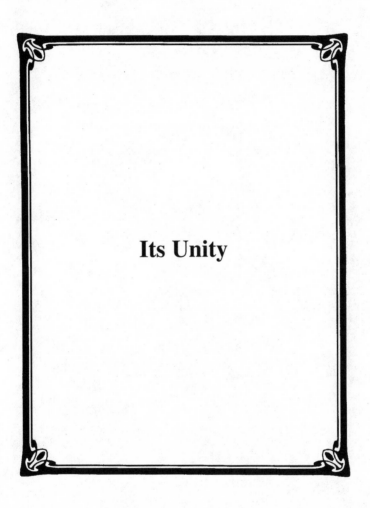

Its Unity

48. The Week of Prayer for Christian Unity †

We have come together in the presence of Almighty God to pray for the recovery of the unity of Christ's Church, and for the renewal of our common life in Jesus Christ in whom we are all made one.

Silence

Let us give heed to the words of Holy Scripture which set forth God's will and purpose for the unity of his Church.

"Hear, O Israel, the Lord our God is one Lord; and you shall love the Lord your God with all your heart, and with all your soul, and with all your mind."
Lord, write your word in our hearts:
That we may know and do your will.

"There is one body, and one Spirit, as there is also one hope held out in God's call to you; one Lord, one faith, one baptism; one God and Father of all, who is over all and through all and in all."
Lord, write your word in our hearts:
That we may know and do your will.

"For Christ is like a single body with its many limbs and organs which, many as they are, together make up one body. For indeed we were all brought into one body by baptism, in the one Spirit, whether we are Jews or Greeks, whether slaves or free, and that one Holy Spirit was poured out for all of us to drink."
Lord, write your word in our hearts:
That we may know and do your will.

"But it is not for these alone that I pray, but for those also who through their words put their faith in me; may they all be one; as you, Father, are in me, and I in you, so also may they be in us, that the world may believe that you have sent me."
Lord, write your word in our hearts:
That we may know and do your will. Amen.

PRAYERS FOR TODAY'S CHURCH*

49. Growing Together in Christ †

Let us thank God that, because we are all made in his image, it is possible for all to be united. Let us thank God for the special unity which those who are new creatures in Christ Jesus can enjoy. Let us ask God to forgive the sin that has destroyed the unity he intended for humanity.
Lord of mercy:
Hear our prayer.

Let us thank God for the growth of understanding between Christians of different outlooks and traditions. Let us thank God for the growth in unity of our local churches. Let us pray that we may grow together in truth and love.
Lord of mercy:
Hear our prayer.

Let us pray that we may learn from Christians of other traditions. Let us pray that they may learn from us. May they and we remember that Jesus prayed for us to be sanctified in truth before he prayed for us to be one. May God so guide us that we might seek unity through the truth.
Lord of mercy:
Hear our prayer.

Let us pray for our own church, that we and all its members may be filled with the spirit of faith, hope and love, and so attain to that unity which will lead people to acknowledge the truth of the Gospel.
Lord of mercy:
Hear our prayer.

Let us pray for the local community of which we are a part. Let us pray for greater unity between its various sections, interests and age-groups.
Lord of mercy:
Hear our prayer.

Let us pray for the unity of our country, for a greater understanding and sympathy between the young and those who are older, between employers and those they employ, between migrant workers and their host communities, and between the Church and those who have rejected institutional Christianity.
Lord of mercy:
Hear our prayer.

Finally let us pray for the unity of the world, for reconciliation, peace and compassion between rich and poor, white and non-white, capitalist and communist, and those nations which have long been embattled one against the other.
Lord of mercy:
Hear our prayer.

Silence

Lord Jesus Christ, you said to your apostles,
"Peace I give to you;
my own peace I leave with you":
Regard not our sins, but the faith of your Church,
and give to us the peace and unity of that heavenly City,
where with the Father and the Holy Spirit you live and reign,
now and for ever. Amen.

PRAYERS FOR TODAY'S CHURCH
AND THE BOOK OF COMMON PRAYER 1979

50. The Ecumenical Church

God has so adjusted the body, that there may be no discord in the body, but that the members may have the same care for one another. If one member suffers, all suffer together; if one member is honored, all rejoice together.

Now you are the body of Christ and individually members of it. Therefore let us pray:

For the whole Church of Christ, scattered abroad on six continents, and bearing many names, that it may no longer be torn asunder, divided in itself, or weak, but may become a glorious Church, without spot or blemish, fulfilling your perfect will:
Your will be done in your Church, we pray, O Lord.

For the churches that are passing through times of suffering and persecution, that their faith and courage may not fail nor their love grow cold:
Save them and us, we pray, O Lord.

For the churches that are strong in faith, that they may abound in grace and in knowledge and love of you:
Use them and us, we pray, O Lord.

For all weak and struggling churches, that they may persevere and be strong, overcoming those forces which hinder their growth or threaten their existence:
Sustain them and us, we pray, O Lord.

For the newer churches of Asia, Africa, and the islands of the sea, that they may grow into the full stature of the completeness of Christ, bringing new treasures into the Church of the ages:
Direct their steps and ours, we pray, O Lord.

For the older churches of the East and the West, that they may increase in wisdom and humility, and find new ways to make the message of the gospel understood in the world of today:
Renew them and us, we pray, O Lord.

For our fellowship as Christians, that we may hold fast to the truth, be delivered from all error, and walk with one another in the way of love and unity:
Teach us and guide us, we pray, O Lord.

For the ecumenical councils of churches, that through them Christians may more quickly overcome their reluctance to cooperate with one another, transcend their differences, and be knit together in a fellowship of understanding and love:
Draw all churches nearer to one another, we pray, O Lord.

Silence

O sovereign and almighty God,
bless all people and all your flock.
Give your peace and your love
to us your servants
that we may be united in the bond of peace,
in one body and one spirit,
in one hope of our calling,
in your divine and boundless love,
for the sake of Jesus Christ,
the great Shepherd of the sheep. Amen.

THE BOOK OF PRAYERS FOR CHURCH AND HOME*

51. The Various Christian Communions

Let us give thanks to God for the gifts and graces of each branch of the one great family of Christians.

For the Roman Catholic Church: its glorious traditions, its disciplines of holiness, its worship, rich with the religious passion of the centuries; its noble company of martyrs, teachers, and saints:
We thank you, O Lord, and bless your holy name.

For the Eastern Orthodox Church: its secret treasures of mystical experience; its venerable liturgy; its regard for life in community, and its common will as a source of authority:
We thank you, O Lord, and bless your holy name.

For the Congregationalist concern for the rightful independence of the soul and of the group:
We thank you, O Lord, and bless your holy name.

For the Baptist emphasis on personal regeneration and the conscious relation of the mature soul to the Lord:
We thank you, O Lord, and bless your holy name.

For the powerful ability of Methodists to awaken the conscience of Christians to social evils; and for their emphasis upon the witness of experience and the fruits of the disciplined life:
We thank you, O Lord, and bless your holy name.

For the Presbyterian reverence for the sovereignty of God and their confidence in God's faithfulness to his covenant; for their sense of the moral law, expressing itself in constitutional government:
We thank you, O Lord, and bless your holy name.

For the Quaker witness to the perpetual real presence of the inner light in every human soul, and for their faithful continuance of a free prophetic ministry and Christian non-violence:
We thank you, O Lord, and bless your holy name.

For the Lutheran devotion to the grace of God and the Word of God, enshrined in the ministry of Word and Sacraments:
We thank you, O Lord, and bless your holy name.

For the Anglican Church: its reverent and temperate ways, through its Catholic heritage and its Protestant conscience; its yearning over the divisions of Christendom, and its longing to be used as a house of reconciliation:
We thank you, O Lord, and bless your holy name.

For the numberless Free Churches, many humble and without splendor, in slum or rural isolation, speaking the gospel to those unwelcome or uninspired in other congregations:
We thank you, O Lord, and bless your holy name.

O God, grant to all these families within your one great Church that, as they come from east and west and north and south to sit down in your kingdom, each may lay at your feet that special grace and gift with which you have endowed it; in Christ's name we pray. *Amen.*

THE STUDENT PRAYER BOOK*

52. Affirmations and Thanksgivings For Use at Ecumenical Gatherings †

The Leader says:

We are the people of God,
and we are one in Christ.
We are one in Christ.

We are in a new age,
and our unity is made more clear,
an indication of our Lord's intention
that all be one in him.
We are one in Christ.

Challenged by our world,
and alive within it,
we rejoice to discover our common concerns,
and are heartened by our common devotion.
We are one in Christ.

Yet it is not that our oneness comes only as we renounce our inheritance.
It is rather that we come, as the Magi,
each with our gift to the Lord
whose body is the Church,
and each with our saints:

One of the Reformed tradition says:

We give Calvin, and Knox, and Wesley.
We give order, and simplicity, and justice.
And we are grateful for the gift.

One of the Anglican tradition says:

We give Cranmer, and Hooker, and Temple.
We give liturgy, and moderation, and social concern.
And we are grateful for the gift.

One of the Baptist tradition says:

We give Williams, and Moody, and Graham.
We give emotion, and fervor, and freedom.
And we are grateful for the gift.

One of the Lutheran tradition says:

We give Luther, and Bach, and Bonhoeffer.
We give theology, and music, and piety.
And we are grateful for the gift.

One of the Roman Catholic tradition says:

We give Augustine, and Aquinas, and John XXIII.
We give structure, and heritage, and renewal
And we are grateful for the gift.

One of the Orthodox tradition says:

We give Chrysostom, and Basil, and Berdyaev.
We give continuity, and mystical vision, and life in community.
And we are grateful for the gift.

The Leader says:

We come with these gifts,
with our talents and our vocations,
as we are in the Lord.
And as we are now, we pray.

For this, our oneness in Christ:
Lord, we thank you.

For the hope of the city of God:
Lord, we thank you.

For the determination to be found
as free men and women before you:
Lord, we thank you.

For faith that trusts in you alone:
Lord, we thank you.

For the continuing renewal of your Church:
Lord, we thank you.

For all the kinds of Christians
we are grateful,
acknowledging the Spirit's work in our distinctions,
and praying for the grace to perceive
the divisiveness that pride creates.
In that we are separated sisters and brothers
by reason of our own fault,
perpetuating the sins of the centuries:
Forgive us, dear Lord,
and unite us in your love.
Amen.

CARL T. UEHLING

53. An Act of Dedication

The members of the community face one another across the center aisle or stand in a large circle around the altar or the font, with two leaders saying,

1:      Let us make a common act of dedication.

      Silence

      In the first century, Paul said to the Church at Rome:
      "All of us, in union with Christ, form one body, and as parts of it we belong to each other.

2:      "The life and death of each of us has its influence on others; if we live, we live for the Lord; and if we die, we die for the Lord, so that alive or dead we belong to the Lord."
      We hear your truth, Lord. Help us to do it.

1:      In the first century, Paul said to the Church at Corinth:
      "Now together you are Christ's body; but each of you is a different part of it.

2:      "If one part is hurt, all parts are hurt with it. If one part is given special honor, all parts enjoy it."
      We hear your truth, Lord. Help us to do it.

1:      In the first century, Paul said to the Church in Galatia:
      "My brothers and sisters, serve one another in works of love.

2:      "If you go snapping at each other and tearing each other to pieces, you had better watch out or you will destroy the whole community."
      We hear your truth, Lord. Help us to do it.

1:      In the first letter of John, it is said:
      "We have passed out of death and into life. Of this we can be sure, because we love our brothers and sisters in Christ.

2:      "Our love is not to be just words or mere talk, but something real and active; only by this can we be certain that we are children of the truth."
      We hear your truth, Lord. Help us to do it.

1:      In this century, Dietrich Bonhoeffer has said:
        "It is grace, nothing but grace, that we are allowed to live in
        community with fellow Christians.

2:      "We belong to one another only through and in Jesus Christ."
        We hear your truth, Lord. Help us to do it.

1:      Jesus said, "You must love the Lord your God with all your heart,
        and with all your soul, and with all your mind, and with all your
        strength.

2:      "And you must love your neighbor as yourself."
        We hear your truth, Lord. Help us to do it. Amen.

HORACE ALLEN

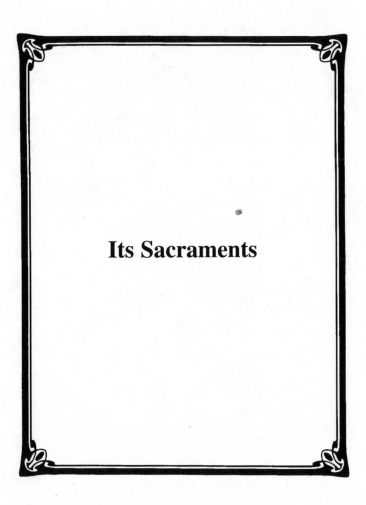

Its Sacraments

54. Enrolling Candidates for Baptism

The Candidates stand together at the front of the church while the person appointed leads the litany.

In peace let us pray to the Lord, saying "Lord, have mercy."

For these catechumens, that they may remember this day on which they were chosen for Baptism, and remain ever grateful for this heavenly blessing, let us pray to the Lord.
Lord, have mercy.

That they may use this [Lenten] season wisely, joining with us in acts of self-denial and in performing works of mercy, let us pray to the Lord.
Lord, have mercy.

For their teachers, that they may make known to those whom they teach the riches of the Word of God, let us pray to the Lord.
Lord, have mercy.

For their sponsors, that in their private lives and public actions they may show to these candidates a pattern of life in accordance with the Gospel, let us pray to the Lord.
Lord, have mercy.

For their families and friends, that they may place no obstacles in the way of these candidates, but rather assist them to follow the promptings of the Spirit, let us pray to the Lord.
Lord, have mercy.

For this congregation, that [during this Lenten season] it may abound in love and persevere in prayer, let us pray to the Lord.
Lord, have mercy.

For our Bishop[s], _____, and for all the clergy and people, let us pray to the Lord.
Lord, have mercy.

For all who have died in the hope of the resurrection, and for all the departed, let us pray to the Lord.
Lord, have mercy.

In the communion of [_____ and of] all the saints, let us commend ourselves, and one another, and all our life, to Christ our God.
To you, O Lord our God.

Silence

The Presiding Minister says the following prayer with hands extended over the candidates:

Immortal God, Lord Jesus Christ, the protector of all who come to you, the life of those who believe, and the resurrection of the dead: We call upon you for these your servants who desire the grace of spiritual rebirth in the Sacrament of Holy Baptism. Accept them, Lord Christ, as you promised when you said, "Ask, and it will be given you; seek, and you will find; knock, and it will be opened to you." Give now, we pray, to those who ask, let those who seek find, open the gate to those who knock; that these your servants may receive the everlasting benediction of your heavenly washing, and come to that promised kingdom which you have prepared, and where you live and reign for ever and ever. *Amen.*

THE BOOK OF OCCASIONAL SERVICES

55. For Catechumens Preparing for Baptism

Let us now pray for *these persons* who *are* to receive the Sacrament of new birth.

Deliver *them,* O Lord, from the way of sin and death.
Lord, hear our prayer.

Open *their* hearts to your grace and truth.
Lord, hear our prayer.

Fill *them* with your holy and life-giving Spirit.
Lord, hear our prayer.

Keep *them* in the faith and communion of your holy Church.
Lord, hear our prayer.

Teach *them* to love others in the power of the Spirit.
Lord, hear our prayer.

Send *them* into the world in witness to your love.
Lord, hear our prayer.

Bring *them* to the fullness of your peace and glory.
Lord, hear our prayer.

Grant, O Lord, that all who are baptized into the death of Jesus Christ your Son may live in the power of his resurrection and look for him to come again in glory; who lives and reigns now and for ever. *Amen.*

THE BOOK OF COMMON PRAYER 1979

56. For Those To Be Baptized

Lord Jesus Christ, you desire that everyone who follows you shall be born again by water and the Spirit: Remember your servants who *tomorrow* are to be baptized in your Name.

By their names, Lord:
Grant that you will know them, and call them to a life of service.

By their names, Lord:
Grant that they may become the persons you created them to be.

By their names, Lord:
Grant that they may be written for ever in your Book of Life.

Through the water of their baptism, Lord:
Grant that they may be united with you in your death.

Through the water of their baptism, Lord:
Grant that they may receive forgiveness for all their sins.

Through the water of their baptism, Lord:
Grant that they may have power to endure, and strength to have victory in the battle of life.

As members of your Church, Lord:
Grant that they may rise to a new life in the fellowship of those who love you.

As members of your Church, Lord:
Grant that they may suffer when another suffers, and when another rejoices, rejoice.

As members of your Church, Lord:
Grant that they may be your faithful soldiers and servants until their life's end.

Through the abiding presence of your Spirit, Lord:
Grant that they may lead the rest of their lives according to this beginning.

Through the abiding presence of your Spirit, Lord:
Grant that when they pass through the dark waters of death, you will be with them.

Through the abiding presence of your Spirit, Lord:
Grant that they may inherit the kingdom of glory prepared for them from the foundation of the world.

To you, Lord Christ, with the Father and the Holy Spirit, be honor and glory in the Church, now and for ever. Amen.

THE BOOK OF OCCASIONAL SERVICES

57. The Renewal of Baptismal Vows

Through the Paschal mystery, dear friends, we are buried with Christ by
Baptism into his death, and raised with him to newness of life. I call upon
you, therefore, to renew the solemn promises and vows of Holy Baptism,
by which we once renounced Satan and all his works, and promised to
serve God faithfully in his holy catholic Church.

Do you reaffirm your renunciation of evil and renew your commitment to
Jesus Christ?
I do.

Do you believe in God the Father?
I believe in God, the Father almighty, Creator of heaven and earth.

Do you believe in Jesus Christ, the Son of God?
I believe in Jesus Christ, his only Son, our Lord.
He was conceived by the power of the Holy Spirit
*   and born of the Virgin Mary.*
He suffered under Pontius Pilate, was crucified, died, and was buried.
He descended to the dead.
On the third day he rose again.
He ascended into heaven, and is seated at the right hand of the Father.
He will come again to judge the living and the dead.

Do you believe in God the Holy Spirit?
I believe in the Holy Spirit, the holy catholic Church,
the communion of saints, the forgiveness of sins,
the resurrection of the body, and the life everlasting.

Will you continue in the apostles' teaching and fellowship, in the breaking
of bread, and in the prayers?
I will, with God's help.

Will you persevere in resisting evil and, whenever you fall into sin, repent
and return to the Lord?
I will, with God's help.

Will you proclaim by word and example the Good News of God in Christ?
I will, with God's help.

Will you seek and serve Christ in all persons, loving your neighbor as
yourself?
I will, with God's help.

Will you strive for justice and peace among all people, and respect the dignity of every human being?
I will, with God's help.

The Celebrant concludes the Renewal of Baptismal Vows with these words:

May Almighty God, the Father of our Lord Jesus Christ, who has given us a new birth by water and the Holy Spirit, and bestowed upon us the forgiveness of sins, keep us in eternal life by his grace, in Christ Jesus our Lord. *Amen.*

THE BOOK OF COMMON PRAYER 1979*

58. Baptism in the Spirit

Lord and life-giving Spirit, who brooded over the waters when first the world began:
Make us dead to sin but alive to God.

Who led your people out of slavery through the waters of the Red Sea and into freedom through the waters of the Jordan:
Make us dead to sin but alive to God.

Who overshadowed Mary of Nazareth and caused her to be the mother of God's only Son:
Make us dead to sin but alive to God.

Who anointed Jesus as Messiah as he was baptized by John in the Jordan:
Make us dead to sin but alive to God.

Who raised Jesus from the grave and proclaimed him Son of God in all his power:
Make us dead to sin but alive to God.

Who appeared in tongues of flame at Pentecost:
Make us dead to sin but alive to God.

Who charges the waters of baptism through and through with power to give new life:
Make us dead to sin but alive to God.

Lord, hear our prayer:
Let our cry come to you.

Let us pray:

Almighty and everlasting God, who out of pure mercy decreed both the creation and the renewal of the world, be present and active in the sacraments which you have instituted for our salvation. Send forth the Spirit of adoption in full measure that those who are born of water and the Spirit may live under the power of that same Spirit all the days of their life and so arrive safely in their heavenly home; through Jesus Christ our Lord. *Amen.*

PRAY LIKE THIS

59. Offertory Prayers

These prayers may be used as the offering of money is presented and the Bread and Wine placed on the Table and made ready.

At the presentation of the money-offering

Blessed are you, Lord, God of all creation.
Through your goodness we have this money to offer, the fruit of our labor and of the skills you have given us.

Take us and our possessions to do your work in the world.
Blessed be God for ever.

At the presentation of the Bread

Blessed are you, Lord, God of all creation.
Through your goodness we have this bread to offer, which earth has given and human hands have made.

It will become for us the bread of life.
Blessed be God for ever.

At the presentation of the Wine

Blessed are you, Lord, God of all creation.
Through your goodness we have this wine to offer, fruit of the vine and work of human hands.

It will become our spiritual drink.
Blessed be God for ever.

THE ANGLICAN CHURCH OF THE PROVINCE OF SOUTHERN AFRICA AND THE ENGLISH TRANSLATION OF THE ROMAN MISSAL, 1973*

60. The Sacrament of Unity
- A Communion Litany -

Let us pray, giving thanks to the Lord who bestows on us the great mystery of his love in this Eucharistic meal.

Silence

Because the bread is one, we, though many, are one body, all of us who partake of the one bread.
We are one in his body and one in his love.

This is my body which shall be given up for you; do this in remembrance of me.
We are one in his body and one in his love.

A new commandment I give you, that you love one another; that as I have loved you, you also love one another.
We are one in his body and one in his love.

As the Father has loved me, I also have loved you. Abide in my love.
We are one in his body and one in his love.

Do not labor for the food that perishes, but for that which endures to life everlasting, which the Son of Man will give you.
We are one in his body and one in his love.

I am the bread of life. All who come to me shall not hunger, and all who believe in me shall never thirst.
We are one in his body and one in his love.

Now you are the body of Christ, and each of you individually a member of it.
We are one in his body and one in his love. Amen.

SCRIPTURE SERVICES

61.   A Thanksgiving for the Bread of Life

Be praised, Lord,
by parents
who set on the table each day
the fruit of their work:
bread of a life of contentment,
bread of a life full of difficulties,
so that their children might grow to adulthood.
Praise and glory be yours, for ever.

Be praised, Lord,
by the poor who each morning
must beg again for
the bread of tears and misery
and who sometimes taste human compassion
in a loaf offered to them and shared.
Praise and glory be yours, for ever.

Be praised, Lord,
by the radical reformers of society
who offer heart and life
so that their poor brothers and sisters
might one day taste abundantly
the bread earned by their own sweat.
Praise and glory be yours, for ever.

Be praised, Lord,
by engineers and technicians
serving in poor nations
so that a more productive and well-tended earth
might yield a plentiful harvest of wheat and rice and beans.
Praise and glory be yours, for ever.

Be praised, Lord,
for your presence
alongside parents of families,
alongside beggars, engineers and reformers.
Your presence is mysterious and difficult to grasp,
and yet so strong and real
that we can derive life from it,
just as we live by eating bread.
Praise and glory be yours, for ever.

Be praised, Lord,
by your Son, Jesus Christ,
in a way surpassed by no other.
He multiplied bread for the poor
and took his place at table with sinners.
Then on the night before his passion,
at that moment, in order to become the least among us all,
he became bread pulled apart and broken,
passed from hand to hand and shared.
Praise and glory be yours, for ever. Amen.

PRAYERS IN COMMUNITY

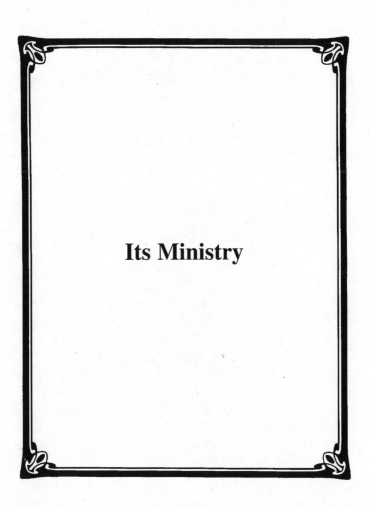

Its Ministry

62. Our Ministry as Servants

This may be led by two voices.

1:    Be generous and share your food with the poor. You will be blessed for it.   (Proverbs 22:9)
The Lord calls us to be servants. Let us rejoice!

2:    If you oppress poor people, you insult the God who made them; but kindness shown to the poor is an act of worship.   (Proverbs 14:31)
The Lord calls us to be servants. Let us rejoice!

1:    Defend the rights of the poor and the orphans; be fair to the needy and the helpless.   (Psalm 82:3)
The Lord calls us to be servants. Let us rejoice!

2:    A good person knows the rights of the poor, but wicked people cannot understand such things.   (Proverbs 29:7)
The Lord calls us to be servants. Let us rejoice!

1:    Treat foreigners as you would your own, and love them as you love yourselves.   (Leviticus 19:34a)
The Lord calls us to be servants. Let us rejoice!

2:    Do not follow the majority when they do wrong, or when they give testimony that perverts justice.   (Exodus 23:2)
The Lord calls us to be servants. Let us rejoice!

1:    Speak up for people who cannot speak for themselves. Protect the rights of all who are helpless.   (Proverbs 31:8)
The Lord calls us to be servants. Let us rejoice!

2:    Speak for them and be a righteous judge. Protect the rights of the poor and needy.   (Proverbs 31:9)
The Lord calls us to be servants. Let us rejoice!

Silence

Lord, help us love you with all our heart, soul, strength, and mind, and our neighbors as ourselves. We rejoice that we are able to love, because you first loved us; through Christ our Lord. Amen.

BREAD FOR THE WORLD

63. Your Will Be Done

Let us pray to the Father, asking for grace to drink the cup which God offers us.

Silence

With Christ our Brother we hear the call. With him we answer:
Father, your will be done!
Father, your will be done in us!

Make us strong with the faith of our father Abraham.
Father, your will be done in us!

Make us bold with the courage of Moses, the leader of your people.
Father, your will be done in us!

Enlighten us with the wisdom of Samuel, ruler and judge over Israel.
Father, your will be done in us!

Give us the spirit of discernment and decision so that we may work in your service with the authority of the great king David.
Father, your will be done in us!

Make us alive, as you did Isaiah the prophet, with a sense of your holy presence.
Father, your will be done in us!

Give us, as you gave to John the Baptist, a love of poverty and self-effacement in our labors for the spread of your kingdom.
Father, your will be done in us!

Make us great-hearted, like Paul, so that we may be all things to all people, in Christ Jesus.
Father, your will be done in us!

Shape us, transform us, even as you made the Virgin Mary a perfect instrument in your hands.
Father, your will be done in us!

Let us pray, giving thanks to the Lord for having chosen us for a special role and vocation in the Church.

Silence for personal prayer

O Lord our God, you have chosen us from before the foundation of the world and blessed us with every spiritual blessing. Grant, we pray, that, having been made new through the mystery of our redemption, we may respond fully to the gift of our holy election and restore all people, all things, and ourselves to you; through Christ our Lord. *Amen.*
Lord, what will you have me do?

You have not chosen me, but I have chosen you, and have appointed you that you should go and bear fruit, and that your fruit should remain. *Thanks be to God! Amen.*

SCRIPTURE SERVICES

64. A Litany of the Apostles

Lord Jesus, we remember before you those you called to be your disciples and trained to become your apostles.
They were all of them laypeople, Lord, but you chose them for the extension of your ministry as prophet, priest, and king.

We remember Peter, that strange, uncouth rock made of such shifting sand.
Help us, O Lord, like Peter, to find in you the Christ, the Son of the living God.

We remember Andrew, evangelist extraordinary, who was always bringing someone to you.
Unlock our lips, O Lord, that, like Andrew, we may learn to talk about you with skill and grace.

We remember James and John, "Sons of Thunder," willing vehicles of a mother's ambition.
Chasten and refine our ambitions, O Lord, that, like them, we may learn at last to seek only your will.

We remember Philip, slow of wit, big of heart.
Remind us, O Lord, that you place more stock in our hearts than in our wits.

We remember Thomas, the skeptic, who ached because he wanted so badly to believe.
As you did for Thomas, O Lord, convict us of the power and sufficiency of your resurrection.

We remember Matthew, prosperous, despised, an outcast in the midst of his own people.
Let us not forget, O Lord, that with you no human label ever sticks.

We remember James, your brother, perhaps your rival in your family.
Impress upon us, O Lord, the rightful claim of family ties, and yet their insignificance compared with your claim on us.

We remember Simon, the Zealot.
Keep all of our lesser loyalties, O Lord, even our love of country, subordinate to our loyalty to you.

We remember -we barely remember- your obscure disciples, Thaddeus and Bartholomew.
You know why you chose them, Lord, and, like millions of other obscure disciples, they served you well.

And we remember Judas, though we wish we could forget him.
But we dare not forget him, because he is flesh of our flesh and bone of our bone, and because your love reached out and included even him.

Silence

Lord, we thank you for the whole company of your apostles, and for your continuing invitation to discipleship. Amen.

MODELS FOR MINISTERS I*

65. Thanksgiving for the Ministry of the Laity †

Let us thank God for those persons who have responded to Christ's call to serve him in the world.
Lord, we know that you call us to serve our neighbor in love, not only in church, but also in the world in which we live.

For those who minister to the sick as medical personnel, or through hospital visitation and volunteer work:
We give you thanks, O Lord.

For those who help with the education of our children, both salaried staff and volunteer aides:
We give you thanks, O Lord.

For those who are actively involved in the political process of our community, state, and nation:
We give you thanks, O Lord.

For those who work for social justice, fair housing, and equal opportunity for both sexes and all races:
We give you thanks, O Lord.

For those who visit the lonely and the shut-in, and for those who find time to listen to the troubled and distressed:
We give you thanks, O Lord.

For those who serve through Meals on Wheels and for those who offer counsel and support at walk-in centers or anonymously over the phone:
We give you thanks, O Lord.

For those who work to make our community a safe and pleasant place to live - engineers, contractors, architects, fire and police personnel:
We give you thanks, O Lord.

For those who work with our children and youth through scouting, tutorial programs, athletic groups, and teen centers:
We give you thanks, O Lord.

For those who seek both to glorify you and to help their neighbor through their work:
We give you thanks, O Lord.

For those who serve as homemakers, providing care, nourishment, and a secure haven for families:
We give you thanks, O Lord.

For all those who labor and whose efforts are often unseen and unsung, but who contribute significantly to Christ's ministry in the world:
We give you thanks, O Lord.

We pray for all who labor faithfully day in and day out.
Work through us and help us always to work for you.

Let us thank God for the love we have experienced in Christ Jesus, which motivates and empowers us to serve others in his name.
O Lord, we recall the words of your Son when he said,
"I came not to be served, but to serve."
He saw our needs, and he ministered to us in love.
We thank you for calling us to follow in his footsteps.
We ask you to keep our eyes open to the possibilities around us,
and to grant us strength and courage, and the willingness
to continue to serve Christ and all our neighbors.
In Christ's name we pray. Amen.

MELVIN VOS
-MONDAY'S MINISTRIES

66. A Thanksgiving for Music and Musicians

O God our Father, we thank you for music and its wondrous power to touch and heal and strengthen; under its spell the closed doors of the human spirit are unlocked and our hearts are moved to respond to you in worship. We praise you for this most precious gift.

Silence

Let everything that lives praise the Lord.
Thanks be to God!

We thank you for all those who, entrusted with this gift, have "composed musical tunes and set forth verses in writing"; living on among us in their works, they have wonderfully enriched our lives and exalted you in the liturgy of your Church. We praise you for all faithful singers of your song.

Silence

Let everything that lives praise the Lord.
Thanks be to God!

We thank you for all who teach in conservatories and schools of sacred music, interpreting music born in the souls of others and bringing gifts to fruition in many generations of students. We praise you for what they, receiving generously from you, have shared generously with others.

Silence

Let everything that lives praise the Lord.
Thanks be to God!

And lastly we thank you for all who day by day enable us to sing your song in many ways and many places, accompanying it on organ and guitar and trumpet, leading it with the beauty of the solo voice, enriching it with new forms of music, patient scholarship and gifted teaching. We praise you for their ministry and gratefully ask your blessing on them this day.

Silence

Let everything that lives praise the Lord.
Thanks be to God! Amen.

JEFFERY W. ROWTHORN

67. For Theological Seminaries

During the times of silence specific people may be remembered or mentioned aloud by name.

O God of truth, ever beckoning us to loftier understanding and deeper wisdom, we seek your will and implore your grace for all who share the life of divinity schools and seminaries in our day, knowing that, unless you build among us, we who teach and learn will labor but in vain.

Silence

For the men and women who teach, that they may together bring fire and vision to a common task, knowing one field yet eager to relate it to all others; just in their academic demands, yet seeing each student as a child of God; fitted to teach not only by great learning but by great faith in humankind and in you, their God:
In them and in us, O God, kindle your saving truth.

Silence

For deans and presidents, trustees and development officers, and all others who point the way for theological education in our day, that their chief concern be not budgets and buildings and prestige, but men and women freed to know your whole will and roused to serve you in your Church:
In them and in us, O God, kindle your saving truth.

Silence

For janitors and maids, for cooks and keepers of the grounds, for those who prepare our food and wash our dishes, and for the host of other workers and suppliers whose faithfulness ministers to our common life:
In them and in us, O God, kindle your saving truth.

Silence

For parents and givers of scholarships, who support theological students, that they may not desire for them more income, or social acceptance, or glory of family or of donor, but look rather for new breadth of intelligence, the spirit made whole, and devoted Christian service in life:
In them and in us, O God, kindle your saving truth.

Silence

For the students themselves, that their confusion may be brief, their perspective constantly enlarged, and their minds and spirits alert to all that chapel and classroom, library and fieldwork assignment can mean in their lives:

In them and in us, O God, kindle your saving truth.

Silence

For every member of the community of learning and of service, that with them we may be aware of your Holy Spirit leading us all into truth, and may grasp here your special intention for all our learning and striving:

In them and in us, O God, kindle your saving truth.

Silence

We know, O heavenly Father,
that a seminary education is but the willing and planning
of many men and women,
each sought by your great love.
Grant that we who would earnestly serve you
may witness in the world to the reality of your gospel,
as it is shown forth in Christ Jesus our Lord. Amen.

JOHN OLIVER NELSON
-THE STUDENT PRAYER BOOK

68. A Litany for Ordinations

For use at Ordinations or on Ember Days or other appropriate occasions.

God the Father:
Have mercy on us.

God the Son:
Have mercy on us.

God the Holy Spirit:
Have mercy on us.

Holy Trinity, one God:
Have mercy on us.

We pray to you, Lord Christ.
Lord, hear our prayer.

For the holy Church of God, that it may be filled with truth and love, and
be found without fault at the Day of your Coming,
we pray to you, O Lord.
Lord, hear our prayer.

For all members of your Church in their vocation and ministry, that they
may serve you in a true and godly life,
we pray to you, O Lord.
Lord, hear our prayer.

For ____, our ____, and for all other ministers, that they may be filled with
your love, may hunger for truth, and may thirst after righteousness,
we pray to you, O Lord.
Lord, hear our prayer.

For ____, chosen to serve as ____ in your Church,
we pray to you, O Lord.
Lord, hear our prayer.

That *he* may faithfully fulfill the duties of this ministry, build up your
Church, and glorify your Name,
we pray to you, O Lord.
Lord, hear our prayer.

That by the indwelling of the Holy Spirit *he* may be sustained and encouraged to persevere to the end,
we pray to you, O Lord.
Lord, hear our prayer.

For his family [or the members of *his* household *or* community], that they may be adorned with all Christian virtues,
we pray to you, O Lord.
Lord, hear our prayer.

For all who fear God and believe in you, Lord Christ, that our divisions may cease and that all may be one as you and the Father are one,
we pray to you, O Lord.
Lord, hear our prayer.

For the mission of the Church, that in faithful witness it may preach the Gospel to the ends of the earth,
we pray to you, O Lord.
Lord, hear our prayer.

For those who do not yet believe, and for those who have lost their faith, that they may receive the light of the Gospel,
we pray to you, O Lord.
Lord, hear our prayer.

For the peace of the world, that a spirit of respect and forbearance may grow among nations and peoples,
we pray to you, O Lord.
Lord, hear our prayer.

For those in positions of public trust, especially _____, that they may serve justice and promote the dignity and freedom of every person,
we pray to you, O Lord.
Lord, hear our prayer.

For a blessing upon all human labor, and for the right use of the riches of creation, that the world may be freed from poverty, famine, and disaster,
we pray to you, O Lord.
Lord, hear our prayer.

For the poor, the persecuted, the sick, and all who suffer; for refugees, prisoners, and all who are in danger; that they may be relieved and protected,
we pray to you, O Lord.
Lord, hear our prayer.

For ourselves; for the forgiveness of our sins, and for the grace of the Holy Spirit to amend our lives,
we pray to you, O Lord.
Lord, hear our prayer.

For all who have died in the communion of your Church, and those whose faith is known to you alone, that, with all the saints, they may have rest in that place where there is no pain or grief, but life eternal,
we pray to you, O Lord.
Lord, hear our prayer.

Rejoicing in the fellowship of the ever-blessed Virgin Mary, *blessed* _____, and all the saints, let us commend ourselves, and one another, and all our life to Christ our God.
To you, O Lord our God.

Lord, have mercy.
Christ, have mercy.
Lord, have mercy.

The Leader concludes with a suitable Collect and the People respond "Amen."

THE BOOK OF COMMON PRAYER 1979

69. Veni Creator

Come, Holy Ghost, our souls inspire:
And lighten with celestial fire.

Thou the anointing Spirit art:
Who dost thy sev'nfold gifts impart.

Thy blessed unction from above:
Is comfort, life, and fire of love.

Enable with perpetual light:
The dullness of our blinded sight.

Anoint and cheer our soilèd face:
With the abundance of thy grace.

Keep far our foes, give peace at home:
Where thou art guide, no ill can come.

Teach us to know the Father, Son:
And thee, of both, to be but One,

That through the ages all along:
This may be our endless song:

Praise to thy eternal merit,
Father, Son, and Holy Spirit. Amen.

LATIN, 9TH CENTURY
-TRANSLATED BY JOHN COSIN*

70. For a New Ministry

Representatives of the congregation and of the clergy of the diocese stand before the bishop with the new minister. Any of the presentations that follow may be added to, omitted, or adapted, as appropriate to the nature of the new ministry, and to the order of the minister In the absence of the bishop, the deputy substitutes the words given in parentheses.

Representatives of the congregation present a Bible, saying:

_____, accept this Bible, and be among us *(or* be in this place) as one who proclaims the Word.
Amen. And may the Lord be with you.

The Bishop presents a vessel of water, saying:

_____, take this water, and help me (help the Bishop) baptize in obedience to our Lord.
Amen. And may the Lord be with you.

Others present a stole or some other symbol, saying:

_____, receive this *stole,* and be among us as a pastor and priest.
Amen. And may the Lord be with you.

Others present a book of prayers or some other symbol, saying:

_____, receive this *book,* and be among us as a *man* of prayer.
Amen. And may the Lord be with you.

Others present olive oil or some other symbol, saying:

_____, use this *oil,* and be among us as a healer and reconciler.
Amen. And may the Lord be with you.

If the new minister is the rector or vicar of the parish, a Warden may now present the keys of the church, saying:

_____, receive these keys, and let the doors of this place be open to all people.
Amen. And may the Lord be with you.

Representative clergy of the diocese present the Constitution and Canons of this Church, saying:

_____, obey these Canons, and be among us to share in the councils of this diocese.
Amen. And may the Lord be with you.

Other Representatives of the congregation present bread and wine, saying:

_____, take this bread and wine, and be among us to break the Bread and bless the Cup.
Amen. And may the Lord be with you.

The Bishop then says:

_____, let all these be signs of the ministry which is mine and yours (the Bishop's and yours) in this place.
Amen. And may the Lord be with you.

The Bishop then presents the new minister to the congregation, saying:

Greet your new *Rector.*

When appropriate, the family of the new minister may also be presented at this time.

The Congregation expresses its approval. Applause is appropriate.

The Bishop greets the new minister.

The new Minister then says to the people:

The peace of the Lord be always with you.
And also with you.

The new Minister then greets other members of the clergy, family members, and the congregation. The People greet one another.

THE BOOK OF COMMON PRAYER 1979

71. A Litany of Farewell

Good Christian people, I bid you now pray for the saving presence of our living Lord

In this world:
He is risen.

In this Church:
He is risen.

In this community:
He is risen.

In this parish:
He is risen.

In the hearts of all faithful people:
He is risen.

But especially I bid you pray and give thanks for _____ who is *(are)* now leaving our community.

For expectations not met:
Lord, have mercy.

For grievances not resolved:
Lord, have mercy.

For wounds not healed:
Lord, have mercy.

For anger not dissolved:
Lord, have mercy.

For gifts not given:
Lord, have mercy.

For promises not kept:
Lord, have mercy.

And now for this portion of your lifelong pilgrimage which you have made with these people in this place:
Thanks be to God.

For friendships made, celebrations enjoyed, and for moments of nurture:
Thanks be to God.

For wounds healed, expectations met, gifts given, promises kept:
Thanks be to God.

For bread and wine, body and blood:
Thanks be to God.

For all the thoughtful, little unheralded things done to make the day better for someone:
Thanks be to God.

And so, to establish a home in another place with other members of the family of Christ:
Go in peace.

To continue the journey with new friends and new adventures, new gifts to give and to receive:
Go in peace.

To offer wisdom and experience, competence and compassion, in the vocation to which you are called:
Go in peace.

With whatever fears, whatever sadness, whatever excitement, whatever dreams may be yours:
Go in peace.

With our faith in you, our hope for you, and our love of you:
Go in peace.

Here the People may add their awn petitions.

The Lord watch between us while we are absent one from another - in the Name of the Father, and of the Son, and of the Holy Spirit.
Go in peace. Amen.

HENRY L. H. MYERS

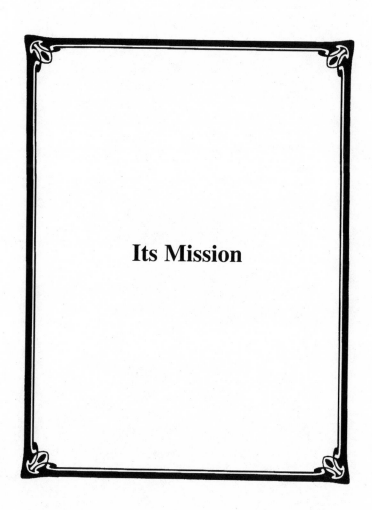

Its Mission

72. A Cycle of Intercessions for the Mission of the Church

These litanies may be used separately or as a cycle of prayer on the seven days of the week.

Monday

Almighty Father, you give us life
as you give life to all people.
You call us into the Church
that with men and women
of different races, colors, and languages,
different experiences and different traditions,
we may be one body
to the glory of Christ on earth.
Help us to be what you have called us to be.

You are the giver of life.
Father, renew us by your Spirit.

Father of all, you give us
wealth in the earth and in the oceans,
forests and fertile plains,
air to breathe, water to drink,
and all that is needful for human life.
We pray for those who know little of your bounty,
for whom the earth is a cruel desert
and existence a constant struggle
against overwhelming odds.
We acknowledge that their burdens should be our burdens;
we acknowledge that we share a common humanity.

You are the giver of life.
Father, renew us by your Spirit.

Father, you have so made us that we need one another,
but because we do not know how to love everyone,
you tell us to start with the sister or brother at our side.
We pray for any from whom we are estranged. Bless them,
and bless us in our future relationships with them.
We pray for our families, our friends,
and all whom we meet day by day . . .
In their particular needs we ask you to bless them.

You are the giver of life.
Father, renew us by your Spirit.

Father, you are present in every part of human experience.
We hold before you
the infant lying in a mother's arms,
the young lovers planning together their first home,
the sick and infirm battling with weakness and incapacity,
the dying, soon to experience your new creation.

You are the giver of life.
Father, renew us by your Spirit.

Eternal Father, we remember before you
those who have passed from this world . . .
As we all received from you the gift of life,
so we pray that you will bring us to the life eternal.

You are the giver of life.
Father, renew us by your Spirit.
Amen.

Tuesday

We pray for the Church,
where all too often, like Cain,
we have made the worship offered by our brother
a cause for hostility and division.
We pray that our Lord may bind us together,
teaching us to value the richness of our diversity
and to rejoice in every fresh glimpse of God's glory
seen through traditions other than our own.

Lord, teach us to love:
That we may be children of God.

We pray for those lands where brother and sister fight sister and brother,
divided by arbitrary borders, ideology or religion.
We pray for those lands where extremes of wealth and poverty
are bitterly divisive.
We pray for those lands where power is grossly abused
and the dispossessed bear the heaviest burden.

Lord, teach us to love:
That we may be children of God.

We pray for all who have been nourished on bitterness
and fed with the wrongs suffered by earlier generations.
We pray for all who have grown to hate people
instead of hating that which evil has done to people.
We pray for the young who are impatient for change
and the not so young who resist all change.

Lord, teach us to love:
That we may be children of God.

We commend to God any special needs known to us . . .
As we remember the sick, the sorrowful, and all who are in any distress,
let us also remember that God has supremely made himself known to us as
Savior and calls us to share in God's rescuing work.

Lord, teach us to love:
That we may be children of God.

Lord, we would heal and not destroy.
Teach us the discipline of obedience to the commandment
"You shall love your neighbor as yourself,"
and give us the fortitude to go on obeying to the end.

Lord, teach us to love:
That we may be children of God.

Let us remember before God those who have died . . .
Lord, we are all sinners and utterly dependent on your grace.
We praise you for the forgiveness of sins
by which men and women are enabled
to rise from death to eternal life.

Lord, teach us to love:
That we may be children of God.
Amen.

Wednesday

Lord Jesus, you have faced temptation, you know how difficult it can be to
distinguish between vision and mirage, between truth and falsehood.

Lord, help us when we are tempted:
And save us when we fall.

Help us in the Church —
When we confuse absence of conflict with the peace of God.
When we equate the shaping of ecclesiastical structures with serving you in
the world.
When we imagine that our task is to preserve rather than to put at risk.
When we behave as though your presence in life were a past event rather
than a contemporary encounter.

Lord, help us when we are tempted:
And save us when we fall.

Help us in the world —
When we use meaningless chatter to avoid real dialogue.
When we allow the image presented by the media to blind us to
the substance that lies behind it.
When we confuse privilege with responsibility and claim rights
when we should be acknowledging duties.
When we allow high-sounding reasons to cover evil actions.

Lord, help us when we are tempted:
And save us when we fall.

We pray for our families and our friends and hold them before you in our
thoughts . . .
We especially pray for any who may be under particular pressures and
stress at this time . . .

Lord, help us when we are tempted:
And save us when we fall.

Lord Jesus, you have passed through the test of suffering
and are able to help those who are meeting their test now.
We pray for all who suffer . . .
We especially pray for those who suffer through their own folly or the folly
or malice of others . . .

Lord, help us when we are tempted:
And save us when we fall.

Before the throne of God, where we may find mercy and timely help,
we remember those who have departed this life . . .
Dying, Christ broke the power of sin and death
that we might enter with him into the life eternal.

Lord, help us when we are tempted:
And save us when we fall.
Amen.

Thursday

Lord, we often fold our hands in prayer,
when we should really jump for joy
because you come to us as rescuer, as Savior,
cleaning up the mess we make of our lives,
putting together what we pull apart.

Tell out, my soul, the greatness of the Lord.
Rejoice, my spirit, in God my Savior.

We pray for the Church.
You have called us to have a part in its life
and, despite our failures, you have not cast us off.

Tell out, my soul, the greatness of the Lord.
Rejoice, my spirit, in God my Savior.

We know that much of the Church's life and witness
looks silly and weak in the eyes of the world at large,
but you still use its foolishness to shame worldly wisdom
and its weakness to witness against the abuse of power.

Tell out, my soul, the greatness of the Lord.
Rejoice, my spirit, in God my Savior.

We pray for those who cry desperately for salvation,
    for tyranny to be overthrown,
    for the despised to be given dignity,
    for the poor to receive a proper share of the earth's resources.
You are the source of hope and the inspiration to action.

Tell out, my soul, the greatness of the Lord.
Rejoice, my spirit, in God my Savior.

We bring you particular needs . . .
With confidence we share these with you
for you are the God who lives among us.

Tell out, my soul, the greatness of the Lord.
Rejoice, my spirit, in God my Savior.

We pray for our families . . .
Your human life brought both pain and joy to your earthly relatives.
Help us also to know you in both the joys and the pains of family life.

Tell out, my soul, the greatness of the Lord.
Rejoice, my spirit, in God my Savior.

We remember those who have died ...
Through our sorrow and sense of loss we are glad
for the promise that there shall be an end to death,
and to mourning and crying and pain;
for the old order has passed away.

Tell out, my soul, the greatness of the Lord.
Rejoice, my spirit, in God my Savior.
Amen.

Friday

Lord Jesus, in a dark hour
you spoke of the gift of peace;
we beg that gift for ourselves, that we may have
the inner serenity that cannot be taken from us.
Then we may be messengers of your peace
to a strife-torn world.

Give peace in our time, Lord.
Help us to live in peace.

We pray for those who are fighting,
injury, disfigurement, and death their constant companions,
nerves and bodies strained beyond endurance,
the streams of compassion drying up within them,
their only goal the destruction of the "enemy."
Whatever the color of their skin - we pray for them.
Whatever the sound of their tongue - we pray for them.
Whatever the insignia they wear - we pray for them.

Give peace in our time, Lord.
Help us to live in peace.

We pray for all who have been broken in battle;
for those who weep and those who can no longer weep;
for those who feel the anguish and for those who have lost the capacity to
feel;
for all prisoners - and all prison guards;
for those who exist in war-torn lands and for those who no longer have a
homeland.

Give peace in our time, Lord.
Help us to live in peace.

We pray for all who stir up strife;
for all who make a profit out of the misery of others;
for all who are led into vice as they seek a momentary forgetfulness;
for all who believe that war is inevitable.

Give peace in our time, Lord.
Help us to live in peace.

The desire to press self-interest is deeply rooted in us.
We defend our attitudes when we should be ashamed of them.
We compare the noblest aspects of our own cause with the basest of that of
our opponents.
We are reluctant to admit that our own selfish desires could contribute to
the miseries of others.

Give peace in our time, Lord.
Help us to live in peace.

We bring to you particular needs . . .
and we remember those who have died . . .

Give peace in our time, Lord.
Help us to live in peace.
Amen.

Saturday

Spirit of power,
we find it hard to come together in the Church
even within a single congregation.
How shall we learn to be one family,
loving and serving the whole of humankind?
Lead us into such unity of purpose

that we may receive power:
not the power to threaten or destroy,
but the power to restore waste places.
Use us to declare your glory
that blind eyes may see, deaf ears hear,
and the cynical be brought to faith.

Spirit of the Living God,
Hear our prayer.

Spirit of truth,
we live in a modern Babel
where words are used to conceal meaning
rather than make it plain.
Lead the peoples of the world into such a love of truth
that nation may speak with nation,
not seeking to confuse
but to understand and to be understood,
whereby trust is created, out of which
a truly international community may be born.

Spirit of the Living God,
Hear our prayer.

Creator Spirit,
you give to the old the capacity
to dream dreams and to the young to see visions,
but because we exalt ourselves and our desires
to the place that is yours alone,
our visions are visions of horror
and our dreams nightmares.
Raise up artists and prophets among us
with the will and the ability
to inspire and cleanse our society,
to set our hearts aflame and turn our eyes to the heights.

Spirit of the Living God,
Hear our prayer.

Source of all comfort, we pray for the lonely, the sick, the sad,
the bereaved and all who suffer or are ill at ease . . .
We claim for them the gift of your peace,
that their troubled hearts may be set at rest
and their fears banished.

Spirit of the Living God,
Hear our prayer.

Giver of life, we remember those who have died . . .
May they enter into the Kingdom
where your presence is all in all.

Spirit of the Living God,
Hear our prayer.
Amen.

Sunday

Crucified and risen Lord,
we pray for the Church.
Save us from dawdling by an empty tomb.
Save us from bondage to the past.
Save us from the hypnotic fascination of decay and death
and make your Church to know your resurrection life.
May we follow where you lead
and live for you in today's world.

The Lord is risen.
He is risen indeed.

Savior Christ, we pray for the whole human family.
Hanging on the cross,
you gave hope to a rebel at your side
and prayed for those who condemned you to that violent death.
We too live amid violence,
the violence of subversion, of repressive government,
and all the subtle violence by which the powerful
seek to impose their will on the weak.
None of us is free from its taint.
You alone can give victory over the violence of the world
and of our hearts.
Save us, Lord.
Give us the will and the power to share your victory.

The Lord is risen.
He is risen indeed.

Living Lord, we pray for our society,
entombed in material possessions
and oppressed with ever-changing fears.
Many know no better hope than that things may get no worse
and that they may enjoy a few years of quiet retirement before the end.
Release us from this living death.
Cause us to live with the life you alone can give.

The Lord is risen.
He is risen indeed.

Lord, you know what it is to suffer pain, degradation, and rejection and to
die an outcast.
We pray for all who suffer . . .
May they know you as one who shares their agony
and enables them to share your triumph.

The Lord is risen.
He is risen indeed.

With thanksgiving for the life that was given
and joyous hope of the life that is yet to be,
we remember those who have died . . .
As in Adam all die,
so in Christ will all be brought to life.

The Lord is risen.
He is risen indeed.
Amen.

THE DAILY OFFICE REVISED*

73. For the Church of Christ

O Christ the Rock, on which your people, as living stones joined together, grow into a spiritual house;
Defend your Church, we pray.

O Christ the Vine, of which your people are the branches;
Defend your Church, we pray.

O Christ the Head of the Body, of which your people are the members;
Defend your Church, we pray.

O Christ our Prophet, you teach the way of God in truth;
Defend your Church, we pray.

O Christ our Priest, you offered yourself upon the Cross, and now make intercession for us to the Father;
Defend your Church, we pray.

O Christ our King, you reign over all the earth, and make us citizens of your heavenly kingdom;
Defend your Church, we pray.

O Christ, you sent the Holy Spirit upon the Church, clothing it with power from on high;
Defend your Church, we pray.

We pray to you, Lord Christ.
Lord, hear our prayer.

That we may be devoted to the apostles' teaching and fellowship, to the breaking of bread and the prayers,
Lord, hear our prayer.

That we may make disciples of all nations, baptizing them in the Name of the Father, and of the Son, and of the Holy Spirit,
Lord, hear our prayer.

That you will fulfill your promise to be with us always, even to the ages of ages,
Lord, hear our prayer.

That you will sustain all members of your holy Church, that in our vocation
and ministry we may truly and devoutly serve you,
Lord, hear our prayer.

That you will bless the clergy of your Church, that they may diligently
preach the Gospel and faithfully celebrate the holy Sacraments,
Lord, hear our prayer.

That you will heal the divisions in your Church, that all may be one, even
as you and the Father are one,
Lord, hear our prayer.

Arise, O God, maintain your cause;
Do not forget the lives of the poor.

Look down from heaven, behold and tend this vine;
Preserve what your right hand has planted.

Let your priests be clothed with righteousness;
Let your faithful people sing with joy.

The Lord be with you.
And also with you.

Let us pray.

(Silence)

Let your continual mercy cleanse and defend your Church, O Lord;
and, because we cannot continue in safety without your help,
protect and govern us always by your goodness;
through Jesus Christ our Lord,
who lives and reigns with you and the Holy Spirit,
one God, for ever and ever. Amen.

THE BOOK OF OCCASIONAL SERVICES

74. For the Renewal of the Church

Let us pray to the Lord and Giver of life that the Church of God may be renewed and strengthened for its mission in our day.

(Silence)

That the Church may become alive again with the fire of its first charity, fearless of danger and reckless unto death, in the splendor of that Life which is the light of the world,
Holy Spirit, hear us.

That the Church may be worthy of its liberty, persistent in reform, active in benevolence, trusting the people, and ever faithful to the Jerusalem which is above, and free, and the mother of us all,
Holy Spirit, hear us.

That the old may dream dreams, and the young see visions; that its sons and daughters may prophesy, bearing eager witness of its beauty to the world,
Holy Spirit, hear us.

That all its members, putting self aside, disinterested and pure in heart, may seek and find God, and rejoice in the truth,
Holy Spirit, hear us.

That its ministers may be good and wise, strong and courageous, competent in their work, and faithful in their witness,
Holy Spirit, hear us.

That its bishops, full of insight and imagination, may venture great things, not exercising dominion, but serving as true leaders of the people,
Holy Spirit, hear us.

That its councils and conventions may be keen to go forward, filled with wisdom, eager to rebuild the walls of Jerusalem,
Holy Spirit, hear us.

That its scholars may have disciples, its prophets hearers, its saints imitators, and all its pioneers many anxious to follow in their steps,
Holy Spirit, hear us.

That we may forsake that love of party which keeps us from loving one another; and so, coming together in friendship, we may find the overpowering love of God, which shall knit us all together in one united Church,
Holy Spirit, hear us.

And, finally, that the Church, with love recovered in its midst, may teach all to love one another, and all nations to dwell together in helpfulness and friendship, reconciled and redeemed,
Holy Spirit, hear us.

Father, be with us all.
Christ, be with us all.
Holy Spirit, be with us all.
Be with us, Holy God, now and evermore.

God, our Shepherd, give to the Church a new vision and a new charity, new wisdom and fresh understanding, the revival of its brightness and the renewal of its unity; that the eternal message of your Son may be hailed as the good news of the new age; through him who makes all things new, even Jesus Christ our Lord.
Amen.

THE KINGDOM, THE POWER AND THE GLORY

75. For All Manner of Churches

Lord Jesus, Head of the Church, your Body:
We thank you for your ecumenical Church -
suffering, militant, and triumphant at the last.

We thank you for powerhouses of spiritual energy within your Church: for
Catholic retreat centers, Orthodox monasteries, and evangelical communities
like Iona in Scotland and Taizé in France.
Help them by their example to put energy and spirit
into our witness also.

We thank you for rural churches, serving farming communities and
providing much strength for those on whom we all depend.
Help them to find new ways of joint service
and to avoid the pitfall of self-pity.

We thank you for churches in small towns, focal points in their peoples'
striving for the enhancement of their common life.
Help them to keep in touch with the problems and needs of your world,
reaching out with a will to learn and to love.

We thank you for churches in commuter suburbs: for their ministry to
whole families and for their deep interest in family wholeness.
Help them to avoid the illusion of independence and of self-sufficiency
and remind them of their mission to the cities.

Lord, we thank you for city churches, fighting for their life, and making the
changes necessary to work with new people, people moving in and moving
out, all your children, all loved by you.
Help such churches to be versatile,
adaptable, imaginative, resourceful.

We thank you for specialized churches, experimental churches, churches
where Christians unlike us, who feel unaccepted by us or who cannot
themselves accept us, are seeking you.
Help them to find you, and strip us and them of truculence and hate, that
we may find each other in you.

We thank you for churches which do not seem like churches at all: for Christians meeting for Bible study in a living room, Christians gathering secretly to celebrate the Eucharist, Christians meeting at great peril to themselves in many parts of your world.
Help them to be aware of the world-wide communion
of Christians who care for them and pray for them always.

Lord Jesus, Head of the Church, your Body:
We thank you for your ecumenical Church—
suffering, militant, and triumphant at the last. Amen.

MODELS FOR MINISTERS I*

76. For the Diocese

Let us pray for the Church in this diocese.

Pour your abundant blessing, O Lord, on your servant _____, Bishop of
this diocese, that *he* may be guided and guarded day by day in leading and
serving those committed to *his* charge:
Hear us, good Lord.

Bless the Cathedral of _____ in _____, and shed your grace upon its Dean
and clergy and all its staff, that they may make it a true mother church to
the diocese:
Hear us, good Lord.

Direct the hearts and minds of all who assist the Bishop in the
administration of the diocese:
Hear us, good Lord.

Bless all the Clergy of the diocese, that they may be faithful stewards of
your mysteries, and carry forward the salvation of people everywhere:
Hear us, good Lord.

Grant your abundant blessing to all who minister in our cities, that they
may pursue their task with steadfastness and love:
Hear us, good Lord.

Bless all who work in the small towns and villages of the diocese, that they
may be sustained and guided in the special circumstances of their life and
ministry:
Hear us, good Lord.

Call to the work of ministry men and women who are full of the Holy
Spirit and of faith, and endue them with the spirit of power, and of love,
and of a sound mind:
Hear us, good Lord.

Bless all who are engaged in training candidates for the ministry in
universities, seminaries and divinity schools:
Hear us, good Lord.

Hallow the life and work of every Liturgical Assistant, that the worship of
the Church may be enriched, and your people strengthened:
Hear us, good Lord.

Guide and uphold Lay Missioners, and all who are engaged in the work of evangelism:
Hear us, good Lord.

Grant to all Churchwardens and Vestrymembers grace to execute their trust with loyalty and devotion:
Hear us, good Lord.

Inspire all Choir Directors, Organists and Choirmembers, that they may lead the praises of your people with joy and understanding:
Hear us, good Lord.

Prosper the work of all who teach and learn in our Sunday Schools, that our children may grow up in your faith and fear, and in the knowledge and love of Christ:
Hear us, good Lord.

Guide those who are responsible for managing the Diocesan Conference Center at _____, that it may minister to the needs of clergy and laity alike:
Hear us, good Lord.

Fill with your spirit all who serve on our diocesan councils and committees, that they may ever seek the advancement of your kingdom and have a right judgment in all things:
Hear us, good Lord.

Bless all religious communities that by their life and prayers, and their understanding of your word, they may strengthen and enrich your Church:
Hear us, good Lord.

Bless all the societies and guilds in the diocese, especially _____, that their members may be strong in bearing witness to the truth with faith and courage:
Hear us, good Lord.

Give us all a more earnest spirit of prayer, hospitality and self-denial, that those who do not know you may be brought to share in the blessings we so richly enjoy:
Hear us, good Lord.

Move the hearts of your people to be faithful stewards, giving willingly and regularly for the work of the Church, especially in _____, that the progress of the Gospel may be not hindered:
Hear us, good Lord.

Grant that our work for the Church at home may be matched by ever greater zeal for the extension of your kingdom overseas:
Hear us, good Lord.

O God, by your grace you have called us in this diocese to a goodly fellowship of faith. Grant that your Word may be truly preached and truly heard, your Sacraments faithfully administered and faithfully received. By your Spirit, fashion our lives according to the example of your Son, and grant that we may show the power of your love to all among whom we live; through Jesus Christ our Lord. Amen.

EMBER PRAYERS
AND THE BOOK OF COMMON PRAYER

77. Women of Power

Holy Spirit, Life-giver, we recall before you this day those women, known and unknown, who have used the power and gifts you gave them to change the world for good. Grant that, with their example in mind, we may find that same power in ourselves and use our gifts to build your kingdom of justice and peace.

We recall Eve, symbol of that ability to create which all human beings enjoy.
We pray for her power of creativity.

We recall Sarah, who with Abraham answered God's call to leave her homeland and place her faith in a covenant with the Lord.
We pray for her power of faith.

We recall Hagar, who shunned oppression and exploitation, and dared to talk to the Lord and give a name to God.
We pray for her power to face the unknown courageously.

We recall Esther and Deborah, who saved a nation through their acts of valor.
We pray for their power of will to act for the good of many.

We recall Mary, Mother of God, who became God's accomplice in setting all people free.
We pray for her power of trust and self-giving.

We recall Mary Magdalene and the other women, who faced disbelief when they announced Jesus' resurrection.
We pray for their power to believe in the face of skepticism.

We recall Phoebe and Priscilla, and the other women who were leaders of the early Church.
We pray for their power to spread the Gospel and to inspire communities of faith.

We recall Hilda and Julian and Hildegard, abbesses and mystics who kept faith and knowledge alive.
We pray for their power of leadership.

We recall Teresa of Avila and Catherine of Siena who challenged corruption and renewed the Church.
We pray for their power of intelligence and candor.

We recall Sojourner Truth, Harriet Tubman and Elizabeth Cady Stanton, liberators and prophets of the nineteenth century.
We pray for their power of conviction carried into action.

We recall our mothers and grandmothers whose lives gave shape to ours.
May the power at work in them and in all women of faith pass now to us.
Come, Holy Spirit, come and work in us as you worked in them. Amen.

ECUMENICAL ACT: AFFIRMING LIFE
ON INTERNATIONAL WOMEN'S DAY*

78. God with a Woman's Face

God of the poor,
come to us as a devout woman offering two mites.

God of the lost,
come to us as a prudent woman seeking a hidden coin.

God of the outsider,
come to us as an alien woman begging for the crumbs from our table.

God of the sick,
come to us as a bleeding woman grasping for a healing touch.

God of the condemned,
come to us as a judged woman fallen before her accusers.

God of the hurt,
come to us as a beautiful woman washing our feet with her hair.

God of the dying,
come to us as a mourning woman grieving for her brother.

Compassionate God,
Open our hearts to receive you as you visit us in women who have been
filled with your Spirit.

*You have blessed us all with dreams of a common future and gifts for a
common life; in all things keep us faithful to the message of your Gospel,
so that, as women and men together, we may bear witness to your love in
Christ Jesus. Amen.*

KATHY GALLOWAY*

79. Dedication to God's Design †

Let us kneel and offer ourselves to God that we may know how to take our share in God's design for the world.

Let us pray.

(Silence)

That we may put ourselves alongside our fellows and see the Christian faith and life from their point of view:
Lord, hear our prayer.

That the Church may be aware of the rapid rate of change both in the thought of men and women and in their social circumstances:
Lord, hear our prayer.

For the wisdom of the Holy Spirit in the large-scale and complex problems of society and work today, which require corporate judgments and solutions:
Lord, hear our prayer.

That in the choices facing us today, in situations partly good and partly evil, we may be granted the insights of the Holy Spirit, and guided to make decisions which will forward your will:
Lord, hear our prayer.

That you will grant to Christians working in big organizations the faith to share in some small way your active concern for the good ordering of people's lives and the supplying of their needs:
Lord, hear our prayer.

That we may see in our daily work the opportunity to serve you through the truth of our insights, the honesty of our service, and our concern for our fellow-workers:
Lord, hear our prayer.

That you will bless those groups of Christians who are trying to discover how they may best exercise Christian vocation through their professions:
Lord, hear our prayer.

That our local churches may no longer be seen as arks of safety, but as powerhouses of grace for the invading forces of your Kingdom:
Lord, hear our prayer.

That you will bless and guide all lay movements which seek to advance your Kingdom in special spheres of work or in particular neighborhoods:
Lord, hear our prayer.

That you will guide our local churches to face the challenge of these movements, to learn from them and to offer them understanding and grateful fellowship:
Lord, hear our prayer.

That you will enable the clergy to bring the light of your truth to your people and the grace of the sacraments to their strengthening:
Lord, hear our prayer.
Amen.

PRAYERS FOR TODAY'S CHURCH

80. The Spirit of Jesus

Each section may be used separately, or the whole may be used as one continuous litany.

1. In the Ministry of Jesus

Holy Spirit,
who came upon the Virgin Mary
so that she became the mother of Jesus,   (Luke 1:34)
    we pray to you:
Open our hearts to your word,
help us to receive Jesus, the Word of God.

Holy Spirit,
who came upon Zechariah, Elizabeth, Simeon,   (Luke 1:41, 67)
and Anna, and helped them recognize the Messiah,   (Luke 2:26)
    we pray to you:
Enlighten the eyes of our hearts
so that we may know how to recognize Jesus, the Lord.

Holy Spirit,   (Matthew 3:16)
who came upon Christ Jesus   (Mark 1:10)
when he was baptized in the waters of the Jordan,   (Luke 3:22)
    we pray to you:
Baptize us in the fire of your love
so that the Father may say to each of us: (Matthew 3:17)
"You are my beloved;   (Luke 3:22)
on you my favor rests."

Holy Spirit,   (Matthew 4:1)
who led Christ Jesus   (Mark 1:12)
out into the desert of temptation,   (Luke 4:1)
    we pray to you:
Give us the strength
to conquer in ourselves the power of evil.

Holy Spirit,
who sent Christ Jesus   (Matthew 12:18-21)
to carry the Good News to the poor,   (Luke 4:18-19)
    we pray to you:
Help us to continue your work
by serving the poor, our brothers and sisters.

Holy Spirit,
who spoke the truth by the mouth of despised disciples, (Matthew 10:20)
      we pray to you:
Place in us your words of wisdom;   (Luke 13:11)
help us to conquer evil by good.   (Romans 12:21)

2. In the Acts of the Apostles

Spirit of Jesus,   (Acts 2:1-11)
poured out in flames of fire upon your disciples   (Acts 4:31)
on the day of Pentecost,
      we pray to you:
Set afire the hearts of your faithful
so that they will announce in all the languages of the world
the wonders of the salvation of God.

Holy Spirit,
who led the deacon Philip on the road from Gaza
to the meeting with the eunuch of the queen of Ethiopia
and had him announce the Good News of Jesus,   (Acts 8:26-40)
      we pray to you:
Lead your missionaries
toward all those who are seeking the truth.

Holy Spirit,
who built up the infant churches   (Acts 9:31)
and filled them with your consolation,
      we pray to you:
Make the Kingdom of God on earth
grow by your joy and your peace.

Holy Spirit,
who called Paul and Barnabas
to their mission among the pagans   (Acts 13:4)
and filled them with the joy
of announcing the Good News,   (Acts 13:52)
      we pray to you:
Today bring to life fervent witnesses for Christ.

Holy Spirit,
who helped the apostles at the council of Jerusalem
and inspired their decisions, (Acts 15:28)
    we pray to you:
Enlighten those in authority
that their ministry
will be of service to their brothers and sisters. (Acts 20:28)

Holy Spirit,
who pointed out the way for your disciples
to announce the Gospel, (Acts 16:6-8)
    we pray to you:
As in the time of the apostles,
guide today's messengers of the Good News.

3. In the Life of the Church

Spirit of Jesus,
you pour the love of God into our hearts; (Romans 5:5)
    we pray to you:
Enflame all our lives
with the fire of your love.

Holy Spirit,
you raised Christ Jesus from the dead; (Romans 8:11)
    we pray to you:
Stamp upon us the seal of eternal life.

Spirit of Jesus,
you make us holy temples
to the glory of the Father;
    we pray to you:
Help us to glorify God in our bodies. (I Corinthians 6:19-20)

Holy Spirit,
you distribute your gifts
for the common good of the whole Church; (I Corinthians 12:4-11)
    we pray to you:
Let the variety of gifts and of ministries
strengthen the unity of the whole body
that all may be loved in the Church
for the special work they accomplish.

Holy Spirit,
in you we have been baptized
to form only one Body;   (I Corinthians 12:13)
    we pray to you:
Gather together all Christians
in the unity of your Church.

Spirit of Jesus,
wherever you reign,   (II Corinthians 3:17)
there freedom triumphs;
    we pray to you:
Lead us to the complete truth,   (John 16:13)
so that your truth will make us free.   (John 8:32)

Spirit of truth,   (John 14:17)
whom the Father sends in the name of the Son,
    we pray to you:
Recall to our memories the words of Jesus   (John 14:26)
and keep them in our hearts.
Amen.

LUCIEN DEISS   From *Come, Lord Jesus,* ©1976, 1981 by Lucien Deiss
Reprinted with permission.

81. The Work of the Spirit

O Lord, who hast set before us the great hope that thy kingdom shall come on earth, and hast taught us to pray for its coming, make us ever ready to thank thee for the signs of its dawning, and to pray and work for that perfect day when thy will shall be done on earth as it is in heaven.

For the work of thy Spirit within and beyond the bounds of thy visible Church,
We thank thee, O Lord.

For the work of thy Spirit in the history of the world, through peaceful advance, and through pain and tumult,
We thank thee, O Lord.

For the work of thy Spirit in the history of our own country, through its heroes and leaders, in politics, law, and industry,
We thank thee, O Lord.

For the work of thy Spirit in science and commerce, in literature and art,
We thank thee, O Lord.

For the work of thy Spirit in the slow triumph of truth over error,
We thank thee, O Lord.

For the work of thy Spirit in the growing desire for unity and harmony, between people of every class and nation,
We thank thee, O Lord.

For the work of thy Spirit in the spread of education, and in the development of a fuller life for individuals, with healthier surroundings and better conditions,
We thank thee, O Lord.

For the work of thy Spirit in the deepening sense of human worth and in the growing respect for womanhood and childhood,
We thank thee, O Lord.

For the work of thy Spirit in the Church, which will not cease till it joins all nations and kindreds and tongues and peoples into one great family, to thy praise and glory,
We thank thee, O Lord. Amen.

THE KINGDOM, THE POWER AND THE GLORY

82. The Fruits of the Spirit

Leader 1:
Jesus said, "This is my Father's glory, that you bear fruit in plenty and so be my disciples." Let us pray for a new heart and a new spirit, that we may show forth the fruits of the Spirit abundantly in our lives.

Silence.

Create in us a clean heart, O God,
And renew a right spirit within us.

Leader 1:
We pray for the fruit of the Spirit which is love, that we may cherish our sisters and brothers in the one family of Christ throughout the world;

Leader 2:
And for the fruit of the Spirit which is patience, that all who shepherd the flock of Christ may with wisdom and forbearance lead us in the way we should go.

Leader 2:
If the Spirit is the source of our life,
let the Spirit also direct our course.

Leader 1:
We pray for the fruit of the Spirit which is self-control that all the leaders of the nations may exercise power with restraint and authority with compassion;

Leader 2:
And for the fruit of the Spirit which is peace, that we may work untiringly for understanding, cooperation and harmony among the nations of the world.

Leader 2:
If the Spirit is the source of our life,
· *let the Spirit also direct our course.*

Leader 1:
We pray for the fruit of the Spirit which is joy, that we may delight in the beauty of God's creation and the diversity of God's children;

Leader 2:
And for the fruit of the Spirit which is goodness, that we may commend the hope of the Gospel to others by the generosity and integrity of our lives.

Leader 2:
If the Spirit is the source of our life,
let the Spirit also direct our course.

Leader 1:
We pray for the fruit of the Spirit which is kindness, that we may care for all whose lives are closely linked with ours;

Leader 2:
And for the fruit of the Spirit which is gentleness, that we may seek out and serve the sick and the handicapped, the lonely and the needy.

Leader 2:
If the Spirit is the source of our life,
let the Spirit also direct our course.

Leader 1:
We pray for the fruit of the Spirit which is faithfulness, that we may be worthy of our heritage in Christ Jesus and show forth the faith of those who have gone before us in living words and loving deeds.

Silence.

Everliving God, whose will it is that all should come to you through your Son Jesus Christ: Inspire our witness to him, that all may know the power of his forgiveness and the hope of his resurrection; who lives and reigns with you and the Holy Spirit, one God, now and for ever. Amen.

JEFFERY W. ROWTHORN*

PRAYER
AND
THE
LOCAL COMMUNITY

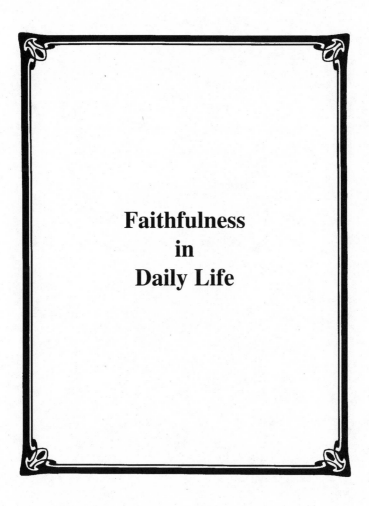

**Faithfulness
in
Daily Life**

83. For Disciples

Jesus said: "Whoever among you wants to be great must become the servant of all. For the Son of Man himself has not come to be served but to serve, and to give his life to set many others free."
Master, we hear your call;
Lord Jesus, help us to follow.

Jesus said: "Unless you change your whole outlook and become like little children, you will never enter the kingdom of heaven."
Master, we hear your call;
Lord Jesus, help us to follow.

Jesus said: "Blessed are the poor in spirit, for theirs is the kingdom of heaven. Blessed are the meek, for they shall inherit the earth."
Master, we hear your call;
Lord Jesus, help us to follow.

Jesus said: "You must love your enemies, and do good without expecting any return and without giving up hope on anyone; so will you be children of the Most High, because God indeed is kind to the ungrateful and wicked. Be compassionate, as your Father is compassionate."
Master, we hear your call;
Lord Jesus, help us to follow.

Jesus said: "This is my Father's glory, that you may bear fruit in plenty and so be my disciples. If you dwell in me, as I dwell in you, you will bear much fruit; for apart from me you can do nothing."
Master, we hear your call;
Lord Jesus, help us to follow.

Jesus said: "There is no greater love than this, that you should lay down your life for your friends. This is my commandment; love one another, as I have loved you."
Master, we hear your call;
Lord Jesus, help us to follow.

Jesus said: "All power in heaven and on earth has been given to me. You, then, are to go and make disciples of all the nations and baptize them in the name of the Father, and of the Son, and of the Holy Spirit. Teach them to observe all that I have commanded you. And remember, I am with you always, even to the end of the world."
Master, we hear your call;
Lord Jesus, help us to follow.
Amen.

CONTEMPORARY PRAYERS FOR PUBLIC WORSHIP

84. The Mind of Christ

"Let your bearing towards one another arise out of your life in Christ Jesus." (Philippians 2:5)

Let us then remember Jesus:
who, though he was rich, yet for our sakes became poor and dwelt among us;
who was content to be subject to his parents, the child of a poor couple's home.
May this mind be in us that was in Christ Jesus.

Who lived for nearly thirty years an ordinary life, earning his living with his own hands and refusing no humble tasks;
whom the common people heard gladly, for he understood their ways.
May this mind be in us that was in Christ Jesus.

Let us remember Jesus:
who was mighty in deed, healing the sick and the disordered, using for others the powers he would not invoke for himself;
who refused to force anyone's allegiance.
May this mind be in us that was in Christ Jesus.

Who was Master and Lord to his disciples, yet was among them as their companion and as one who served;
whose meat was to do the will of the Father who sent him.
May this mind be in us that was in Christ Jesus.

Let us remember Jesus:
who loved people, yet retired from them to pray, rose a great while before day, watched through a night, stayed in the wilderness, went up into a mountain, sought a garden;
who, when he would help a tempted disciple, prayed for him.
May this mind be in us that was in Christ Jesus.

Who prayed for the forgiveness of those who rejected him, and for the perfecting of those who received him;
who observed good customs, but defied conventions which did not serve the purposes of God;
who hated sin because he knew the human cost of pride and selfishness, of cruelty and impurity, and still more the cost to his Father in heaven.
May this mind be in us that was in Christ Jesus.

Let us remember Jesus:
who believed in people to the last and never despaired of them;
who through all disappointment never lost heart;
who disregarded his own comfort and convenience, and thought first of
others' needs, and though he suffered long, was always kind.
May this mind be in us that was in Christ Jesus.

Who, when he was reviled, reviled not again, and when he suffered,
threatened not;
who humbled himself and carried obedience to the point of death, even
death on the cross, and endured faithful to the end.
May this mind be in us that was in Christ Jesus.

O Christ, our only Savior, so come to dwell in us that we may go forth with
the light of your hope in our eyes, and with your faith and love in our hearts.
Amen.

THE KINGDOM, THE POWER AND THE GLORY

85. The Greatest of These Is Love
-I Corinthians 13

Love is patient and kind.

O God, help us to be patient with people,
even when they are foolish and annoying;
and help us to be as kind to others
as we would wish them to be to us.

Love is not jealous or boastful.

O God, help us never to grudge other people
their possessions or successes,
and keep us from all pride and conceit,
that we may never boast of what we are,
or have, or have achieved.

Love is not arrogant or rude.

O God, make us at all times courteous,
and no matter who the other person is,
help us never to look on anyone with contempt.

Love does not insist on its own way; it is not irritable or resentful.

O God, help us not to be irritable
and difficult to live with,
nor to resent criticism or rebuke,
even when we do not deserve it.

Love does not rejoice at wrong, but rejoices in the right.

O God, help us never to find pleasure in any wrong thing,
but to find happiness only in doing the right,
and in helping others to do it.

Love bears all things.

O God, help us to bear insults and slights,
and never to grow bitter.

Love believes all things.

O God, help us never to lose faith
in Jesus our Lord.

Love hopes all things.

O God, help us never to despair,
however dark and difficult and discouraging life may be.

Love endures all things.

O God, help us to stick it out to the end,
and never to give in.

Love never ends. For faith, hope, and love abide, these three; but the greatest of these is love.

O God, you are love;
help us to show your love to others each day of our lives.
This we ask for your love's sake. Amen.

WILLIAM BARCLAY
-EPILOGUES AND PRAYERS

86. Hearing and Heeding

Jesus Christ said, Do not lay up for yourselves treasures on earth, but lay up for yourselves treasures in heaven.
O God, incline our hearts to follow in this way.

Jesus Christ said, Seek first the kingdom of God and his righteousness.
O God, incline our hearts to follow in this way.

Jesus Christ said, Do good and lend, hoping for nothing in return.
O God, incline our hearts to follow in this way.

Jesus Christ said, Love your enemies.
O God, incline our hearts to follow in this way.

Jesus Christ said, Watch and pray, that you do not enter into temptation.
O God, incline our hearts to follow in this way.

Jesus Christ said, Fear not, only believe.
O God, incline our hearts to follow in this way.

Jesus Christ said, Except you turn again and become as little children, you shall not enter into the kingdom of heaven.
O God, incline our hearts to follow in this way.

Jesus Christ said, Ask and it shall be given you; seek, and you shall find; knock, and it shall be opened to you.
O God, incline our hearts to follow in this way. Amen.

JOHN BAILLIE

87. For Spiritual Growth

As our knowledge grows larger,
increase our love of the truth.

As our arms grow stronger,
increase our respect for love.

As our world grows smaller,
increase our sense of community.

As our nation grows more divided,
increase our efforts for unity.

As our neighborhood grows more impersonal,
increase our attempts to know each other.

As our families grow up,
increase our interests in others.

As our freedoms grow greater,
increase our powers of self-control.

As our material comforts grow in number,
increase our interest in things of the spirit.

As our institutions grow more complex,
increase our concern for the individual.

As our laws grow more complicated,
increase our hopes for justice.

As our future grows more uncertain,
increase our appreciation for the present.

As our bodies grow older,
increase our faith in the one eternal God. Amen.

LARRY HARD

88. For God's Presence at All Times

Let us pray, asking the Lord to make his presence known to us.

(Silence)

When we lose sight of the power you hold as Lord and Master of history -
Stay with us then, O Lord.

When we fail to recognize your presence in the events of our daily life -
Stay with us then, O Lord.

When we do not remember that it is necessary for us to suffer and die with
you so as to share your glory -
Stay with us then, O Lord.

When we make our minds dull and foolish so that we do not understand the
word that you speak to us -
Stay with us then, O Lord.

When we are tempted to think of your Church as a mere set of restrictions
and obligations which weigh upon us -
Stay with us then, O Lord.

When we are inclined not to face the real situations that arise in our lives,
but prefer to turn from them and from seeking your holy will in them -
Stay with us then, O Lord.

When our feelings tell us that the trials you send us are a sign that you have
abandoned us -
Stay with us then, O Lord.

When our emotions deceive us into thinking that evils are not evil because
you permit them -
Stay with us then, O Lord.

When our need for material security makes us confuse good providence
with greed -
Stay with us then, O Lord.

When our impulse to show our love for others degenerates into selfish
attempts to satisfy our own passions -
Stay with us then, O Lord.

When the representatives of your holy authority are seen by us as merely human, and not as the bearers of your will for us -
Stay with us then, O Lord.

When the day of our life on earth draws towards evening and the hand of death tightens its grip upon us -
Stay with us Lord, then and forever. Amen.

SCRIPTURE SERVICES

89. A Litany of the Tongue ✝

O God, you have given power to our tongues to create light or darkness in the lives of our friends; help us to keep watch over our words.

Let the words of my mouth, and the meditation of my heart, be acceptable in your sight, O Lord, my Strength and my Redeemer.

From backbiting and talebearing, from uncharitable judgement, from flattery and scandal, from deliberate lie and subtle insincerity, guard our wayward tongues.

Let the words of my mouth, and the meditation of my heart, be acceptable in your sight, O Lord, my Strength and my Redeemer.

We humbly confess before you the harm done by our hasty speech. We have discouraged those we might have helped, embittered those we might have sweetened, exasperated those we might have pacified, depressed those we might have gladdened, misguided those we might have led. Convert, we entreat you, our disordered and ill-tempered tongues.

Create in me a clean heart, O God, and renew a right spirit within me.

Let all bitterness and anger and evil-speaking be put away from us, together with all malice.

Create in me a clean heart, O God, and renew a right spirit within me.

Use our tongues for noble ends. To hearten the dismayed, illumine the benighted, strengthen the weak, comfort the sad; to bring light out of darkness, friendship out of enmity, and joy out of pain.

Guide our lips, O Lord.

May good causes, hard beset by many enemies, be strengthened by our forthright speech. Let not unpopularity affright us nor cowardice detain us from the stout utterance of our best convictions. May no right be denied to anyone, no hopeful movement of your purpose fail for want of our supporting word.

Guide our lips, O Lord.

Forasmuch as we must speak to our own hearts before we can speak to others, watch the inner conversation of our souls. Let not the rudder of our tongues turn the ship of our own spirits into perverse courses. Free our self-communion from every crooked way; let our inner meditation enlighten our outward speech, and may we so wisely talk to ourselves that we can persuasively talk to others.

Have mercy on us, O Lord, and grant us these blessings. Amen.

HARRY EMERSON FOSDICK

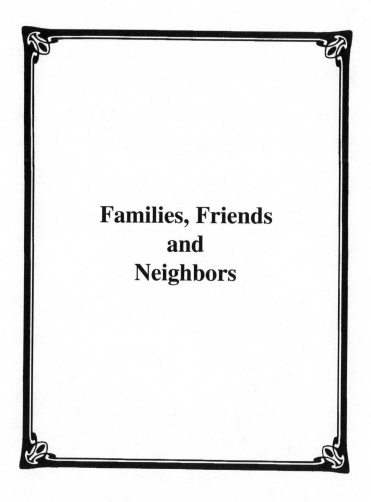

**Families, Friends
and
Neighbors**

90. Men and Women †

A woman: God, whose likeness and image we are,

A man: you have made us male and female,

A woman: ordained that our very life
come from the union of the sexes,

A man: and fashioned our world in such a way
that this distinction
is within its very structure.

All: *For what we are,*
we give you thanks.

A woman: For tenderness and gentleness and pity,
for the love of beauty
and order and tranquility,
and for the instinct to give shelter
and nourish and enfold,

All: *For all that is of woman,*
we give you thanks.

A man: For decisiveness and action and strength,
for the love of precision
and accomplishment and endeavor,
and for the instinct to protect
and lead and determine,

All: *For all that is of man,*
we give you thanks.

A woman: And yet, Lord,
women can also be strong.
Why must we be treated as if we were weak
and incompetent and unworthy?

A man: And, Lord,
men can also love beauty.
Why must we be treated as if we were weak
and insensitive and unfeeling?

All:	*Help us, Lord, to see ourselves as complete persons,*
	and give us the sense to allow others
	to be themselves.

A woman:	Set women free
	from the expectations of others
	and the chains of tradition
	and the pressures of society.

A man:	Set men free
	from their need to dominate
	and their fear of change
	and their pride.

All:	*Help us, Lord, to be completely human*
	by allowing us to be sexually complete.

A woman:	Let women continue to cherish
	homes and families,
	recipes and fashions.

A man:	Let men continue to work with
	their hands and minds,
	concerned for athletics
	and tools and motors.

All:	*So may it be, Father,*
	that as we are, we praise you
	by coming together in the order of your creation,
	each adding our sexuality
	and our being as humans,
	created by you for your world.

A woman:	Increase our respect and regard one for another,

A man:	and teach us to gain from each other
	that our lives may be fulfilled,

All:	*For we pray in the name of Jesus.*
	Amen.

CARL T. UEHLING

91. For a Couple on Their Wedding Day

Eternal God, creator and preserver of all life, author of salvation, and giver of all grace: Look with favor upon the world you have made, and for which your Son gave his life, and especially upon this man and this woman whom you make one flesh in Holy Matrimony.
Lord, in your mercy,
Hear our prayer.

Give them wisdom and devotion in the ordering of their common life, that each may be to the other a strength in need, a counselor in perplexity, a comfort in sorrow, and a companion in joy.
Lord, in your mercy,
Hear our prayer.

Grant that their wills may be so knit together in your will, and their spirits in your Spirit, that they may grow in love and peace with you and one another all the days of their life.
Lord, in your mercy,
Hear our prayer.

Give them grace, when they hurt each other, to recognize and acknowledge their fault, and to seek each other's forgiveness and yours.
Lord, in your mercy,
Hear our prayer.

Make their life together a sign of Christ's love to this sinful and broken world, that unity may overcome estrangement, forgiveness heal guilt, and joy conquer despair.
Lord, in your mercy,
Hear our prayer.

Bestow on them, if it is your will, the gift and heritage of children, and the grace to bring them up to know you, to love you, and to serve you.
Lord, in your mercy,
Hear our prayer.

Give them such fulfillment of their mutual affection that they may reach out in love and concern for others.
Lord, in your mercy,
Hear our prayer.

Grant that all married persons who have witnessed these vows may find their lives strengthened and their loyalties confirmed.
Lord, in your mercy,
Hear our prayer.

Grant that the bonds of our common humanity, by which all your children are united one to another, and the living to the dead, may be so transformed by your grace, that your will may be done on earth as it is in heaven; where, O Father, with your Son and the Holy Spirit, you live and reign in perfect unity, now and for ever. *Amen.*

THE BOOK OF COMMON PRAYER 1979

92. In Praise of Marriage †

Thanksgiving for Marriage

(Everyone stands and a husband and wife lead an Act of Thanksgiving for Marriage. The people make their reply loudly and with enthusiasm.)

Husband:　　Let us thank God for our wedding day.

　　All:　　*Thanks be to God.*

　　Wife:　　Let us thank God for the wonder of falling in love and making love.

　　All:　　*Thanks be to God.*

Husband:　　Let us thank God for our wives.

Husbands:　　*Thanks be to God.*

　　Wife:　　Let us thank God for our husbands.

　Wives:　　*Thanks be to God.*

Husband:　　Let us thank God for our homes.

　　All:　　*Thanks be to God.*

　　Wife:　　Let us thank God for our children.

　　All:　　*Thanks be to God.*

Husband:　　Let us thank God for our friends.

　　All:　　*Thanks be to God.*

　　Wife:　　Let us thank God for everything.

　　All:　　*Thanks be to God.*

Reaffirmation of Marriage Vows

(The people are seated.)

Husband:	Listen to what St. Paul has to say about marriage, and how he sees in it a mirror of Christ's love for his Church.
Wife:	"Husbands, love your wives, as Christ also loved the Church and gave himself up for it, to consecrate it, cleansing it by water and word, so that he might present the Church to himself all glorious, with no stain or wrinkle or anything of the sort, but holy and without blemish."
Husband:	"In the same way, men also are bound to love their wives, as they love their own bodies. In loving his wife a man loves himself. For no one ever hated his own body; on the contrary he provides and cares for it; and that is how Christ treats the Church, because it is his Body, of which we are living parts."
Wife:	Thus it is that (in the words of Scripture): "A man shall leave his father and mother and shall be joined to his wife, and the two shall become a single body." It is a great truth that is hidden here.
Husband:	"I for my part refer it to Christ and to the Church, but it applies also individually: each of you must love his wife as his very self";
Wife:	"And the woman must see to it that she pays her husband all respect."

(Everyone stands for the Reaffirmation of the Marriage Vows.)

Husband:	I call upon the husbands here to reaffirm their marriage vows, saying with me:
Husbands:	*I reaffirm my solemn promise to my wife to have and to hold, for better, for worse; for richer, for poorer; in sickness and in health; to love and to cherish, till death us do part.*
Wife:	I call upon the wives here to reaffirm their marriage vows to their husbands.

| Wives: | *I reaffirm my solemn promise to my husband to have and to hold, for better, for worse; for richer, for poorer; in sickness and in health; to love and to cherish, till death us do part.* |

Blessing of Married Couples

| Minister: | May God the Father, who at creation ordained that man and woman become one flesh, keep you one. *Amen.* |

May God the Son, who adorned this manner of life by his first miracle, at the wedding in Cana of Galilee, be present with you always. *Amen.*

May God the Holy Spirit, who has given you the will to persevere in your love and in your covenant with each other, strengthen your bond. *Amen.*

And may God the Holy Trinity, the source of all unity, bless you this day and for ever. *Amen.*

PRAYERS FOR TODAY'S CHURCH
AND THE BOOK OF OCCASIONAL SERVICES*

93. Fathers

Alleluia! happy the man who dreads the Lord
By joyfully keeping the commandments.
Alleluia! He is happy indeed.

Children of such men will be powers on earth,
Descendents of the upright will always be blessed.
Alleluia! He is happy indeed.

Everything will prosper in his family,
For his virtue will never falter.
Alleluia! He is happy indeed.

Giving light to good men in a dark world,
He is merciful, tender-hearted, virtuous.
Alleluia! He is happy indeed.

Interest is not charged by this good man,
Justly he conducts all his business.
Alleluia! He is happy indeed.

Kept safe by virtue, he stands for ever,
Leaving behind him an imperishable memory;
Alleluia! He is happy indeed.

Maintaining his confidence in the Lord,
Never needing to fear bad news,
Alleluia! He is happy indeed.

Outfacing fear with firmness of heart, until
Patience is rewarded by the downfall of enemies.
Alleluia! He is happy indeed.

Quick to be generous, he gives to the poor;
Right conduct for him is no passing fancy.
Alleluia! He is happy indeed.

Such men as this will always be honored,
Though this fills the wicked with fury,
Alleluia! He is happy indeed.

Until, grinding their teeth, they waste away,
Vanishing like their empty aspirations.
  Alleluia! Happy the man who dreads the Lord
  by joyfully keeping the commandments. Amen.

PSALM 112*

94. Mothers †

God of grace and love, we pray for your richest blessing upon all mothers:

Loving God, we thank you that Jesus enjoyed a mother's love and grew up within a family.
Thanks be to God!

We thank you for the homes where we were born and for the care and affection of our mothers.
Thanks be to God!

We thank you if we are still privileged to enjoy the warmth and security of family life.
Thanks be to God!

We pray for all mothers today:

For expectant mothers, especially those awaiting the birth of their first child;
We pray to you, O Lord.

For those who have young children and who get tired and harassed with so much to do;
We pray to you, O Lord.

For those with difficult homes, whose children are more of a problem than a blessing;
We pray to you, O Lord.

For those with difficult husbands, who find it hard to be constant and loving;
We pray to you, O Lord.

For those who find it hard to make ends meet, or who go short themselves for the sake of their families;
We pray to you, O Lord.

For those who are nearly at the end of their tether;
We pray to you, O Lord.

For those who are anxious because their children are growing up and seem to be growing away from them;
We pray to you, O Lord.

For those who feel a sense of emptiness as their children marry and leave home;
We pray to you, O Lord.

For those mothers who are trying to make Christ real to their families;
We pray to you, O Lord.

For those who do not know him as their Savior, nor how to cast their care on him;
We pray to you, O Lord.

For those who are elderly and may feel unwanted;
We pray to you, O Lord.

For those have no husband to share their responsibilities - the widowed, the divorced, and the unmarried mother,
We pray to you, O Lord.

We pray also for those who have been denied the privilege of motherhood, those who cannot have children of their own, and those who have never had the opportunity to marry,
We pray to you, O Lord.

Lastly, we pray for those closest to us; may we love and care for them as we ourselves have been loved and helped. We ask it for your love's sake. *Amen.*

CHRISTOPHER IDLE AND JOHN D. SEARLE
-PRAYERS FOR TODAY'S CHURCH

95. Friendship †

O gracious Spirit, who hast tempered the rigor of this present world with the loveliness of friendship, we rejoice in our friends.
Thanks be to thee, O Lord.

For the encouragement of their love, the support of their confidence, the faithfulness of their counsel, and the warmth of their affection,
Thanks be to thee, O Lord.

For those most singular and blessed gifts of friendship - power to keep faith with our own souls; to walk cleanly amid the soil and bravely amid the disheartenment of life; to believe in our best in the face of failure, and in extremities to be of excellent hope,
Thanks be to thee, O Lord.

For friends, living on earth and departed hence, whose love has been our peace and strength; for the beauty of their lives through which thou hast shined upon us like the sun through eastern windows; and for thy Christ who called us not servants, but friends,
Thanks be to thee, O Lord.

Because our sins hurt not ourselves only, but our friends, we are ashamed and penitent. For hasty temper and thoughtless word, for lack of kindliness and understanding, and for all disloyal dealing, open or secret, whereby we have betrayed those who trusted us,
We repent before thee, O Lord.

We stand in awe before our power to sway the lives and control the happiness of those who love us. For all misuse of friendship to untoward ends, for unbelief that mars the faith of friends, for low tastes which drag them down, for miserable moods which cloud their skies, and for all unworthy living which roughens their spiritual journey,
We repent before thee, O Lord.

Because friendship is so excellent a grace, widen its domain, we beseech thee. Reclaim from violence and strife the relationships of races and nations; redeem them from suspicion and prejudice to good will and trust. O Sun of Righteousness, shine on our fierce and wayward world, and lighten its path to closeness and unity in thee.
Lord, have mercy upon us and grant us this blessing.

Make our human friendships, we beseech thee, a revelation to our souls of thine unfailing love. Despite the mysterious dealings of thy Providence, may we walk by faith in thy friendliness. Enfold us in thy grace, support us by thy power, establish us in thy fellowship, and grant us the crown of life, that we should ever be the friends of God.

Lord, have mercy upon us and grant us this blessing. Amen.

HARRY EMERSON FOSDICK

96. The Various Ages of Life †

Leader: We come from the various ages of our lives, Father,
offering what we are,

All: *and asking that your love*
will continue,
age after age,
year after year.

A child: Be with your people who are children.
Help their teachers and parents.
Keep them from harm and danger.
Make them strong and wise and happy.

All: *Father, may your love continue with us year after year.*

An
elderly
person: Be with your people who are old.
Give them patience for their infirmities,
and companions for their lonely hours.
Give them new evidence of your love,
and teach them to trust you
above all others.

All: *Father, may your love continue with us year after year.*

A young
person: Be with your people who are young.
Encourage their enthusiasm,
resolve their doubts and anxieties,
and lengthen their perspectives.

All: *Father, may your love continue with us year after year.*

A person
in mid-life: Be with your people in mid-life.
Help them to deal with their fears
for themselves and their families.
Preserve them from boredom,
selfishness and indulgence,
and other bad fruits
of our affluent society.

All: *Father, may your love continue with us year after year.*

Leader:	See us in our stages in life, Father,
	and come to us in our needs.
	Show us how we need each other,
	and the ways in which we can come together.

All:	*Lord, help us to meet each other's needs.*

A Child:	Give those of us who are children
	the love of those who might be
	our grandparents.
	We need the time they can give to us,
	and their love.

All:	*Lord, help us to meet each other's needs.*

An elderly person:	Give those of us who are old
	young children whom we might spoil
	with our love.
	We need their smiles and joy,
	their innocent view of life.

All:	*Lord, help us to meet each other's needs.*

A young person:	Give those of us who are young
	the friendship of those who might be
	our parents.
	We need their interest in our lives,
	their counsel and advice.

All:	*Lord, help us to meet each other's needs.*

A person in mid-life:	Give those of us who are in mid-life
	the young whom we might see
	as though seeing ourselves.
	We need their carefree confidence,
	their newer ways of thinking and doing.

All:	*Lord, help us to meet each other's needs.*

Leader:	Our times are in your hands, Father,
	and a thousand years in your sight
	are like a day.

You know that the youngest among us
will become the oldest,
that even the oldest is but a child
before you.

All: *Help us to see what we need from one another,*
         and how we can help one another,
         after the example of Jesus Christ, your Son, our Lord,
         who lives and reigns with you
         and the Holy Spirit,
         one God now and for ever. Amen.

CARL T. UEHLING

97. On Growing Old

Holy Trinity, One God,
gateway to eternity,
Help us to your kingdom.

Lord,
our thoughts are as hard to communicate
as they were when we were children.
We talk,
sometimes endlessly, we fear,
and the expressions on the faces of listeners
show that they do not hear.
Preoccupied,
they wait to leave us.
Holy Trinity, One God,
gateway to eternity,
reunite us in your kingdom.

But it need not be a sorrow
to find ourselves alone.
We need some time
to rearrange our memories
and discard mistaken choices,
so that what we keep
to bring to you
may be named the best we knew.
Holy Trinity, One God,
gateway to eternity,
perfect us for your kingdom.

And yet,
our losses we recall with pain.
With the ache in our bones
comes an aching longing
to hear again a familiar laugh,
to feel the tenderness,
to share.
Lord, save us from living on memory.
You have the company of those we loved.
You share it now.
To be old is to miss those with whom we learned our sharing.

Holy Trinity, One God,
gateway to eternity,
fill us with longing for your kingdom.

Still, Lord, we must not
neglect the present.
Today may be the last we have
to enjoy
the manner in which morning sunlight comes,
and evening shadows lengthen;
to smile at friends;
to read a printed page.
Let some wisdom
we did not know before
strike at our hearts with
leaping recognition.
Yes!
Holy Trinity, One God,
gateway to eternity,
prepare us for your kingdom.

Tonight our souls may be required of us.
Holy Trinity, One God,
gateway to eternity,
welcome us to your kingdom.
Amen.

KAY SMALLZRIED

98. For the Elderly

We remember before you, O Lord, with gratitude, with shame, and with renewed concern, the many millions of older people in this country. We pray for them, and especially for the elderly in this community.

(Silence)

The wisdom and experience that they have acquired in so many ways over so many years;
   This we remember with gratitude.

The time they devote to loving and spoiling and listening to the young;
   This we remember with gratitude.

Their adaptability to changing circumstances in a time when nothing seems to be permanent or dependable;
   This we remember with gratitude.

Their appreciation for nature, their love of travel, their curiosity and zest for life;
   This we remember with gratitude.

Their courage in facing physical disability, suffering, and the approach of death;
   This we remember with gratitude.

(Silence)

Our ignoring of their opinions and of their contributions so that they feel useless and unwanted;
   This we remember with shame.

Our confining of them, the old with the old, in nursing homes and institutions;
   This we remember with shame.

Our letting them live on shrinking incomes and on inadequate food;
   This we remember with shame.

Our failure to design or adapt our churches so that they may enter and move about in them with ease;
   This we remember with shame.

Our letting them die slow and desperate deaths in unheated, unvisited apartments;
This we remember with shame.

(Silence)

Almighty God, help us with renewed concern to celebrate and use the vast treasure of wisdom, knowledge and experience that comes with the living out of many years.

Quicken us with compassion that we may make this community and this nation a place where people of every age, however old, however weak, may be accorded all the justice, all the dignity, and all the worth that is theirs by right as children of your one family on earth; through Jesus Christ our Lord. Amen.

JEFFERY W. ROWTHORN

99. For Children at Risk

Leader 1:   Tortured by hunger and thirst,
Leader 2:   ravaged by disease and pollution;

Save all your children, Lord.

Leader 1:   Savaged by the brutalities of war,
Leader 2:   victimized by violence and abuse;

Save all your children, Lord.

Leader 1:   Broken by exploitative child labor,
Leader 2:   stunted by suffering;

Save all your children, Lord.

Leader 1:   Thwarted by prejudice,
Leader 2:   deprived of beauty, joy and laughter;

Protect all your children, Lord.

Leader 1:   Uprooted by famine, war and disaster,
Leader 2:   burdened by the debts of preceding generations;

Protect all your children, Lord.

Leader 1:   Aged before they could be young,
Leader 2:   denied freedom, justice and peace;

Protect all your children, Lord.

Leader 1:   Nurtured and guided with love and understanding,
Leader 2:   provided with food and clothing and shelter;

Care for all your children, Lord.

Leader 1:   Enriched by a safe and clean environment,
Leader 2:   empowered by education and opportunity,

Care for all your children, Lord.

| Leader 1: | Welcomed and honored in our midst, |
| Leader 2: | brought to know and to love you as their Savior; |

Care for all your children, Lord. Amen.

MARY FORD-GRABOWSY*

100. Litany for Youth

All: *O God, we are your children; help us to know that we are never forgotten, never deserted, always forgiven, always loved.*

Leader 1: O God, we have meant to serve you better than we do, but we have not.

Leader 2: We have dreamed dreams of all that we would do for you, and we have seldom even started.

All: *O God, we are your children; help us to know that we are never forgotten, never deserted, always forgiven, always loved.*

Leader 1: O God, the whole world lies before us. We have many choices, and we are often confused.

Leader 2: Help us to choose wisely those things that will affect all our lives - the things we study, the people we marry, the work we do.

All: *O God, we are your children; help us to know that we are never forgotten, never deserted, always forgiven, always loved.*

Leader 1: O God, we know that you are greater than we can imagine. We know that we were made in your image, but we think small thoughts of you and big thoughts of ourselves.

Leader 2: Help us to know you as that Spirit which reaches from the smallest blade of grass to the farthest star; that Love which is so great that it leans down from heaven to help us in our every action.

All: *O God, we are your children; help us to know that we are never forgotten, never deserted, always forgiven, always loved.*

Leader 1: O God, we know that you are not just the God of our denomination, our country, our friends and family, but we find it hard to act as if we really believed it.

Leader 2: We say that all people are brothers and sisters, but we forget that members of one family are often very different. We try to ignore the differences in our customs and beliefs. Help us to understand them instead of pretending they don't exist, and to respect all ways of worshipping and serving you.

All: *O God, we are your children; help us to know that we are never forgotten, never deserted, always forgiven, always loved.*

Leader 1: O God, we find fault with Christianity without ever really trying it. We lose our tempers over customs that seem old-fashioned and neglect the truth hidden under them.

Leader 2: O Father, help us to know that you made us and all the world, and that you love your creation.

Leader 1: O Christ, help us to know that you came to us because we have not the strength to go to you, and that you come to us still.

Leader 2: O Holy Spirit, help us to know that you are within each one of us, ready to teach if we are ready to learn.

All: *O God, we are your children; help us to know that we are never forgotten, never deserted, always forgiven, always loved.*

Leader 1: O God, we know that you are not just in church, in saintly people or in great actions, but we forget.

Leader 2: Help us to see you in our enemies as well as in our friends.

Leader 1: Help us to be patient with our families when they do not understand us, to learn to look for things to love in unattractive people, to forgive those who hurt us and to ask forgiveness when we hurt others.

Leader 2: Help us to laugh at ourselves and so begin to learn humility. Help us to praise you in everything we do, and for everyone we meet.

All: *O God, we are your children; help us to know that we are never forgotten, never deserted, always forgiven, always loved.*

Leader 1: O God, we want peace and we are very afraid. We are afraid of pain and terror, of war and chaos and things we have not known.

| Leader 2: | We are afraid, too, of little things, of being thought foolish and laughed at, of having those we love think badly of us, of failing some test the world has set us, but we do not fear you, God, nor trust you very much, because you are not real enough to us. |

| All: | *O God, we are your children; help us to know that we are never forgotten, never deserted, always forgiven, always loved.* |

| Leader 1: | O God, help us to learn to know you, to know that you were at our beginning and will be at our end, that you call to us now and will call through whatever comes to us all our lives long. |

| Leader 2: | O Christ, our friend as well as our judge, our companion in temptation, in suffering and in love, help us to know you and to love you by walking in the path that you have made for us. |

| All: | *O God, we are your children; help us to know that we are never forgotten, never deserted, always forgiven, always loved.* |

| Leader 1: | O God, take us by the hand and forgive us when we fall. |

| Leader 2: | Lift us up and help us to try again. |

| All: | *O Father, strengthen us;*
O Christ, walk with us;
O Holy Spirit, teach us;
for we are your children,
never forgotten, never deserted,
always forgiven, always loved.
Amen. |

AVERY BROOKE

101. The Right Time to Be Different

God of wisdom, help us to know the right time to be different.

As Noah ignored the laughter of the world,
may we follow your will in spite of ridicule.

As Joseph resisted the invitation of Potiphar's wife,
may we control the power of sex in our lives.

As Daniel risked his life for the right to worship,
may we grow day by day in our personal devotion.

As Amos fearlessly pointed to the sins and failures of his time,
may we speak for rightness, justice, and love.

As David accepted the challenge all others shunned,
may we meet the fearful decisions of life.

As Elizabeth's baby leaped for joy at the coming of the Lord,
may we find excitement in your nearness.

As Mary kept those things and pondered them in her heart,
may we take time to meditate on your love.

As Stephen prayed for those who stoned him,
may we learn the virtue of a forgiving heart.

As Peter was taught not to call anything unclean that you have made clean,
may we conquer prejudice and hatred for your sake.

As Paul responded eagerly to the battle of the Christian life,
may we willingly walk in the Spirit.

As the Son of Man came not to be served but to serve,
*may we give of our life and time and money for the physical and spiritual
good of others.*
Amen.

ELMER N. WITT
-TIME TO PRAY

102. At a High School Baccalaureate

Each section may be used separately, or the whole may be used as one continuous litany.

Leader 1:   Lord, it is your will for us to welcome new freedoms.

Leader 2:   We welcome new freedom to embark on a career,
              freedom to earn our own money, or train to earn it,
              freedom to spend our money, or save it,
              freedom to fashion new routines,
              freedom to plan leisure,
              freedom to bear new responsibilities,
              freedom to make fresh meaning out of life.

Leader 1:   We welcome new freedom to grow into the world you have given us,
              to travel to the destination you have prepared for us,
              to meet and serve the people you have waiting for us.

Leader 2:   In the challenge of freedom

Graduates: *Equip us.*

Leader 1:   In the decisions of freedom

Graduates: *Direct us.*

Leader 2:   In the art of freedom

Graduates: *Discipline us.*

Leader 1:   In the dangers of freedom

Graduates: *Protect us.*

Leader 2:   In the raptures of freedom

Graduates: *Steady us.*

Leader 1:	In the life of freedom
Graduates:	*Give us joy.*
Leader 2:	In the use of freedom
Graduates:	*Grant us wisdom.*
Leader 1:	Against all the victimization of the world,
Graduates:	*the Son has set us free, and we are free indeed.*
Leader 2:	So in the freedom of the Son,
Graduates:	*we shall make money honestly,* *we shall make love honorably,* *we shall make time for those who need us,* *we shall make friends of our enemies,* *we shall make amends right away,* *we shall make God supreme,* *for God's service in the world is perfect freedom.* *Amen.*

PAUL KIMBER AND OTHERS
-WORSHIP FOR TODAY

103. Students Around the World

Let us pray for the students of the world.

(Silence)

For those who are persecuted and imprisoned for their faith,
Lord, hear and help.

For those who live in constant fear,
Lord, hear and help.

For those who are ill or hungry or cold,
Lord, hear and help.

For those who are in despair at the collapse of false hopes,
Lord, hear and help.

For those who are blinded by this world's success, that they may come to
know the love of God,
Lord, hear and help.

For those who are lonely, that they may find comfort in the Gospel,
Lord, hear and help.

(Silence)

Let us pray for those in revolutionary situations, that they may confess their
faith in the hour of trial and show forth a true picture of community in
Christ,
Lord, hear and help.

For those in newly independent countries, that they may seize with zeal the
great opportunities open to them to bring their people closer together,
Lord, hear and help.

For those who have civil strife raging in their countries, that they may be
comforted in the face of the terrors surrounding them, and thereby be
strengthened to comfort others by word and deed,
Lord, hear and help.

(Silence)

Let us pray for those of us who find our work too difficult,
Lord, hear and help.

For those who do not give of their best in their work,
Lord, hear and help.

For those who are oppressed by the fear of failure in examinations,
Lord, hear and help.

For those who are perplexed and cast down by the struggle to understand the world in which they live,
Lord, hear and help.

(Silence)

Let us pray for those whose work is a joy to them, that they may be strengthened and enabled to communicate their joy to others,
Lord, hear and help.

For those who are engaged in the work of research and discovery, that their minds may be enlightened continually to see more of your glory,
Lord, hear and help.

For those who are leaders in the student community, that their influence may be for good,
Lord, hear and help.

(Silence)

Let us pray to God for all who teach and have the care of students in educational institutions,
Lord, hear and help.

For those who work under great difficulties of time and lack of materials,
Lord, hear and help.

For those who find hostility, misunderstanding, and rivalry among their colleagues,
Lord, hear and help.

(Silence)

Let us pray for those who distort the truth in the interests of false ideologies,
Lord, hear and help.

For those who are presumptuous, bitter, or indifferent, that they may come
to unite with others in mutual respect and Christian love,
Lord, hear and help.

For those who have a vision of their responsibility, that they may be given
the wisdom and strength to discharge it effectively,
Lord, hear and help.

(Silence)

Let us pray to God for the student Christian groups throughout the world,
that they may be living, worshiping, and witnessing communities in the
universities and schools of the world,
Lord, hear and help.

For college chaplains and all who work in Christ's name with students,
Lord, hear and help.

For all seekers after truth, that their minds may be enlightened, and their
wills strengthened to follow the truth disclosed.
Lord, hear and help.

(Silence)

*May the God of hope fill us with all joy and peace in believing, that we
may abound in hope through the power of the Holy Spirit. Amen.*

THE STUDENT PRAYER BOOK

104. For Those Who Teach

Leader: St. Paul wrote: "If it is teaching, let us give all that we have to our teaching."

Jesus said, "Whoever among you wants to be great must become the servant of all; for the Son of Man himself has not come to be served, but to serve."

Teachers: *Our purpose is not to become the God of the classroom,*
nor to make our class the pride of the school,
nor to make our school the showcase of the city.
We serve children because they will grow into adults;
because their minds and spirits are hungry,
we shall feed them.

Leader: Jesus said, "I am come that they may have life."

Teachers: *We teach for their sake, that they may know God's world;*
knowing, that they may delight and worship in it;
delighting, that their lives may find free service and full
expression in it.

Leader: Jesus was born in a borrowed crib, accepted friendship from his disciples, ointment from Mary, and the Cross from his enemies. All these he touched with a new glory.

Teachers: *Our selves and our gifts we offer for his service.*
We do not want to be envious of the talents of our colleagues,
but to be glad about our own gifts.
Accept and glorify our gifts, O Lord.

Leader: Jesus said that happiness belonged to the humble-minded, the meek, the merciful, the sincere, those hungry and thirsty for goodness.

Teachers: *Let us share this happiness,*
by reassessing ourselves and our work, and by being ready
to alter what is wrong;
by learning from the experience and character of other people;
by co-operating freely with those in authority over us,
remembering the particular responsibilities they always bear;
by having the grace to be open to advice and, if necessary,
correction from those under us.

Leader:	Jesus had all things committed to him by the Father, but wrapped himself with a towel and washed the feet of the disciples.
Teachers:	*Help us, O Lord, to accept the mundane things that sometimes gall our spirits: duties at lunchtime or recess; extra work for a sick colleague or a student teacher; visits by inspectors and health workers.*
Leader:	Jesus welcomed children with their mothers and blessed them. He said, "Let them come, for of such is the Kingdom of heaven."
Teachers:	*Grant that we may share your compassion, Lord, and therefore your patience with awkward children or difficult parents.*
Leader:	Jesus said, "My peace I give to you."
Teachers:	*Enable us to work from your peace;* *to have confidence for the moment, and not hunger restlessly for results;* *to give each hour its full value as part of the whole education of the child;* *and when the day ends with frayed nerves, still to be wise in the use of time and temper.*
Leader:	Jesus, you say to us, "Come, follow me";
Teachers:	*Keep us, through the Holy Spirit's work, in the thrill and awe of our calling, for the sake of your Kingdom.* *Amen.*

FRANK GODFREY
-WORSHIP FOR TODAY

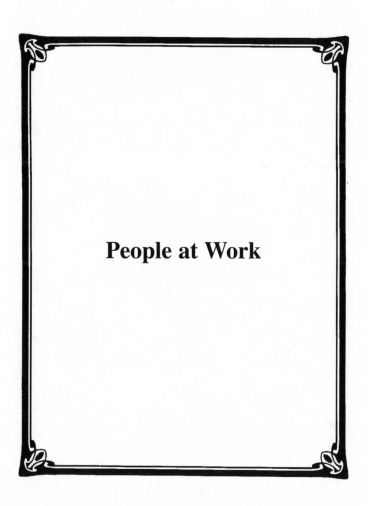

People at Work

105. God of the World Around Us

Leader and People:

>*God of concrete, God of steel,*
>>*God of piston and of wheel,*
>*God of pylon, God of steam,*
>>*God of girder and of beam,*
>*God of atom, God of mine,*
>>*all the world of power is thine!*

Leader:
O God our Father,
We praise you because we see you in the wonders of this universe - in the
life-giving sun by day, in the moon and the galaxies of stars by night, in the
immensities of space and the beauty of nature and the marvels of energy;
We acknowledge you and praise you as the Lord of all creation.

We praise you because we see you in the development of humanity, the
growth of nations, and the movements of peoples;
We acknowledge you and praise you as the Lord of all history.

>*God of Turk and God of Greek,*
>>*God of ev'ry tongue we speak,*
>*God of Arab, God of Jew,*
>>*God of ev'ry race and hue,*
>*God who knows no bound'ry line,*
>>*all the world of men is thine!*

We praise you because we see you leading people to discover the meaning
and purpose of existence;
We acknowledge you and praise you as the Lord of truth and life.

We praise you because we see you at work in men and women who put to
good use the raw material of creation, who experiment, plant, and build,
who manufacture, produce and use all that is entrusted to us;
We acknowledge you and praise you as the Lord of agriculture and industry.

>*Lord of science, Lord of art,*
>>*Lord of map and graph and chart,*
>*Lord of physics and research,*
>>*Word of Bible, Faith of Church,*
>*Lord of sequence and design*
>>*all the world of truth is thine!*

We praise you because we see you incarnate and revealed in Jesus, the carpenter of Nazareth, in whom all human labor is made sacred;
We acknowledge you and praise you as the Lord of all work.

We praise you because we see you helping people to be in contact with one another and to transport to one another the products of their work;
We acknowledge you and praise you as the Lord of communications and trade.

> *Lord of cable, Lord of rail,*
>> *Lord of interstate and mail,*
> *Lord of rocket, Lord of flight,*
>> *Lord of soaring satellite,*
> *Lord of lightning's vivid line,*
>> *all the world of speed is thine!*

We praise you because we see you cooperating with people in their work, seeking to make things of true value, reconciling differences between management and workers, and bringing peace to the world of industry;
We acknowledge you and praise you as the Lord of reconciliation.

We praise you because we see condemned on the Cross, on which Jesus was killed, selfishness, pride, the avoidance of responsibility, hard-heartedness and cowardice; and see exalted, as the one hope of all, the love that seeks to save and be spent in the service of others, the love that sacrifices, the love that unites, and the love that conquers.
We acknowledge you and praise you as the Source and Lord of love.

> *God whose glory fills the earth,*
>> *gave the universe its birth,*
> *loosed the Christ with Easter's might,*
>> *saves the world from evil's blight,*
> *claims us all by grace divine,*
>> *all the world of love is thine!*

WORSHIP FOR TODAY
HYMN STANZAS BY RICHARD G. JONES*

106. For Those We Depend On

Heavenly Father: we pray today for the many people who serve us through their work. Let us remember them.

Silence

We acknowledge in gratitude those who hallow their work by helpfulness:
    receptionists, secretaries, clerks, custodians;
    doctors, nurses, nurses' aides, surgeons, orderlies;
    chaplains, pastors, educators, postal clerks;
    judges, politicians, and delivery people.
Help them find joy in service, O Lord:
And give us gratitude and appreciation for all they do for us.

But work is not always satisfying. Let us remember those who do not enjoy what they do.

Silence

We pray for
    people who are not suited to the jobs they are given;
    people caught in a web of dishonesty;
    people whose initiative is thwarted and who only follow orders;
    employers and employees who do not know how to relate to each other;
    people who feel they are victims of "the system";
    people who are too tired to do their best;
    people who exploit others.
Hear our prayers for them, O Lord:
And give us understanding and compassion in all we do for them.

Some work done for us each day is dangerous. Let us remember the men and women who protect our lives.

Silence

We pray for members of our Armed Forces;
    for fire fighters and police and members of the Coast Guard;
    for bus drivers, railroad engineers, jet pilots, and air traffic controllers;
    for ambulance drivers and paramedics and rescue personnel.
Protect them and us in the face of danger, O Lord:
And give us all care and concern for each other's life and well-being. This we pray in Jesus' name. Amen.

MODELS FOR MINISTERS I*

107. Our Daily Work †

Let us remember that God's first recorded command was to work. Let us ask God's forgiveness for the times when we have considered our work as drudgery rather than as a gift from God.
Lord, in your mercy:
Hear our prayer.

Let us pray for all employers that they may carry out their responsibilities with justice and integrity. Let us pray for the members of this congregation who are employers.
Lord, in your mercy:
Hear our prayer.

Let us pray for all employees that they may do good and honest work. Let us pray for the members of this congregation who are employed by others.
Lord, in your mercy:
Hear our prayer.

Let us pray for the unions, thanking God for all that has been achieved in getting better working conditions and fairer wages for workers. Let us pray for union leaders and shop stewards that they may exercise their great powers wisely and responsibly.
Lord, in your mercy:
Hear our prayer.

Let us pray for those with whom we have relationships through their work or through ours. Let us pray for our colleagues at work and for due appreciation of those who serve us week by week.
Lord, in your mercy:
Hear our prayer.

Let us pray for those whose work is dull and monotonous; for those whose work is dangerous; for those whose work causes them to be separated from their families for long periods; and for those whose work brings them into situations where they are greatly tempted.
Lord, in your mercy:
Hear our prayer.

Let us pray for those who cannot work; for those who cannot find employment; for those who cannot obtain work because they are discriminated against; for those who are disabled; and for those who have retired.
Lord, in your mercy:
Hear our prayer. Amen.

PRAYERS FOR TODAY'S CHURCH

108. For Those Who Work

Leader 1: O Lord God: you are ever at work in the world for us and
for all humankind;
guide and protect all who work to get their living.

Leader 2: We pray for those who plow the earth,
for those who tend machinery;
Work with them, O God.

Leader 1: For those who sail deep waters,
for those who venture into space;
Work with them, O God.

Leader 2: For those who work in offices and warehouses,
for those who labor in stores or factories;
Work with them, O God.

Leader 1: For those who work in mines,
for those who buy and sell;
Work with them, O God.

Leader 2: For those who entertain us,
for those who broadcast or publish;
Work with them, O God.

Leader 1: For those who keep house,
for those who train children;
Work with them, O God.

Leader 2: For all who live by strength of arm,
for all who live by skill of hand;
Work with them, O God.

Leader 1: For all who employ or govern;
Work with them, O God.

Leader 2: For all who excite our minds with art, science, or learning;
Work with them, O God.

Leader 1: For all who instruct,
for writers and teachers;
Work with them, O God.

Leader 2:	For all who serve the public good in any way by working; *Work with them, O God.*
Leader 1:	For all who labor without hope, for all who labor without interest; *Great God, we pray your mercy, grace, and saving power.*
Leader 2:	For those who have too little leisure, for those who have too much leisure; *Great God, we pray your mercy, grace, and saving power.*
Leader 1:	For those who are underpaid, for those who pay small wages; *Great God, we pray your mercy, grace, and saving power.*
Leader 2:	For those who cannot work, for those who look in vain for work; *Great God, we pray your mercy, grace, and saving power.*
Leader 1:	For those who trade on the troubles of others, for profiteers, extortioners, and greedy people; *Great God, we pray your mercy, grace, and saving power.*
Leader 2:	Work through us and help us always to work for you in Jesus Christ our Lord. *Amen.*

THE WORSHIPBOOK

109. A Thanksgiving for Work

Leader 1:   For the work of our lives we give you thanks, O Lord, and praise.

Leader 1:   For the work of our hands;
Leader 2:   For the work of our minds;
Leader 3:   For the work of our hearts,
We give you thanks, O Lord, and praise.

Leader 1:   For the enlightening work of teachers, librarians, researchers and scholars;
Leader 2:   For the healing work of doctors, nurses and counselors;
Leader 3:   For the creative work of artists, musicians, painters and sculptors,
We give you thanks, O Lord, and praise.

Leader 1:   For the precise work of engineers, scientists and computer specialists;
Leader 2:   For the nurturing work of homemakers, parents and guardians;
Leader 3:   For the wise work of grandparents and retirees,
We give you thanks, O Lord, and praise.

Leader 1:   For the proclaiming work of writers, photographers, editors and publishers;
Leader 2:   For the trustworthy work of accountants, bankers, lawyers, politicians and salespeople;
Leader 3:   For the faith-filled work of ministers, ordained and lay,
We give you thanks, O Lord, and praise.

Leader 1:   For the protective work of police, fire fighters and military personnel;
Leader 2:   For the dedicated work of secretaries, receptionists and bookkeepers;
Leader 3:   For the compassionate work of volunteers, young and old,
We give you thanks, O Lord, and praise.

Leader 1:   For the judicious work of managers, administrators, directors and supervisors;
Leader 2:   For the fruitful work of farmers, fisherfolk, growers and gardeners;
Leader 3:   For the steadfast work of those who manufacture products and household goods,
We give you thanks, O Lord, and praise.

Leader 1:	For the constructive work of builders, surveyors, architects, masons and carpenters;
Leader 2:	For the efficient work of those who transport people and things by bus and train, plane and taxi, truck and boat;
Leader 3:	For the hospitable work of cooks, waiters and waitresses, cashiers, and hotel and motel workers,
	We give you thanks, O Lord, and praise.

Leader 1:	For the clarifying work of those who work with television, radio and news media;
Leader 2:	For the dependable work of telephone and postal workers;
Leader 3:	For the good work of all who labor for the common good,
	We give you thanks, O Lord, and praise.

Leader 1:	For our work which sheds light on the darkness;
Leader 2:	For our work which creates order from chaos;
Leader 3:	For our work which builds peace out of hostility,
	We give you thanks, O Lord, and praise.

Leader 1:	For our work which serves others;
Leader 2:	For our work which empowers others;
Leader 3:	For our work which inspires others,
	We give you thanks, O Lord, and praise.

Silence.

For all work on our part, and the part of others, which builds your Kingdom here on earth, we give you thanks, O Lord, and praise. Amen.

DAVID AND ANGELA KAUFFMAN

110. For the Unemployed

Lord God, have mercy on us for our ignorance and greed which have brought to millions unemployment in the midst of plenty.

From any sense of our own virtue at some gesture of charity to the unemployed,
Good Lord, deliver us.

From luxury and display, while many have nowhere to lay their heads,
Good Lord, deliver us.

From heedless comfort in the security of our homes, while families of the poor are evicted from their homes, their children and furniture upon the street,
Good Lord, deliver us.

From methods of private or public relief which save the bodies of men and women but destroy their inmost spirit; from hurting the finer sensibilities of those in need, robbing them of their pride and self-respect,
Good Lord, deliver us.

From false notions that by preaching we can save people's souls, while unemployment breaks their hearts, unbalances their minds, destroys their homes, tempts them beyond measure, visits want and disease upon their children, turns their heart to bitterness, hatred, and rebellion, or to hopelessness, despair, and death,
Good Lord, deliver us.

From ever forgetting the forlorn figures of the homeless and the unemployed, and from failure to see that our social fabric is as shabby as their clothes,
Good Lord, deliver us.

From satisfaction with any revival of trade or renewed prosperity while multitudes still can find no work,
Good Lord, deliver us.

That our conscience may know no rest until unemployment is abolished,
We entreat you, good Lord.

That you will guide us quickly to that good life in which there shall be peace and a generous sharing in labor, leisure and joy by all your children,
We entreat you, good Lord.

(Silence)

O God, the Lord of the vineyard, you do not wish any to stand idle in the marketplace; hear our prayer for the multitudes without employment or assurance of livelihood, and in your loving wisdom show us the right ways to help and heal all our distress; through Jesus Christ our Lord.
Amen.

THE STUDENT PRAYER BOOK

111. For Farmers and Their Families

Let us give thanks to God:

For the wonder of the changing seasons and the ever-new miracle of life
stirring in field and forest,
We give you thanks, O God.

For the privilege of sharing with you in the act of creating the good things
of earth for your children, and for your nearness in all the phases of
agricultural life,
We give you thanks, O God.

For the Christ of the country road, who walked and served in the
countryside of Galilee, and who today walks the backroads of the world in
comradeship with those who till the soil,
We give you thanks, O God.

For the coming of seed-time, for good soil, for abundant rains,
We give you thanks, O God.

For the friendship which prompts farmers to share tools and labor,
We give you thanks, O God.

For neighbors who help when sickness or death, old age or new life come
to us,
We give you thanks, O God.

For better seeds, better methods, county agents and other helps to us who
farm the land,
We give you thanks, O God.

For the Grange and other community associations,
We give you thanks, O God.

For the blessings of sleep and the renewed strength of awakening in the
morning,
We give you thanks, O God.

That you will grant us a vision of the earth redeemed and used as a sacred
trust for the welfare of all your great family on earth,
We ask you to hear us, O Lord.

That you will give us skill in planting and tending our crops and caring for our herds,
We ask you to hear us, O Lord.

That you will give us strength and health and knowledge of your laws so that our bodies may be useful in your service,
We ask you to hear us, O Lord.

That you will bless the rural churches of the world and their ministers, that their fellowship may be enriched and that they may bring their neighbors into lasting fellowship with you,
We ask you to hear us, O Lord.

That you will speedily grant a just and lasting peace in all the earth, that people everywhere may again beat their swords into plowshares and their spears into pruning-hooks, and all live together in harmony and tranquility in the lands you have given them,
We ask you to hear us, O Lord.

That all may share with joy in sowing the seed and reaping the harvest of the Kingdom of God,
We dedicate our hands and our minds, O God.

To a renewed appreciation of the holy earth and its gifts, and to a consecrated stewardship of all its resources, material and human,
We dedicate our hands and our minds, O God.

To comradeship with the rural peoples of the world, and to sharing with them generously all the gifts and graces you have given us,
We dedicate our skills and our lives, O God.

Accept our thanks,
hear our prayers,
and graciously use the gifts of mind, body, and soul
which we now lay upon your altar,
through Jesus Christ our Lord. Amen.

RURAL PEOPLE AT WORSHIP

112. The Presentation of Gifts at Harvest Time

Minister: Let us with gladness present the offerings and oblations of our life and labor to the Lord.

All: *Let us with a gladsome mind*
praise the Lord, for he is kind;
for his mercies aye endure,
ever faithful, ever sure.

The Gift of Bread *(Presented by two fathers)*

Minister: The eyes of all wait upon you, O Lord,

Congregation: *And you give them their food in due season.*

Fathers: We present to God bread, the staff of life, as a token of our gratitude for his sending all things that are needful both for our souls and for our bodies.

Minister: Let us pray for all those whose daily work provides our food and clothing; those who work on land and sea; and let us remember that we do not live by bread alone.

All: *Praise him for our harvest store,*
he hath filled the garner floor;
for his mercies aye endure,
ever faithful, ever sure.

The Gift of Milk *(Presented by two mothers)*

Minister: You open your hand,

Congregation: *And fill all things living with plenteousness.*

Mothers: We present to God this milk as a token of our gratitude for his loving care and as a symbol of human kindness to be shown to children and to the sick.

Minister: Let us pray for all the homes and hospitals in our land, and for our Church as it ministers the milk of God's word, that we may all grow unto salvation.

All:	*All things living he doth feed,*
	his full hand supplies their need;
	for his mercies aye endure,
	ever faithful, ever sure.

The Gift of Fruit and Vegetables *(Presented by three young people)*

Minister:	He brought forth grass for the cattle,
Congregation:	*And green herb for the service of men.*
Young People:	We offer God some of the fruits of the earth as a token of our gratitude and as a symbol of the future entrusted to us.
Minister:	Let us pray for schools, youth organizations, colleges and universities, that young people may grow in the knowledge of our Savior, follow Christ the King, and enthrone him in their hearts for ever.
All:	*He hath bid the fruitful field*
	crops of precious increase yield;
	for his mercies aye endure,
	ever faithful, ever sure.

The Gift of Flowers *(Presented by four children)*

Minister:	Consider the lilies of the field, how they grow;
Congregation:	*Even Solomon in all his glory was not arrayed like one of these.*
Children:	We present these flowers and say "thank you" for all the beautiful things in God's world.
Minister:	Let us pray that the beauties of the earth may teach us the beauty of God's love and goodness, and that we may enable our children to grow up in love and understanding.
All:	*Praise him that he made the sun*
	day by day its course to run;
	for his mercies aye endure,
	ever faithful, ever sure.

The Gifts of Industry *(Presented by three industrial workers)*

Minister: Whatever your hand finds to do,

Congregation: *Do with all your might.*

Workers: We present these gifts to God as a token of our gratitude for all his wondrous gifts of strength and craft and skill.

Minister: Let us pray that in industry and in commerce there may be freedom from distrust, bitterness, and dispute. May we all seek what is just and equal, and may we all live together in unity and love.

All: *God with all-commanding might*
filled the new-made world with light;
for his mercies aye endure,
ever faithful, ever sure.

The Gift of Money *(Presented by two lay leaders of the congregation)*

Minister: Bear one another's burdens,

Congregation: *And fulfill the law of Christ.*

Lay leaders: We present the offerings of this congregation as a token of our possessions which are all a trust from God.

Minister: Let us pray that Christians everywhere may be known for their industry, their right use of leisure, their sacrificial giving, and their honest, kindly dealing with one another, as people striving to love God and their neighbor as themselves.

All: *Let us blaze his name abroad,*
for of gods he is the God;
for his mercies aye endure,
ever faithful, ever sure.

The Gift of Bread and Wine *(Presented by two deacons)*

Minister: As often as you eat this bread, and drink this cup,

Congregation: *You proclaim the Lord's death until he comes.*

Deacons:	We present this bread and this wine, that by participating in the sacrament we may feed on Christ by faith and with thanksgiving.
Minister:	Let us pray that as the wheat scattered over the fields has been harvested into this one loaf, so the Church may be gathered together from the ends of the earth into Christ's kingdom, and that, offering ourselves as a living sacrifice, we may be strengthened to go forth into the world to serve God faithfully.
All:	*And for richer food than this,* *pledge of everlasting bliss;* *for his mercies aye endure;* *ever faithful, ever sure.*
	Glory to our bounteous King; *glory let creation sing;* *for his mercies aye endure;* *ever faithful, ever sure.* *Amen.*

WORSHIP FOR TODAY
HYMN STANZAS BY JOHN MILTON*

113. A Litany of Confession and Compassion at Harvest Time ✝

Surrounded by the beauty of God's creation, let us thank God for all the joy
and wonder that come to us through the appreciation of beauty and color.
Let us pray for those who are blind or whose sight is fading.
Lord, in your mercy:
Hear our prayer.

All the flowers, fruit and vegetables grown in our gardens remind us of the
thousands of people who have no gardens where they can grow things and
few open spaces where their children can play. Let us pray for children
who have never picked a flower from their own garden or who have never
climbed a tree. Let us pray also for parents facing each day the frustration
of living in high-rise apartment buildings or in filthy slums.
Lord, in your mercy:
Hear our prayer.

The abundance of our harvest reminds us that millions never have enough
to eat. Let us ask God's forgiveness for our indifference to the needs of
others and for our forgetting that much of the wealth of this country has
been gained by exploiting others. Let us pray that as a nation and as
individuals we may take seriously our responsibilities for those who are
starving.
Lord, in your mercy:
Hear our prayer.

Today we thank God for the provision of our needs as families and
individuals, but God is also concerned for us as a community. Let us pray
for our common life and for those in positions of leadership and authority
here; let us pray for those who have recently moved here and for those who
find it difficult to accept the changes taking place in our community.
Lord, in your mercy:
Hear our prayer.

The beauty of creation and the abundant provision for our physical needs
remind us to give thanks to God, but millions in our land and across the
seas do not know of God's love for them and have never responded to
Christ's invitation, "Come unto me and I will give you rest." Let us pray

for those who have never entrusted their lives to Christ. Let us pray for ourselves and for all the Missionary Societies as, together, we tell people of the Lord Jesus Christ and of his love for them.
Lord, in your mercy:
Hear our prayer.

Today we have remembered to thank God for his goodness to us, but this reminds us that often we forget to thank him, and that we just take God and his love for granted. Let us ask for God's forgiveness and pray that we may never be complacent about the good things which we enjoy and are called by God to share generously with others.
Lord, in your mercy:
Hear our prayer. Amen.

PETER MARKBY
-PRAYERS FOR TODAY'S CHURCH

**Sickness
and
Healing**

114. For Healing

God the Father, whose will for all is health and salvation;
Have mercy on us.

God the Son, who came that we might have life and have it more
abundantly;
Have mercy on us.

God the Spirit, whose temple our bodies are;
Have mercy on us.

Holy Trinity, in whom we live, and move, and have our being;
Have mercy on us.

Son of David, you healed all who came to you in faith;
Heal your people, Lord.

Son of Man, you sent forth your disciples to preach the Gospel and heal the
sick;
Heal your people, Lord.

Son of God, you pardon our sins and heal our infirmities;
Heal your people, Lord.

Eternal Christ, your abiding Spirit renews our minds;
Heal your people, Lord.

Lord Jesus, your holy Name is a medicine of healing and a pledge of
eternal life;
Heal your people, Lord.

We pray that you will hear us, O Lord; and that you will grant your grace
to make the sick well;
Hear us, and make us whole.

That you will give patience, courage, and faith to all who are disabled by
injury or sickness;
Hear us, and make us whole.

That you will give speedy healing, relief from pain, and fearless confidence
to all sick children;
Hear us, and make us whole.

That you will grant your strengthening presence to all who are about to undergo an operation;
Hear us, and make us whole.

That you will sustain those who face long illness, bearing them up as on eagles' wings;
Hear us, and make us whole.

That you will comfort those who endure continual pain, pouring upon them the sweet balm of your Spirit;
Hear us, and make us whole.

That you will grant to all sufferers the refreshment of quiet sleep;
Hear us, and make us whole.

That you will abide with all who are lonely or despondent, having no one to comfort them;
Hear us, and make us whole.

That you will restore all who are in mental darkness to soundness of mind and cheerfulness of heart;
Hear us, and make us whole.

That by sickness endured and sickness observed you will teach us our mortality, that we may prepare for death with fortitude and meet it with hope;
Hear us, and make us whole.

That you will give your wisdom in ample measure to doctors and nurses, that with knowledge, skill, and patience, they may minister to the sick;
Hear us, and make us whole.

That you will guide by your good Spirit all who search for the causes of sickness and disease;
Hear us, and make us whole.

Jesus, Lamb of God:
Have mercy on us.

Jesus, bearer of our sins:
Have mercy on us.

Jesus, redeemer of the world:
Give us your peace.

Our Father, who art in heaven,
hallowed be thy Name,
thy kingdom come,
thy will be done,
on earth as it is in heaven.
Give us this day our daily bread.
And forgive us our trespasses,
as we forgive those who trespass against us.
And lead us not into temptation,
but deliver us from evil.
For thine is the kingdom, and the power, and the glory,
for ever and ever. Amen.

Almighty God, giver of life and health: your Son came into this ailing world to make your children whole. Send your blessing on all who are sick and on all who minister to them; that when they are restored to health of body and mind, they may give thanks to you in your Church; through the same Jesus Christ our Lord. *Amen.*

MORTON STONE
-PRAYERS, THANKSGIVINGS, LITANIES

115. Christ the Healer

Jesus went on from there and reached the shores of the Sea of Galilee, and went up into the hills. He sat there, and large crowds came to him bringing the lame, the crippled, the blind, the dumb and many others; these they put down at his feet, and he cured them. The crowds were astonished to see the dumb speaking, the cripples whole again, the lame walking and the blind with their sight, and they praised the God of Israel.   *(Matthew 15:29-31)*

Lord Jesus, Son of David and Son of God,
Heal and save us.

Lord Jesus, who bore our griefs and carried our sorrow,
Heal and save us.

Lord Jesus, who went about preaching the Good News and curing all kinds of disease and sickness,
Heal and save us.

Lord Jesus, who raised to life the daughter of Jairus, and the only son of the widow of Nain, and Lazarus whom you loved,
Heal and save us.

Lord Jesus, who cured Simon Peter's mother-in-law of a fever, and the woman suffering from hemorrhages,
Heal and save us.

Lord Jesus, who delivered the Gadarene demoniac, and the tormented daughter of the Canaanite woman,
Heal and save us.

Lord Jesus, who cured the centurion's paralyzed servant, and the dumb epileptic boy,
Heal and save us.

Lord Jesus, who restored the sight of Bartimaeus, the blind beggar of Jericho, and who purified many lepers,
Heal and save us.

Lord Jesus, who cured the man with the withered hand, and who made cripples whole again,
Heal and save us.

Lord Jesus, who commanded your disciples to lay hands on the sick and to anoint them with oil to cure them,
Heal and save us.

Lord Jesus, who ordered your disciples to cast out demons in your name,
Heal and save us.

(Here the sick may be prayed for by name.)

Heavenly Father, giver of life and health: Comfort and relieve your sick servants, and give your power of healing to those who minister to their needs, that they may be strengthened in their weakness and have confidence in your loving care; through Jesus Christ our Lord. Amen.

PRAY LIKE THIS
AND THE BOOK OF COMMON PRAYER 1979

116. A Thanksgiving for Hospitals †

O God, we give you thanks that there are such places as hospitals and infirmaries and nursing-homes, and we remember before you with gratitude and concern all who minister in them to the sick and the needy.

(Silence)

For places
where the ill and the weak and the old
are not looked on as a nuisance,
but where they find
loving care and attention,
We give you thanks, good Lord.

For doctors
who have the skill
to find out what is wrong
and to put it right again,
We give you thanks, good Lord.

For nurses
who throughout the day and night
attend to those in discomfort, distress and pain,
We give you thanks, good Lord.

For all the people
who do the many jobs which have to be done,
if the work of a hospital is to go on:
for technicians, dispensers and dieticians,
We give you thanks, good Lord.

For social workers, nurses' aides, and orderlies,
We give you thanks, good Lord.

For secretaries, typists and clerks,
We give you thanks, good Lord.

For porters and ambulance drivers,
cooks and kitchen maids,
We give you thanks, good Lord.

For hospital chaplains
who bring prayer and sacrament, hope and comfort,
to patients and staff alike,
We give you thanks, good Lord.

For all who visit the sick,
coming because they care and want to help,
We give you thanks, good Lord.

For pharmacologists and all who discover new drugs, new forms of
treatment, new ways to conquer old diseases,
We give you thanks, good Lord.

For health plans and for all who work to make healing fully and freely
available to the sick,
We give you thanks, good Lord.

(Silence)

Almighty God, whose blessed Son Jesus Christ went about doing good,
healing all manner of sickness and all manner of disease among the people:
continue, we pray, his gracious work among us, especially in the hospitals
and nursing-homes of our community. Cheer, heal, and sanctify the sick.
Grant to the physicians, surgeons, and nurses wisdom and skill, sympathy
and patience; and assist with your blessing all who are seeking to prevent
suffering and to forward your good purposes of love; through Jesus Christ
our Lord. *Amen.*

WILLIAM BARCLAY
-PRAYERS FOR HELP AND HEALING

117. In a Time of HIV/AIDS

God the Creator,
have mercy on us.

God the Redeemer,
have mercy on us.

God the Sanctifier,
have mercy on us.

Holy Trinity, one God,
have mercy on us.

Draw near to us, O God,
And sustain us with your Holy Spirit.

Be present in our sickness and pain,
And sustain us with your Holy Spirit.

Hear us when we cry to you,
And sustain us with your Holy Spirit.

Forgive us our transgressions,
And sustain us with your Holy Spirit.

We pray for the abiding presence and comfort of your Holy Spirit;
For it is by grace alone that we shall prosper.

We pray for courage to walk with those who are living with HIV/AIDS;
Encourage our hearts and open our hands.

We pray for those who are afflicted with HIV/AIDS or with any other grief
or trouble;
Give them relief and quietness of spirit.

We pray for all HIV care-givers, hospital workers, and researchers;
*Be with them in their tasks, enliven their minds, and grant them success in
your time.*

We pray for the families, friends, and loved one of persons living with
HIV/AIDS;
Fill them with your healing and redemptive love.

We pray for the frightened, the timid and those who breed fear;
Loosen our bonds and help us to grow more and more into the likeness of Christ.

We pray for the dying;
May they know the light and joy of your presence.

We pray for those who have died of AIDS and for all the departed;
May the angels surround them, and the saints welcome them in peace, and may Christ our Savior keep them safe for ever. Amen.

RANDOLPH LLOYD FREW*

118. Prisoners and Prisons †

We pray first for those who are responsible for the maintenance of law and order in our community; for those who administer justice in the courts; and for those who are the victims of crime, violence and deceit.
Lord, hear us.

We pray for all prisoners, especially for those who are facing long sentences, and those who have lost faith in themselves and others, and have little hope for the future.
Lord, hear us.

We pray for young people; for those who have already come up against the law in juvenile and family courts; for those on probation, and those who are being drawn into crime.
Lord, hear us.

We pray for parents, teachers, youth leaders and clergy, and for all who try to help the young escape from the sordid and the second-rate, and to find a true purpose in life.
Lord, hear us.

We pray for all those who have the custody and care of prisoners; for prison wardens, chaplains and officers; for the Justice Department, and those who shape and direct our correctional institutions.
Lord, hear us.

We pray for all those who have a special concern for the after-care of offenders: probation officers, wardens of halfway houses, and employers of former prisoners.
Lord, hear us.

We pray for those who have been released from prison; those who have managed to make good and those who continue to find the going hard; and we ask that we may learn to be as forgiving of others as we know God to be forgiving of us.
Lord, hear us.

We pray for ourselves as members of the community; and we ask that our rightful respect for law and order may not stifle our compassion and concern for those who have not lived up to the accepted standards of our society.
Lord, hear us.

Lord Jesus, for our sake you were condemned as a criminal: Visit our jails and prisons with your pity and judgement. Remember all prisoners, and bring the guilty to repentance and amendment of life according to your will, and give them hope for their future. When any are held unjustly, bring them release. Forgive us, and teach us to improve our justice. Remember those who work in these institutions; keep them humane and compassionate; and save them from becoming brutal or callous. And since what we do for those in prison, O Lord, we do for you, constrain us to improve their lot. All this we ask for your mercy's sake. *Amen.*

PRAYERS FOR TODAY'S CHURCH
AND THE BOOK OF COMMON PRAYER 1979*

119. For Those Whose Lives Are Difficult

O God, our Father, we pray for those whose life at this time is very difficult.

Those who have difficult decisions to make, and who honestly do not know what is the right thing to do;
Jesus said: "Come to me, all whose work is hard, whose load is heavy, and I will give you rest."

Those who have difficult tasks to do and to face, and who fear that they may fail in them;
Jesus said: "Come to me, all whose work is hard, whose load is heavy, and I will give you rest."

Those who have difficult temptations to face, and who know only too well that they may give in to them, if they try to meet them alone;
Jesus said: "Set your troubled hearts at rest; trust in God always, trust also in me."

Those who have a difficult time coping with life, and who are tempted to suicide;
Jesus said: "Set your troubled hearts at rest; trust in God always, trust also in me."

Those who have a difficult temperament and nature to master, and who know that they can be their own worst enemies;
Jesus said: "Father, if it be your will, take this cup from me; yet not my will but yours be done."

Those who have difficult people to work with, and who suffer unjust treatment, unfair criticism, unappreciated work;
Jesus said: "Father, if it be your will, take this cup from me; yet not my will but yours be done."

Lord, in the midst of our difficulties and among all the changes and chances of this mortal life, help us to remember that you do not faint or grow weary.
For those who wait for the Lord shall renew their strength,
they shall mount up with wings as eagles,
they shall run and not be weary,
they shall walk and not faint. Amen.

WILLIAM BARCLAY
-EPILOGUES AND PRAYERS

120. For Compassion

O Savior of the world, by your cross and passion you have redeemed us:
Save us and help us, we entreat you, O Lord.

From the impatience that prevents us from discerning your purpose in pain and sorrow:
Save us, good Lord.

From refusing to share the suffering of the world, from seeking only comfort and pleasure, from forgetting those in distress, from the selfishness that brings needless grief to others:
Save us, good Lord.

Almighty Father, in the afflictions of your people you are yourself afflicted; hear us as we pray for those who suffer.

Silence

For all who are hindered in the race of life through no fault of their own; for the defective and the delicate, and for those who are disabled:
We entreat you to hear us, good Lord.

For those whose livelihood is insecure; for the hungry, the homeless and destitute; for those who are overworked, downtrodden, and in despair:
We entreat you to hear us, good Lord.

For little children whose surroundings hide from them your love and beauty; for the fatherless and motherless, and for the unwanted:
We entreat you to hear us, good Lord.

For prisoners and captives, and all suffering from oppression:
We entreat you to hear us, good Lord.

For all who are suffering because of their faithfulness to conviction and duty:
We entreat you to hear us, good Lord.

For those who have to bear their burdens alone; for those who are in doubt and anguish of soul; for those who are oversensitive, and for those who suffer through their own wrongdoing:
We entreat you to hear us, good Lord.

For all who do not pray for themselves, and for all who have not the consolation of the prayers of others, and for all whose anguish is unrelieved by the knowledge of your love:
We entreat you to hear us, good Lord.

For the infirm and aged, and all who are growing weary with the journey of life; and for all who are passing through the valley of death:
We entreat you to hear us, good Lord.

For all forgotten by us, but dear to you:
We entreat you to hear us, good Lord.

O God our Father, have regard to our prayers, answer them in your compassion, and make us the channels of your infinite pity and helpfulness. *Amen.*

DEVOTIONAL SERVICES FOR PUBLIC WORSHIP

121. For the Dying

(Also suitable for use on Good Friday evening)

God the Father,
Have mercy on us.

God the Son,
Have mercy on us.

God the Holy Spirit,
Have mercy on us.

Holy, blessed, and glorious Trinity,
Have mercy on us.

God, who took the form of a servant and shared the life of suffering and
sorrow,
Have mercy on us.

God, who bore our weaknesses and healed our sicknesses,
Have mercy on us.

God, who became obedient unto death, even death on a cross,
Have mercy on us.

God, who at the beginning breathed life into man, and appointed the hour
of our death,
Have mercy on us.

Hear our prayers, good Jesus, and grant that, dying to sin here, we may live
for you in heaven:
Good Jesus, hear us.

May we, remaining your faithful soldiers and servants here, receive
hereafter the crown of glory:
Good Jesus, hear us.

May we accept with patience all the pains of death, knowing that you have
borne them all as one of us:
Good Jesus, hear us.

Be with us in the valley of the shadow of death:
Good Jesus, hear us.

Let us not, at our last hour, fall away from you:
Good Jesus, hear us.

Forgive us our sins, and strengthen us with the Bread of Life:
Good Jesus, hear us.

Let us die in your faith and fear, in sure and certain hope of the resurrection
to eternal life:
Good Jesus, hear us.

Deliver us, Lord, at our last hour: as you delivered Enoch and Elijah from
the death which must come to all,
So save and deliver us.

As you delivered Noah from the flood,
So save and deliver us.

As you delivered Job from his affliction,
So save and deliver us.

As you delivered Isaac from the knife,
So save and deliver us.

As you delivered Lot from Sodom,
So save and deliver us.

As you delivered the children of Israel from Pharoah,
So save and deliver us.

As you delivered Daniel from the lions' den,
So save and deliver us.

As you delivered the three young men from the fiery furnace,
So save and deliver us.

As you delivered Esther and her people from the power of Haman,
So save and deliver us.

As you delivered David from Saul and from Goliath,
So save and deliver us.

As you delivered Peter from prison and Paul from his enemies,
So save and deliver us.

As you have always delivered from evil those who put their trust in you,
So save and deliver us.

Deliver us, Lord on that fearful day, when the heavens and the earth shall
pass away, when you shall come to judge the world by fire:
Save and deliver us.

In the day of judgement, when the books are opened, and the dead, great
and small, shall stand before you:
Save and deliver us.

Holy God, holy and strong, holy and immortal:
Have mercy on us.

Jesus, Lamb of God:
Have mercy on us.

Jesus, bearer of our sins:
Have mercy on us.

Jesus, redeemer of the world:
Give us your peace.

Our Father, who art in heaven,
    hallowed be thy Name,
    thy kingdom come,
    thy will be done,
        on earth as it is in heaven.
Give us this day our daily bread.
And forgive us our trespasses,
    as we forgive those who trespass against us.
And lead us not into temptation,
    but deliver us from evil.
For thine is the kingdom, and the power, and the glory,
    for ever and ever. Amen.

Happy are the dead who die in the faith of Christ.
Even so, says the Spirit, for they rest from their labors. Amen.

PRAYERS FOR USE AT THE ALTERNATIVE SERVICES

122. At a Vigil

(when the family and friends of the deceased come together for prayers prior to the funeral)

Dear Friends: It was our Lord Jesus himself who said "Come to me, all you who labor and are burdened, and I will give you rest." Let us pray, then, for our brother (sister) _____, that *he* may rest from *his* labors, and enter into the light of God's eternal sabbath rest.

Receive, O Lord, your servant, for *he* returns to you.
Into your hands, O Lord,
we commend our brother (sister) _____.

Wash *him* in the holy font of everlasting life, and clothe *him* in *his* heavenly wedding garment.
Into your hands, O Lord,
we commend our brother (sister) _____.

May *he* hear your words of invitation, "Come, you blessed of my Father."
Into your hands, O Lord,
we commend our brother (sister) _____.

May *he* gaze upon you, Lord, face to face, and taste the blessedness of perfect rest.
Into your hands, O Lord,
we commend our brother (sister) _____.

May angels surround *him,* and saints welcome *him* in peace.
Into your hands, O Lord,
we commend our brother (sister) _____.

(Silence)

Almighty God, our Father in heaven,
before whom live all who die in the Lord:
Receive our brother (sister) _____
into the courts of your heavenly dwelling place.
Let his *heart and soul now ring out in joy to you,*
O Lord, the living God, and the God of those who live.
This we ask through Christ our Lord.
Amen.

THE BOOK OF COMMON PRAYER 1979

123. At a Funeral or Memorial Service

For our brother (sister) _____, let us pray to our Lord Jesus Christ who said, "I am the Resurrection and I am the Life."

(Silence)

Lord, you consoled Martha and Mary in their distress; draw near to us who mourn for _____, and dry the tears of those who weep.
Hear us, Lord.

You wept at the grave of Lazarus, your friend; comfort us in our sorrow.
Hear us, Lord.

You raised the dead to life; give to our brother (sister) eternal life.
Hear us, Lord.

You promised paradise to the thief who repented; bring our brother (sister) to the joys of heaven.
Hear us, Lord.

Our brother (sister) was washed in Baptism and anointed with the Holy Spirit; give *him* fellowship with all your saints.
Hear us, Lord.

He was nourished with your Body and Blood; grant *him* a place at the table in your heavenly kingdom.
Hear us, Lord.

Comfort us in our sorrows at the death of our brother (sister); let our faith be our consolation, and eternal life our hope.
Hear us, Lord.

(The Leader concludes with one of the following prayers:)

Lord Jesus Christ, we commend to you our brother (sister) _____, who was reborn by water and the Spirit in Holy Baptism. Grant that *his* death may recall to us your victory over death, and be an occasion for us to renew our trust in your Father's love. Give us, we pray, the faith to follow where you have led the way; and where you live and reign with the Father and the Holy Spirit, to the ages of ages. *Amen.*

(or)

Father of all, we pray to you for _____, and for all those whom we love but see no longer. Grant to them eternal rest. Let light perpetual shine upon them. May *his* soul and the souls of all the departed, through the mercy of God, rest in peace. *Amen.*

THE BOOK OF COMMON PRAYER 1979

PRAYER
AND
THE
WORLD COMMUNITY

The Nation

124. For the Nation

(This litany is designed to be used on days of national celebration, or in times of national crisis.)

Mighty God: the earth is yours and the nations are your people. Take away our pride and bring to mind your goodness, so that, living together in this land, we may enjoy your gifts and be thankful.
Amen.

For clouded mountains, fields and woodland; for shoreline and running streams;
for all that makes our nation good and lovely;
We thank you, God.

For farms and villages where food is gathered to feed our people;
We thank you, God.

For cities where people talk and work together in factories, shops, or schools to shape those things we need for living;
We thank you, God.

For explorers, planners, statesmen; for prophets who speak out, and for silent faithful people; for all who love our land and guard our freedom;
We thank you, God.

For vision to see your purpose hidden in our nation's history, and courage to seek it in love given and received;
We thank you, God.

O God: your justice is like rock, and your mercy like pure flowing water. Judge and forgive us. If we have turned from you, return us to your way; for without you we are a lost people.
Amen.

From brassy patriotism and a blind trust in power;
Deliver us, O God.

From public deceptions that weaken trust; from self-seeking in high political places;
Deliver us, O God.

From divisions among us of class or race; from wealth that will not share, and poverty that feeds on the food of bitterness;
Deliver us, O God.

From neglecting rights; from overlooking the hurt, the imprisoned, and the needy among us;
Deliver us, O God.

From a lack of concern for other lands and peoples; from narrowness of national purpose; from failure to welcome the peace you promise on earth;
Deliver us, O God.

Eternal God: before you nations rise and fall; they grow strong or wither by your design. Help us to repent of our country's wrong, and to choose your right in reunion and renewal.
Amen.

Give us a glimpse of the Holy City you are bringing to earth, where death and pain and crying will be gone away, and nations will gather in the light of your presence.
Great God, renew this nation.

Teach us peace, so that we may plow up battlefields and pound weapons into building tools, and learn to talk across old boundaries as brothers and sisters in your love.
Great God, renew this nation.

Talk sense to us, so that we may wisely end all prejudice, and may put a stop to cruelty, which divides or wounds the human family.
Great God, renew this nation.

Draw us together as one people who do your will, so that our land may be a light to nations, leading the way to your promised kingdom which is coming among us.
Great God, renew this nation.

Great God, eternal Lord: long years ago you gave our ancestors this land as a home for the free. Show us there is no law or liberty apart from you; and let us serve you modestly, as devoted people; through Jesus Christ our Lord.
Amen.

THE WORSHIPBOOK

125. In Thanksgiving for Our Country

O eternal God, ruler of all the earth, we bless you for our country.
Bountifully have you given to us, beyond all our deserving. You have
made us heirs of what the untold ages have created: the majesty of upthrust
mountains, the green of wooded hills, the prairies rolling to their far
horizons, the fertile valleys where the rivers run. All that we can
accomplish rests on this which you have freely given. Hear us as we bring
you the tribute of our grateful hearts.

For all the mighty width of land from bordering sea to sea,
We thank you, O Lord.

For endless fields where the grain harvests ripen, for orchards with their
golden fruit,
We thank you, O Lord.

For cattle in the meadows, for wild life in the woods, for the fish in the
ocean and lakes and mountain streams, for the homely creatures of the
farm, and for the infinite beauty of winged birds,
We thank you, O Lord.

For rich ores hidden in the hills, for coal and oil and iron, and for all the
treasures of unnumbered mines,
We thank you, O Lord.

For the strength and skill of all the toiling multitude on whom our life
depends: on farms, in fishing fleets, in factories, and before the fires of
furnaces and mills,
We thank you, O Lord.

For the genius of inventors, for the imagination of engineers, for the daring
of those who have dreamed a mightier civilization and have fashioned their
dreams in stone and steel,
We thank you, O Lord.

For those who laid the railroads and launched the ships, for those who have
built the bridges and lifted the towers of cities to the sky,
We thank you, O Lord.

For all the host of men and women who in industry, in commerce, and in
communications hold the world together because they are dependable at
their daily posts,
We thank you, O Lord.

For all the servants of the mind, for scholars and teachers, for authors and artists, and for all poets in word or deed who reveal the wideness and wonder of the world,
We thank you, O Lord.

Yet we remember that as we have greatly received, so in the same measure we are responsible. Forbid that we should betray our trust, or that the fire which has been passed on to us should perish. Help us to be worthy of our forebears, and of their God.

To all the high desires of the pioneers and prophets,
O God, help us to be faithful.

To their belief in the possibilities of the common people,
O God, help us to be faithful.

To their passion for freedom and their readiness to live and die in its defense,
O God, help us to be faithful.

To their scorn of tyranny, and their trust in ordinary folk to rule themselves,
O God, help us to be faithful.

To their vision of a human commonwealth in which people from many lands might share,
O God, help us to be faithful.

To their release from the prejudices and passions of an old world and their will to build a new,
O God, help us to be faithful.

O God, our mothers and fathers trusted in you
And were not confounded.

They lifted their faces to you
And were not ashamed.

So enlighten us, O Father, and lead us on your redeeming way; through Jesus Christ our Lord. *Amen.*

WALTER RUSSELL BOWIE

126. A Litany of Thanksgiving for All Who Fought Peacefully for Freedom

O God, the Ruler of the nations, we thank you for men and women in our nation's past who fought, bravely and without shedding blood, for many kinds of freedom.
They knew that freedom is indivisible, and that freedom for some demands freedom for all.

We thank you for John Woolman and his fellow Quakers,
Who freed their slaves without approval from anyone except you;

For Harriet Beecher Stowe who, by kindling compassion for "Uncle Tom," set a nation's conscience on edge;
And for Martin Luther King who gave his life for the dream of "Black and White together."

We praise you, Father, for forgotten loners who strove to secure the first rights for workers;
And for great leaders of labor who were able to build upon their vision and their sacrifices.

We give you thanks, Father, for Horace Mann who fought to insure a basic education for every child, regardless of caste or class;
And for John Dewey who saw children not as computers to be programmed but as young persons to be helped to grow.

We praise you, O God, for the pioneers in the struggle for the liberation of women - for Susan B. Anthony, Elizabeth Cady Stanton, and others;
And for the single-minded devotion of many who spent themselves working for the day when every child would be a wanted child.

We praise you, O God, for Christians who loved you enough to realize that others might love you in a different way but love you just as well;
For Roger Williams who struck the first peaceful blow for religious freedom, and William Penn who created a commonwealth where all people could dwell in peace.

We thank you for missionaries who chose to live among Indians, slaves, or alien immigrants, because they wanted to bring them into the mainstream of our society;
And for John R. Mott and others who worked for unity, dramatizing the scandal of our divisions and the enlargement of Christian witness and service which reunion would bring.

For all these peaceful fighters for freedom in our nation's past, we thank you, O Lord;
And we pray that we may take our place alongside them in today's struggles for freedom, justice, and mercy; in the name of Jesus Christ who has set us all free. Amen.

JOHN R. BODO
-MODELS FOR MINISTERS I*

127. ... With Liberty and Justice for All

"And a foreigner you shall not oppress, for you know the heart of the foreigner, seeing that you yourselves were foreigners in the land of Egypt."
Next year let us celebrate in a world where everyone is free.

As we celebrate this year there are millions of poor in our own country; we will not be free until all these are free.
Next year let us celebrate in a world where everyone is free.

This year there are many thousands of migrant workers who are exploited to our selfish advantage and gain.
Next year let us celebrate in a world where everyone is free.

This year we celebrate in a world that fears destruction; we cannot be free until fear is ended.
Next year let us celebrate in a world where everyone is free.

This year we celebrate in a climate of oppression where people lack basic freedoms in [_____] and many other parts of the world.
Next year let us celebrate in a world where everyone is free.

We will not be free until all are free.
Next year let us celebrate in a world where everyone indeed is free. Amen.

LITURGY MAGAZINE*

128. Prayers for a National Holiday

Heavenly Father, we give you thanks for the wonder of creation, for the gifts of human life, and for the blessing of human fellowship.
We thank you, Lord.

For Christ, your living Word, through whom we are taught the perfect way of life and the dignity of service,
We thank you, Lord.

For your Spirit, who offers his gifts to us for the common good,
We thank you, Lord.

For the blessing of community in our nation, and for those who have used your gifts to strengthen and enrich its life,
We thank you, Lord.

For our President, and for all who serve as leaders in this land,
We thank you, Lord.

Grant them, we pray, a vision of your will for your people; wisdom to fulfill their vocation of leadership in a nation of many races; strength and courage to carry out the duties of their calling; and the assurance of your presence, your power, and your love.
Lord, in your mercy
Hear our prayer.

We pray for all who are called to serve in times and places of crisis, in the face of racial and social tensions;
Lord, in your mercy
Hear our prayer.

In the Church's proclamation of the Gospel, we ask for a clear message of your love and power;
Lord, in your mercy
Hear our prayer.

In federal, state and local government, for insight, integrity and courage;
Lord, in your mercy
Hear our prayer.

In the administration of law and in the defense of our people, for justice and humility, fairness and compassion;
Lord, in your mercy
Hear our prayer.

In industry and commerce, in trade and business, for mutual care and
cooperation and a concern for the good of all;
Lord, in your mercy
Hear our prayer.

In art and music, theater and entertainment, sport and leisure, for
recognition that all gifts come from you to give to one another;
Lord, in your mercy
Hear our prayer.

In every mode of communication, in literature and press, radio and
television, for a vision of social good and for service to the truth;
Lord, in your mercy
Hear our prayer.

In education, in family and school and college, for a concern not only with
information but also with maturity and fulfillment of life;
Lord, in your mercy
Hear our prayer.

And finally, in the service of those in need and sickness, anxiety and
suffering, for a community that cares;
Lord, in your mercy
Hear our prayer. Amen.

ADAPTED FROM THE SERVICE FOR THE SILVER JUBILEE OF
QUEEN ELIZABETH II*

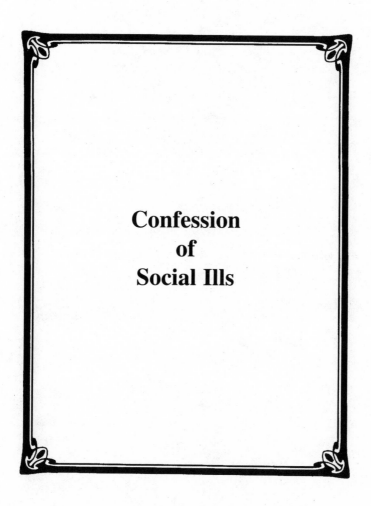

Confession
of
Social Ills

129. For Those Who Hunger

Our Lord Jesus Christ gave himself to those who recognized their need, their hunger, their poverty in and of themselves, and their dependence on God. These were the people most able to receive him and to welcome his message and his word. So today we say: Lord, make us hungry.

For your Word and for your Spirit,	*Lord, make us hungry.*
For the bread of life,	*Lord, make us hungry.*
For understanding and compassion,	*Lord, make us hungry.*
For freedom, justice and peace,	*Lord, make us hungry.*
For an equal sharing of your good gifts,	*Lord, make us hungry.*

Our Lord Jesus Christ said, "If you then, who are evil, know how to give good gifts to your children, how much more will your Father who is in heaven give good things to those who ask him!" So today we turn to the Father once again and say: Lord, fill us.

With your hope and strength,	*Lord, fill us.*
With your boundless love and self-giving,	*Lord, fill us.*
With the power of Christ's death and resurrection,	*Lord, fill us.*
With his sensitivity to the needs of others,	*Lord, fill us.*
With trust in your will to save us all,	*Lord, fill us.*

That all may know you to be their Father and Christ to be the one whom you have sent,
Lord, make us bread broken for others.

That the rights and needs of all may be recognized and provided for,
Lord, make us bread broken for others.

That all may be fed and none go hungry,
Lord, make us bread broken for others.

That all may have life and have it in all its fullness,
Lord, make us bread broken for others.

That we may give thanks to you not only with our lips but in our lives,
Lord, make us bread broken for others.

That your will may be done on earth as it is in heaven,
Lord, make us bread broken for others.

(Silence)

Our Father in heaven,
 hallowed be your Name,
 your kingdom come,
 your will be done,
   on earth as in heaven.
Give us today our daily bread.
Forgive us our sins
 as we forgive those
   who sin against us.
Save us from the time of trial,
 and deliver us from evil.
For the kingdom, the power,
 and the glory are yours,
 now and for ever. Amen.

BREAD FOR THE WORLD

130. For The Lost Ones Among Us

Lord, make us mindful of those who are not like us; those we look at and do not see; those we look at and turn away from.

> *Lord, have mercy on them and us.*

We pray for those who cannot function in our world, by our standards - "For I was a stranger......"

> *Lord, have mercy on them and us.*

We pray for those who are shut away, out of sight, in jails and mental hospitals - "Lord, when did we see you sick or in prison ?"

> *Lord, have mercy on them and us.*

We pray for the homeless, wandering aimlessly on the streets, muttering or ranting - "And the Son of Man had no place to lay his head."

> *Lord, have mercy on them and us.*

We pray for those who sell their blood to survive - "And their blood be on our heads."

> *Lord, have mercy on them and us.*

We pray for those in line outside the soup kitchens - "I have set a table in the presence of my enemies."

> *Lord, have mercy on them and us.*

We pray for those rummaging in trash bins for food or cans - "Lord, when did we see you hungry?"

> *Lord, have mercy on them and us.*

We pray for the customers of Thrift Shops, where we have dumped our stained, out-of-style clothing - "Lord, when did we see you naked?"

> *Lord, have mercy on them and us.*

We pray for the halt, the lame and the blind, who struggle to make their way - "Take up your bed and walk."

Lord, have mercy on them and us.

We pray for those too young to be mothers, with too many children - "Suffer the little ones to come to me, for of such is the kingdom of heaven."

Lord, have mercy on them and us.

We pray for those hustling their talents on the street corner and selling their bodies - "You are forgiven; go and sin no more."

Lord, have mercy on them and us.

We pray for families barely existing in cramped, over-priced, under-furnished apartments - "And there was no room for them in the inn.'

Lord, have mercy on them and us.

We pray for refugees and boat people, risking their lives to find food and freedom and a future - "Enter into the joy of your Lord."

Lord, have mercy on them and us.

We pray for those dying of incurable diseases, shunned and feared and abandoned - "Today you shall be with me in paradise."

Lord, have mercy on them and us.

We pray for the Church and for ourselves that we may see and hear and respond - "Whatever you do for the least of these, you do for me."

Lord, have mercy on them and us. Amen.

MARILYN LOGAN*

131. For the Isolated and the Alienated

My brothers and sisters,
so many men and women
waste away and get shriveled up
in a universe reduced to fit their limited vision.
Let us ask the Spirit of the Lord
to open up their hearts and ours
to a greater and stronger love.
Lord, source of all love,
let us burn with your love.

For families turned in on themselves,
exclusive in their affections,
indifferent to the external world,
that they may notice
the needs and joys which surround them,
let us pray to the Lord.
Lord, source of all love,
let us burn with your love.

For troubled towns
where teenagers rebel
and no longer hope in adults;
for slum neighborhoods
where, with no assistance from the rest of society,
the poor and alienated are dying,
let us pray to the Lord.
Lord, source of all love,
let us burn with your love.

For antagonistic groups, classes, races,
who see their own vengeance and their own security
in absolute, unbending terms;
for politicians
and national and international diplomats,
so that their concern for the common good
may go beyond defense
of the narrow interests of their constituents,
let us pray to the Lord.
Lord, source of all love,
let us burn with your love.

For Christian communities,
entrenched in their dogmas and practices,
that they may guard against seeing an enemy
in someone who disagrees,
a sinner in the unbeliever;
for the most uncompromising among us
in whose eyes every dialogue is already a compromise,
and adaptation to another's viewpoint means
abandoning the truth,
let us pray to the Lord.
Lord, source of all love,
let us burn with your love.

For all of us gathered at the Eucharist,
that throughout the entire world
those who partake of the same bread
and the same communion cup
may become witnesses of the Lord
who made himself all things for all people;
and that each of us may willingly give our life and time
for the happiness of others,
let us pray to the Lord.
Lord, source of all love,
let us burn with your love. Amen.

PRAYERS IN COMMUNITY

132. A Twentieth-Century Litany
for Deliverance

Leader 1:	From the accidents of our history,
Leader 2:	and from the ironies of our history;
All:	*Good Lord, deliver us.*

Leader 1:	From universal education leaving millions unenlightened,
Leader 2:	and from the enlightened betrayed in the maze of their own ingenuities;
All:	*Good Lord, deliver us.*

Leader 1:	From the capitalist destruction of the capitalist ethic,
Leader 2:	and from the socialist rejection of the socialist vision;
All:	*Good Lord, deliver us.*

Leader 1:	From specialists without spirit, and sensualists without heart,
Leader 2:	and from technology become tyranny, and revolution become oppression;
All:	*Good Lord, deliver us.*

Leader 1:	From long lives ending in slow deterioration,
Leader 2:	and good lives ending in sudden assassination;
All:	*Good Lord, deliver us.*

Leader 1:	From Protestants who no longer say, "Here I stand,"
Leader 2:	and from Catholics who no longer cry, "Behold, the Lamb of God,"
Leader 1:	and from churches which no longer preach, "Jesus Christ as Lord, and ourselves as your servants for Jesus' sake";
All:	*Good Lord, deliver us.*
	Good Lord, deliver us.

Leader 2:	Through the accidents and ironies of our history,
All:	*Good Lord, deliver us.*

Leader 1:	Through the short reigns of wise and generous Popes,
Leader 2:	and the long trauma of Vietnam, Watergate and the Cold War;
All:	*Good Lord, deliver us.*

Leader 1:	Through human suffering bringing Christians and Marxists into dialogue,
Leader 2:	and economic pressures bringing workers and employers out of deadlock;
All:	*Good Lord, deliver us.*
Leader 1:	Through fuel shortages requiring us to take other nations seriously,
Leader 2:	and lower speed limits enabling us to take other lives seriously;
All:	*Good Lord, deliver us.*
Leader 1:	Through earthrise seen in awe from the moon,
Leader 2:	and mushroom clouds seen in awe on the screen;
All:	*Good Lord, deliver us.*
Leader 1:	Through finding ourselves called to ministry,
Leader 2:	and finding others ready to minister to us,
Leader 1:	and finding churches ready to change and to die as the price of ministry;
All:	*Good Lord, deliver us.*
	Good Lord, deliver us.
Leader 2:	From subsisting with necessity to living with freedom,
Leader 1:	from the claustrophobia of abundance to the opportunities of shortage;
All:	*Good Lord, deliver us.*
Leader 2:	From human determinism to divine initiative,
Leader 1:	from the Remembrance of Things Past to the City of God
All:	*Good Lord, deliver us.*

> *In the best of times and the worst of times,*
> *in the age of wisdom and the age of foolishness,*
> *in the season of light and the season of darkness,*
> *in the spring of our hope and the winter of our despair,*
> *good Lord, deliver us.*
> *Amen.*

JEFFERY W. ROWTHORN

133. Confession of a Split Personality

We build nuclear bombs to destroy the world,
And we use nuclear power to lighten the darkness.

We have brought many nations together under one roof,
And we have used the United Nations to our own advantage.

We fly faster than the sun,
And we crawl in traffic jams.

We have died in Vietnam,
And we have walked on the moon.

(Silence)

O come, O come, Emmanuel
and ransom captive Israel
that mourns in lonely exile here
until the Son of God appear.

We have beaten people with clubs,
And we have built courtrooms to keep them free.

We care about our brothers and sisters in the ghettos,
And we live in opulent comfort.

We litter the land with garbage,
And we work to conserve its beauty.

We have built schools to educate the young,
And we have made them battlefields for prejudice.

(Silence)

O come, O come, Emmanuel
and ransom captive Israel
that mourns in lonely exile here
until the Son of God appear.

We are rightly proud,
And we are rightly ashamed.

We are able to do all things,
And yet the will to do them is lacking.

In our minds we are God's willing servants, but in our own nature we are
bound fast to the law of sin and death.
Who on earth can set us free from the agony of this condition?

(Silence)

O come, O come, Emmanuel
and ransom captive Israel
that mourns in lonely exile here
until the Son of God appear. Amen.

JEFFERY W. ROWTHORN*

134. A Litany of Modern Ills

From hunger and unemployment, and from enforced eviction:
Good Lord, deliver us.

From unjust sentences and unjust wars:
Good Lord, deliver us.

From neglect by parents, neglect by children, and neglect by callous institutions:
Good Lord, deliver us.

From cancer and stroke, ulcers, madness, and senility:
Good Lord, deliver us.

From famine and epidemic, from overcrowding of the planet, and from pollution of the soil, the air, and the waters:
Good Lord, deliver us.

From segregation and prejudice, from harassment, discrimination, and brutality:
Good Lord, deliver us.

From the concentration of power in the hands of ignorant, threatened, or hasty leaders:
Good Lord, deliver us.

From propaganda, fads, frivolity, and untruthfulness:
Good Lord, deliver us.

From arrogance, narrowness and meanness, from stupidity and pretence:
Good Lord, deliver us.

From boredom, apathy, and fatigue, from lack of conviction, from fear, self-satisfaction, and timidity:
Good Lord, deliver us.

From retribution at the hands of our victims, and from the consequences of our own folly:
Good Lord, deliver us.

From resignation and despair, from cynicism and manipulation:
Good Lord, deliver us.

Through all unmerited suffering, our own and that of others:
Good Lord, deliver us.

Through the unending cry of all peoples for justice and freedom:
Good Lord, deliver us.

Through all concern and wonder, love and creativity:
Good Lord, deliver us.

In our strength and our weakness, in occasional success and eventual failure:
Good Lord, deliver us.

In aloneness and community, in the days of action and the time of our dying:
Good Lord, deliver us.

By the needs of humanity and of the earth, and not by our own merits or deserving:
Good Lord, deliver us.

Deliver us, Good Lord, by opening our eyes and unstopping our ears, that we may hear your word and do your will:
Good Lord, deliver us. Amen.

THE COVENANT OF PEACE
-A LIBERATION PRAYER BOOK

135. A Confession of Wrong in Our Society

All: *Almighty and most merciful Father, we have erred and strayed from thy ways like lost sheep.*

First voice: We have strayed from our own responsibilities to families and communities, thinking that we would thus be free.

All: *We have followed too much the devices and desires of our own hearts.*

Second voice: We have been too sentimental and at the same time have followed too much the logic of our minds; we have built great universities to search out truth, then hidden behind their ivied walls to protect ourselves from strife and danger.

All: *We have offended against thy holy laws.*

First voice: We have allowed our communities and nations to respect selfishness and injustice and have washed our hands of the " due process of law."

All: *We have left undone those things which we ought to have done.*

Second voice: We have been irresponsible in our economic life and allowed unrighteousness to hold sway in politics and the struggle for power,

All: *And we have done those things which we ought not to have done.*

First voice: We have lived at the expense of our poorer brothers and sisters at home and abroad; we have used the terrible destructiveness of science against our enemies,

All: *And there is no health in us.*

Second voice: There is conflict in the depths of our souls which has driven us into sickness of mind and body,

All: *But thou, O Lord, have mercy upon us, miserable offenders.*

First voice: We have considered ourselves untainted by the evils of our modern world.

All: *Spare thou those, O God, who confess their faults.*

Second voice: Be they personal, social, cultural or religious sins,

All: *Restore thou those who are penitent.*

First voice:	Who would change both themselves and their society,
All:	*According to thy promises declared unto mankind in Christ Jesus our Lord,*
Second voice:	Through whom together we are raised up into thy kingdom on earth and in heaven.
All:	*And grant, O most merciful Father, for his sake, that we may hereafter live a godly, righteous and sober life,*
First voice:	Ordered by thy law and freed by thy grace,
All:	*To the glory of thy holy name. Amen.*

THE STUDENT PRAYER BOOK
-AND THE BOOK OF COMMON PRAYER 1928*

136. A Confession of Social Failure †

The confusion of morals —
O Lord, forgive.

The breakdown of social restraints —
O Lord, forgive.

The increase of crime and violence —
O Lord, forgive.

The commercialization of sex —
O Lord, forgive.

The traffic in drugs —
O Lord, forgive.

The exploitation of teenagers —
O Lord, forgive.

The apathy and disenchantment of young people —
O Lord, forgive.

Our loss of vision —
O Lord, forgive.

Our moral cowardice —
O Lord, forgive.

Our failure as parents and adults —
O Lord, forgive.

Our self-seeking and self-indulgence —
O Lord, forgive.

Our love of money and possessions —
O Lord, forgive.

Our connivance at dishonesty and corruption —
O Lord, forgive.

Our unwillingness to serve and give of ourselves —
O Lord, forgive.

Almighty God, have mercy on us, forgive us all our sins through our Lord Jesus Christ, strengthen us in all goodness, and by the power of the Holy Spirit keep us in eternal life. *Amen.*

THE ANGLICAN CATHEDRAL, LIVERPOOL
-PRAYERS FOR TODAY'S CHURCH

137. For the Affluent

O God, we have meant to love and serve you better than we do, but we have not. Our streets are lined with trees, our houses warm, our friends good, our children well-fed. We have meant to thank you with our lives, but we have not.
O God, forgive us and teach us your ways.

We have meant to listen for your voice, but we have been too busy to hear you very often. When we have heard you, we have meant to obey you, but we have forgotten - or at times we have been too afraid.
O God, forgive us and teach us your ways.

We have set up a comfortable family life as our highest goal and closed our eyes to the greater demands of your love. We have filled our lives with too many things to do and too many things to care for.
O God, forgive us and teach us your ways.

We have set ourselves apart from our poorer city neighbors and sometimes we forget that they are even there. We try not to think of the hungry in other lands too often, because there are so many.
O God, forgive us and teach us your ways.

We have lived in anxiety lest our private world explode in pain and terror, and we have looked towards fear and away from you.
O God, forgive us and teach us to hope.

We have considered spending vast sums on weaponry to save us from destruction, but seldom spoken about spending vast sums to feed the poor and hungry.
O God, forgive us and teach us to love.

We have meant to serve you in everything we do, but we have given you only the leftover hour, the spare energy and the momentary prayer.
O God, forgive us and teach us your ways. Amen

AVERY BROOKE

138. "As You Did It to One of the Least of These My Sisters and Brothers, You Did It to Me"

O God, who is old, and lives on fifty dollars a month, in one crummy room and can't get outside,
Help us to see you.

O God, who is fifteen and in the sixth grade,
Help us to see you.

O God, who is three and whose belly aches in hunger,
Help us to see you, as you have seen us in Jesus Christ our Lord.

O God, who sleeps in a bed with your four brothers and sisters, and who cries and no one hears you,
Help us to touch you.

O God, who has no place to sleep tonight except an abandoned car, an alley or deserted building,
Help us to touch you.

O God, who is uneducated, unskilled, unwanted, and unemployed,
Help us to touch you, as you have touched us in Jesus Christ our Lord.

O God, who was laid off last week and can't pay the rent or feed the kids,
Help us to be with you.

O God, who is poor and on welfare and told that you don't want to work,
Help us to be with you.

O God, who is dressed by the suburbs from the church clothing store,
Help us to be with you, as you are with us in Jesus Christ our Lord.

O God, who is chased by the cops, who sits in jail for seven months with no charges brought, waiting for the Grand Jury and no money for bail,
Help us to know you.

O God, who hangs out on the street corners, who tastes the grace of cheap wine and the sting of the needle,
Help us to know you.

O God, who pays too much rent for a lousy apartment because you speak Spanish,
Help us to know you, as you know us in Jesus Christ our Lord.

O God, who is uprooted by Urban Renewal and removed from your neighborhood,
Help us to stand with you.

O God, whose church down the street closed and moved away,
Help us to stand with you.

O God, whose elected leaders only know you exist at election time and represent themselves and not the people,
Help us to stand with you, as you stand with us in Jesus Christ our Lord.

O God, who is poor and has all sorts of programs being planned for you,
Help us to join you.

O God, who is unorganized, and without strength to change your world, your city, your neighborhood,
Help us to join you.

O God, who is fed up with it all and who is determined to do something, who is organizing people for power to change the world,
Help us to join you, as you have joined us in Jesus Christ our Lord. Amen.

ROBERT W. CASTLE, JR.
-PRAYERS FROM THE BURNED-OUT CITY*

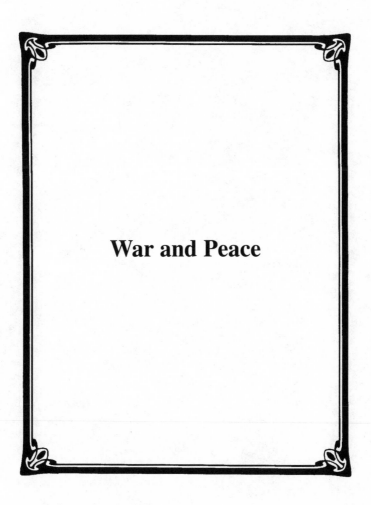

War and Peace

139. For the Abolition of Nuclear Weapons

Leader 1:   Let us accept our calling to be peacemakers in our day and in God's name covenant to work together for the abolition of nuclear weapons.

(Silence)

Leader 1:   Let us covenant together to pray for peace:
to pray that God will hold back nuclear devastation so that we may turn from our folly and live;
to pray for our enemies and in this way bring them closer to us;
to pray that our faith in Christ's victory will triumph over the threat of nuclear war.

All: *Prince of Peace, help us all to pray for peace.*

Leader 2:   Let us covenant together to learn about peace:
to learn what the Bible teaches about peace so that we may study war no more;
to learn what makes for lasting peace between peoples and nations;
to learn what nuclear war would mean for our world and for our children.

All: *Prince of Peace, help us all to learn about peace.*

Leader 1:   Let us covenant together to examine ourselves:
to discover how our lifestyle contributes to greed and hostility and ultimately to war;
to discover how our livelihoods depend increasingly on armaments and preparations for war;
to discover how our faith is compromised as we rely more and more on weapons of destruction.

All: *Prince of Peace, help us all to be honest about ourselves for the sake of peace.*

Leader 2:   Let us covenant together to spread the gospel of peace:
to tell our families and friends about the dangers of nuclear weapons;
to tell our churches about the claims of Christ upon our actions and our lives;
to tell our communities that there can be no protection against a nuclear attack.

All: *Prince of Peace, help us all to be witnesses for peace.*

Leader 1: Let us covenant together to work for peace:
to work to persuade our leaders that nuclear war is an
unthinkable act;
to work to persuade the Church that nuclear war is a sinful
deed;
to work to persuade the world that nuclear war is a
terminal disease.

All: *Prince of Peace, help us all to be peacemakers in our day.*

(Silence)

All: *In God's name we solemnly covenant to work for the
abolition of nuclear weapons and the threat of nuclear
war, and with God's help to seek peace and to pursue it in
every aspect of our lives.
We make this covenant, trusting in the strength of the
Prince of Peace, even Jesus Christ our Lord. Amen.*

SOJOURNERS MAGAZINE*

140. Memorial Day

On this day our memories may be so painful that we cannot live with them.
Yet we cannot, we dare not live without them. Let us pray that we may
never forget, but always remember before God that in his sight war is evil
and that, to all who experience it, war is hell.

(Silence)

For leaders who send the young to war,
that their judgement be sound
and their motives be pure,
we pray to the Lord.
Lord hear our prayer.

For soldiers who lay down their lives for others,
that the love which inspires their sacrifice
may be fulfilled in the love of Christ,
we pray to the Lord.
Lord hear our prayer.

For soldiers who have been maimed or brutalized by war,
that our love for them may make their scars of no consequence
and make their brutality yield to the tenderness of returning love,
we pray to the Lord.
Lord hear our prayer.

For those who have been left behind,
that they may live on the strength of the love that they knew,
we pray to the Lord.
Lord hear our prayer.

For those who suffer most from war,
that the homeless, the orphaned, the hungry, and the innocent
may help us turn from warlike ways to accept God's gift of peace,
we pray to the Lord.
Lord hear our prayer.

(Silence)

Father, help us never to forget that war is evil and war is hell.
Help us to honor its dead and to pray for its victims who live on,
through him who for our sakes laid down his life,
even Jesus Christ our Lord.
Amen.

PRAYERS OF THE FAITHFUL

141. At the Funeral of a Member of the Armed Forces

Let us ask our Father, who has seen his sons and daughters kill each other, to take pity on us, to weep for us and to give _____ new life in Jesus, our risen Lord.

(Silence)

For _____ whom we sent to war, and for all those we sent to die, that they will live on in us, reminding us of the emptiness of hate, and of the peace we cannot seem to attain, let us pray to the Lord.
Lord, hear our prayer.

For _____ ' s family and all the families shattered by war, that they will find in their community the healing strength of your love, let us pray to the Lord.
Lord, hear our prayer.

For _____ ' s friends and for all whose loved ones have been killed in battle, that they will have the courage to continue giving the warmth of their hearts to those who are still alive, let us pray to the Lord.
Lord, hear our prayer.

For the veterans who have returned from World War I, World War II, Korea, Vietnam and Desert Storm, and for all the veterans of the world, that their memory of the act of war will be barren and their anger at the war's carnage will not stop until the world knows peace, let us pray to the Lord.
Lord, hear our prayer.

For those mutilated by war in their hearts and bodies, that they will find hope in him who created them whole, and support from us, our brother's keeper, let us pray to the Lord.
Lord, hear our prayer.

(Silence)

Father, grant to your servant _____, now with you, peace and everlasting life; help us bear our loss, and give us strength to pursue our quest for the unity and harmony of all your children, through Christ our Lord. Amen.

PRAYERS OF THE FAITHFUL

142. World Peace

Remember, O Lord, the peoples of the world divided into many nations and tongues. Deliver us from every evil that gets in the way of your saving purpose; and fulfill the promise of peace to your people on earth, through Jesus Christ our Lord. *Amen.*

(Silence)

From the curse of war and the human sin that causes war;
O Lord, deliver us.

From pride that turns its back on you, and from unbelief that will not call you Lord;
O Lord, deliver us.

From national vanity that poses as patriotism; from loud-mouthed boasting and blind self-worship that admit no guilt;
O Lord, deliver us.

From the self-righteousness that will not compromise, and from selfishness that gains by the oppression of others;
O Lord, deliver us.

From the lust for money or power that drives people to kill;
O Lord, deliver us.

From trusting in the weapons of war, and mistrusting the councils of peace;
O Lord, deliver us.

From hearing, believing, and speaking lies about other nations;
O Lord, deliver us.

From groundless suspicions and fears that stand in the way of reconciliation;
O Lord, deliver us.

From words and deeds that encourage discord, prejudice, and hatred; from everything that prevents the human family from fulfilling your promise of peace;
O Lord, deliver us.

O God our Father: we pray for all your children on earth, of every nation and of every race; that they may be strong to do your will.

(Silence)

We pray for the Church in the world.
Give peace in our time, O Lord.

For the United Nations;
Give peace in our time, O Lord.

For international federations of labor, industry, and commerce;
Give peace in our time, O Lord.

For departments of state, ambassadors, diplomats, and statesmen;
Give peace in our time, O Lord.

For worldwide agencies of compassion, which bind wounds and feed the
hungry;
Give peace in our time, O Lord.

For all who in any way work to further the cause of peace and goodwill;
Give peace in our time, O Lord.

For common folk in every land who live in peace;
Give peace in our time, O Lord.

Eternal God: use us, even our ignorance and weakness, to bring about your
holy will. Hurry the day when all people shall live together in your love;
for yours is the kingdom, the power, and the glory forever. *Amen.*

THE WORSHIPBOOK

143. A Litany of Human Rights

(based on the Universal Declaration of Human Rights adopted on December 10, 1948)

Almighty Lord, by whose holy urging the United Nations in our day, even while disputing with each other, are seeking a new world order of abiding law; grant to your Church everywhere insight to see this as your doing, and vigor to devote heart and mind to this great hope. So may the message of your love, which has freed men and women in every age, pervade and redeem even our halting efforts toward world peace, to the end that all the earth may discover and share the witness of your grace.

We thank you, Lord, for the gifts of wisdom and practicality by which leaders of the nations have set forth precepts to establish righteousness; as we dedicate these precepts anew to your glory, we dedicate ourselves also as instruments of your high purpose, to bring them to sound expression in the life of every nation:
Everyone has the right to life, liberty, and the security of person.
Bless all your people, Lord, that they may know this holy freedom grounded in your gospel.

No one shall be held in slavery or servitude; slavery and the slave trade shall be prohibited in all their forms.
Bless all your people, Lord, that they may know this holy freedom grounded in your gospel.

No one shall be subjected to torture or to cruel, inhuman or degrading treatment or punishment.
Bless all your people, Lord, that they may know this holy freedom grounded in your gospel.

Everyone has the right to recognition everywhere as a person before the law.
Bless all your people, Lord, that they may know this holy freedom grounded in your gospel.

No one shall be subjected to arbitrary interference with privacy, family, home or correspondence, nor to attacks upon honor and reputation.
Bless all your people, Lord, that they may know this holy freedom grounded in your gospel.

Everyone has the right to a nationality.
Bless all your people, Lord, that they may know this holy freedom grounded in your gospel.

Everyone has the right to rest and leisure, including reasonable limitation of working hours and periodic holidays with pay.
Bless all your people, Lord, that they may know this holy freedom grounded in your gospel.

Everyone has the right to a standard of living adequate for the health and well-being of self and of family, including food, clothing, housing and medical care and necessary social services, and the right to security in the event of unemployment, sickness, disability, widowhood, old age or other lack of livelihood in circumstances beyond their control. Motherhood and childhood are entitled to special care and assistance; all children, whether born in or out of wedlock, shall enjoy the same social protection.
Bless all your people, Lord, that they may know this holy freedom grounded in your gospel.

Everyone has the right to education. Education shall be free, at least in the elementary and fundamental stages; elementary education shall be compulsory. Technical and professional education shall be made generally available, and higher education shall be equally accessible to all on the basis of merit.
Bless all your people, Lord, that they may know this holy freedom grounded in your gospel.

Education shall be directed to the full development of the human personality, and to the strengthening of respect for human rights and fundamental freedoms.
Bless all your people, Lord, that they may know this holy freedom grounded in your gospel.

Everyone has the right freely to practice their religion, to participate in the cultural life of the community, to enjoy the arts, and to share in scientific advancement and its benefits.
Bless all your people, Lord, that they may know this holy freedom grounded in your gospel.

Men and women of full age, without any limitations of race, nationality, or religion, have the right to marry and to found a family; the family is the natural and fundamental group unit of society, and is entitled to protection by society and the state.
Bless all your people, Lord, that they may know this holy freedom grounded in your gospel.

All people have duties to the community, in which alone the free and full development of their personalities is possible.
Bless all your people, Lord, that they may know this holy freedom grounded in your gospel.

O God, show us the solemn link between liberties and duties, that our responsibilities may equal our rights in society, and that great eagerness to serve may balance our expectation to be served. So may your kingdom come in freedom and in discipline, and your name be glorified in all justice and truth. *Amen.*

JOHN OLIVER NELSON
-THE STUDENT PRAYER BOOK

144. A Litany of Resolve ✝

(based on the preamble to the United Nations Charter)

It is our resolve to save succeeding generations from the scourge of war, which time and again in this century has brought untold sorrow to humankind.
> *Lord, help us.*

It is our resolve to reaffirm our faith in fundamental human rights, in the dignity and worth of the human person, in the equal rights of men and women and of nations large and small.
> *Lord, help us.*

It is our resolve to establish conditions under which justice and respect for the obligations arising from treaties and other sources of international law can be maintained, and to promote social progress and better standards of life in larger freedom.
> *Lord, help us.*

It is our resolve to unite our strength to maintain international peace and security, and to ensure that armed force shall not be used, save in the common interest.
> *Lord, help us.*

It is our resolve to employ international machinery for the promotion of the economic and social advancement of all peoples.
> *Lord, help us.*

And for these ends it is our resolve to practice tolerance and live together in peace with one another as good neighbors.
> *Lord, help us. Amen.*

THE ANGLICAN CATHEDRAL, LIVERPOOL
-PRAYERS FOR TODAY'S CHURCH

145. Global Responsibility

If the six billion people of the world could be represented in a community of just one hundred people:

Five of them would be United States citizens; the other ninety-five would be citizens of all the other countries.
In Christ there is no east or west,
in him no south or north,
but one great fellowship of love,
throughout the whole wide earth.

The five Americans would own one-half of the money in the world; of the other ninety-five, seventy-five would own virtually nothing at all.
The first commandment is this: You shall love the Lord your God with all
your heart, and with all your soul, and with all your mind, and with all
your strength.

The five Americans would have fifteen times more material possessions than the other ninety-five put together.
And the second is this: You shall love your neighbor as yourself. There is
no other commandment greater than these.

The five Americans would have seventy-two per cent more than the average daily food requirement; two-thirds of the remainder would be below minimum food standards, and many of them would be on a starvation diet.
Then he will say to those at his left hand, Depart from me, you cursed, into
the eternal fire prepared for the devil and his angels; for I was hungry and
you gave me no food, I was thirsty and you gave me no drink . . . Truly, I
say to you, as you did not serve one of the least of these, you did not serve
me. And they will go away into eternal punishment.

A Latin American Cardinal asks: "Do rich Christians know there are seven hundred million illiterates in the Third World, and two hundred million jobless, or that there are three hundred-ninety million near starvation and another one hundred-thirty million undernourished? . . . The rich fail even to suspect the frustrations, resentments, hate, and finally violence engendered by the contrast between those who have so much and the have-nots, between the ever-richer nations and the ever-poorer countries."
And Jesus said to the rich young man, There is still one thing you lack.
Sell all you have and give the money to the poor. It will become treasure
for you in heaven - and come, follow me.

(Silence)

Almighty God, awaken within us that still small voice we call the Christian conscience. Inform it with Scripture, confront it with human needs, quicken it with the compassion of Jesus; instill it with wisdom; and empower it with the Holy Spirit, that it may no longer merely make us feel guilty, but may cause us to spring forth from our beds of lethargy and become living hope and love to the world around us. Amen.

OFFICE OF CREATIVE MINISTRIES
MISSOURI AREA, UNITED METHODIST CHURCH

146. A Litany of Remembrance of All Peoples

Leader: Almighty God, we lift our hopes and prayers to you for all the peoples of the world; you know their condition and need as we do not, and our thoughts of them are poor because we have not cared enough to seek knowledge of them. Accept our prayers as we give expression to the concern in our hearts, and unite our wills with your own mighty intention of good for them.

Voice 1:   We remember in silence before you;
The peoples of Africa and the Middle East, ancient home of kings, birthplace of our culture, lands of bitter wrongs, of ignorance and fear, of disease and death; yet lands of promise, of great rivers and forests, mountains and plains, eager and strong men and women seeking and finding freedom, seeking and finding you.

(Silence)

Leader: Pour out your spirit upon people everywhere;

People: *And hasten the coming of your kingdom.*

Voice 2:   We remember in silence before you;
The peoples of Asia that their divisions may be healed, their emancipation established, and their wisdom increased to accept from other cultures only that which ennobles and exalts.

(Silence)

Leader: Pour out your spirit upon people everywhere;

People: *And hasten the coming of your kingdom.*

Voice 3:   We remember in silence before you;
The peoples of Latin America, struggling upward from ignorance and chaos into swift new achievement and promise, yet hampered by tragic failures of government and of enlightenment, that they may find their destiny anew in your purpose.

(Silence)

Leader: Pour out your spirit upon people everywhere;

People: *And hasten the coming of your kingdom.*

Voice 4:   We remember in silence before you;
The peoples of Europe, many times crushed by war and borne down with old divisions, that as ancient bearers of the message of Christ they may again be inspired by your power in all their common life.

(Silence)

Leader: Pour out your spirit upon people everywhere;

People: *And hasten the coming of your kingdom.*

Voice 5:   We remember in silence before you;
The peoples of the isles and continents of the seas, whose new civilization has sprung up beside ancient tribal ways, that in a day of swift travel and instant communication, they may share only what is deepest and best in the world's ways.

(Silence)

Leader: Pour out your spirit upon people everywhere;

People: *And hasten the coming of your kingdom.*

Voice 6:   We remember in silence before you;
Our own peoples on this continent, proud, tireless, groping for new faith even as they seek to live up to the old; that without condescension and overweening trust in their own powers, they may humbly play their part in your holy pattern for the world's life.

(Silence)

Leader: Pour out your spirit upon people everywhere;

People: *And hasten the coming of your kingdom.*

Leader: Grant, O God, that our imagination may be stretched to enable us to share the poignant needs and vibrant exultation of people everywhere; give us all to dwell in a large place, and make your Church strong in every land, in every tongue, for every people, in Christ Jesus our Lord.

All: *Amen.*

THE STUDENT PRAYER BOOK

147. A Litany of the Circle †

Beloved God, known to our creation by a thousand different names, we
thank you for giving us power through your Spirit to reveal your life to the
world: strengthen, bless and guide all that we do.
Guide us in your grace.

We thank you for your creation, and pray for the earth that you have given
us to cherish and protect; nourish us in your love for all that you have made.
Guide us in your grace.

Every part of this earth is sacred,
Every shining pine needle, every sandy shore.
Every mist in the dark woods,
Every clearing, every humming insect is holy.
The rocky crest, the juices of the meadow, the beasts and all the people,
All belong to the same family.
Teach your children that the earth is our mother;
Whatever befalls the earth befalls the children of the earth.
The water's murmur is the voice of our father's father.
We are part of the earth and the earth is part of us.
The rivers are our brothers; they quench our thirst.
The perfumed flowers are our sisters.
The air is precious,
For all of us share the same breath.
The wind that gave our grandparents breath also receives their last sign,
The wind that gave our children the spirit of life.
This we know, that the earth does not belong to us;
We belong to the earth.
This we know, that all things are connected,
Like the blood which unites one family.
All things are connected;
Our God is the same God, whose compassion is equal for all.
For we did not weave the web of life;
We are merely a strand of it.

Whatever we do to the web
We do to ourselves.

Guide and bless us in our work and in our play, and shape the patterns of
our political and economic life, that all people may share in the fulfillment
of your creative work.
Guide us in your grace.

We thank you for the gift of life, with all its blessings and sorrows. Shield the joyous, and comfort and strengthen those in any need or trouble (especially _____.) Bless those who will be born today and those who will die, that, joining with the company of all your saints, we may rejoice in one unending song of praise.

Guide us in your grace.

These, our prayers and thanksgiving, we offer to you, O God.
Let us give thanks for the web of all of life in the circle that connects us.

Thanks be to God, the God of all, the God known by a thousand names. Amen.

PETER HOLROYD*
BASED ON WORDS OF CHIEF SEATTLE

148. This Fragile Earth, Our Island Home

Leader 1:   Lord, we cry out to you for a reversal in our nation's priorities. As we prepare for war, manufacturing and selling weapons beyond number, our disregard of the needs of the poor breeds violence and despair in our cities. Bring us to repentance and change the hearts of our leaders. Lord, in your mercy,

All: *Hear our prayer.*

Leader 2:   Lord, we cry out to you for all who suffer because conscience has led them to protest. We pray for an end to torture and other violations of human rights in the world. Lord, in your mercy,

All: *Hear our prayer.*

Leader 1:   Lord, we cry out to you that all the nations will stop the making and testing of nuclear weapons, as their contribution to total disarmament and lasting peace. Lord, in your mercy,

All: *Hear our prayer.*

Leader 2:   Lord, we cry out to you to hold back the 50,000 nuclear weapons that now exist from bringing about nuclear disaster and destruction. Lord, in your mercy,

All: *Hear our prayer.*

Leader 1:   Lord, we cry out to you for all the victims of this nuclear age; recalling the horrors of Hiroshima and Nagasaki, we pray for those who suffer from the radiation effects, the trauma, and the memories of those two nightmare events. Lord, in your mercy,

All: *Hear our prayer.*

Leader 2:   Lord, we cry out to you for those who earn their livelihood in war-related industries or professions. Show them how to break free from their involvement with the way of death. Lord, in your mercy,

All: *Hear our prayer.*

Leader 1:   Lord, we cry out to you for the victims of nuclear testing around the world, especially in Nevada and Utah and in the Marshall Islands of the South Pacific. Be with them as

they struggle against the continued abuse of their
homelands.
Lord, in your mercy,

All: *Hear our prayer..*

Leader 2:   Lord, we cry out to you for the native people who have
been forced to give up tribal lands for the testing and
storage of nuclear weapons, especially the people of the
Sioux in South Dakota and the aborigines of Australia.
Lord, in your mercy,

All: *Hear our prayer.*

Leader 1:   Lord, we cry out to you for the many nations of the world
who grow ever poorer under the domination of the
superpowers and their all-consuming military expenditures.
Lord, in your mercy,

All: *Hear our prayer.*

Leader 2:   Lord, we cry out to you for those who are threatened by
the poisoning of the environment, especially those who
have to live their lives beside factories, toxic waste dumps
and nuclear power plants.
Lord, in your mercy,

All: *Hear our prayer.*

Leader 1:   Lord, we cry out to you for ourselves that we may be
better stewards and protectors of the earth's resources and
more mindful of the environment which our children and
our children's children will inherit.
Lord, in your mercy,

All: *Hear our prayer.*

Leader 2:   Lord, we cry out to you for the whole human race,
potential victims of environmental catastrophes. In the
midst of our fear, be present with us to grant us peace;
sustain us in faith and hope and love, and empower us to
act for the well-being of this fragile earth, our island home.

All: *This, Lord, is our cry,*
this, Lord, is our prayer:
peace on the earth and peace in the heavens.
Amen, amen.
Throughout all ages, amen.

SOJOURNERS FELLOWSHIP*

149. God of the Coming Age

Leader: God of the coming age,

Men: *With eager longing*
   all creation waits for transformation;

Women: *In ardent hope*
   we yearn for our redemption.

Leader: Powerful Presence of God, we ask for hope, for ability
   to believe beyond the evidence,
   to wait with patience when the cause seems lost,
   to hold with steady confidence the dream
   of a world made healthy and whole.

God of the coming age,

Men: *With eager longing*
   all creation waits for transformation;

Women: *In ardent hope*
   we yearn for our redemption.

Leader: Merciful Presence of God, we ask forgiveness.
   Too much we have given our allegiance
   to governments and corporations.
   Too often we have trusted commentators
   and journalists.

God of the coming age,

Men: *With eager longing*
   all creation waits for transformation;

Women: *In ardent hope*
   we yearn for our redemption.

Leader: Too completely we have served the interests
   of earth's old administration,
   corrupt and soon to fall from power.
   Too little have we given ourselves to the
   causes that promise a world of equity and peace.

God of the coming age,

Men: *With eager longing*
                all creation waits for transformation;

Women: *In ardent hope*
                we yearn for our redemption.

Leader: Life-giving Presence of God, we ask for signs
            of the age to come:
a new generation of leaders in the struggle for peace;
a way of balancing the earth's food and its peoples'
            longing for daily bread.

God of the coming age,

Men: *With eager longing*
                all creation waits for transformation;

Women: *In ardent hope*
                we yearn for our redemption.

Leader: We ask for a cleansing of humanity's patterns
            so that rivers are clean again
            and the air made fit to breathe again;
the breaking of the power of sickness
            and calamity, of oppression and cruelty,
so that all may come to fullness of life.

God of the coming age,

Men: *With eager longing*
                all creation waits for transformation;

Women: *In ardent hope*
                we yearn for our redemption.

All: Amen.

KEITH WATKINS
BASED ON ROMANS 8:18-25*

150. Christian Hope †

The Christian hope is to live with confidence in newness and fullness of life, and to await the coming of Christ in glory, and the completion of God's purpose for the world.

This is our hope.

Earth's scattered isles and contoured hills,
which part the seas and mold the land,
and vistas newly seen from space
that show a world awesome and grand,
all wondrously unite to sing:
take heart, take hope, the Lord is King!

We believe that Christ will come in glory to judge the living and the dead, raising us from death in the fullness of our being, that we may live with him in the communion of the saints.

This is our hope.

God's judgment passed on social ills
that thwart awhile his firm intent,
the flagging dreams of weary folk
whose brave new world lies torn and rent,
in painful form their message bring:
take heart, take hope, the Lord is King!

We believe in everlasting life, that new existence in which we are united with all the people of God, in the joy of fully knowing and loving God and each other.

This is our hope.

The constant care which Israel knew
alike in faith and faithlessness,
the subtle providence which guides
a pilgrim Church through change and stress,
inspire us gratefully to sing:
take heart, take hope, the Lord is King!

Our assurance as Christians is that nothing, not even death, shall separate us from the love of God which is in Christ Jesus our Lord.

This is our hope.

The light which shines through noble acts,
the quest for truth dispelling lies,
the grace of Christ renewed in us
so love lives on and discord dies,
all blend their song, good news to bring:
take heart, take hope, the Lord is King!
Amen.

THE BOOK OF COMMON PRAYER 1979
HYMN STANZAS BY JEFFERY W. ROWTHORN*

Acknowledgments

The numbers below refer to the litanies as noted in this collection.

ABINGDON PRESS -- for 125, from *Lift Up Your Hearts* by Walter
Russell Bowie. Copyright renewal © 1984 by Mrs. Jean B. Evans,
Mrs. Elizabeth Chapman, and Mrs. Walter Russell Bowie, Jr.
Used by Permission of Publisher, Abingdon Press.

ACTA PUBLICATIONS -- for 109, copyright © 1992 ACTA Publications,
4848 N. Clark St., Chicago, IL 60640 (312) 271-1030. Used by
permission of ACTA Publications.

AGRICULTURAL MISSIONS INC. -- for 111, from *Rural People at
Worship*, compiled by Edward K. Ziegler and published by
Agricultural Missions Inc., New York, 1943.

HORACE J. ALLEN, JR. -- for 53. Used by permission of Professor
Allen, Division of Religious & Theological Studies, Boston University.

ALLYN & BACON PUBLISHING -- for 51, 67, 103, 110, 135, 143, 146,
from *The Student Prayer Book* by J. Oliver Nelson, copyright ©
1953 by Haddam House, Inc.

AUGSBURG FORTRESS -- for 2: "Prayer of the Church" is reprinted
from *Lutheran Book of Worship*, copyright © 1978, by permission of
Augsburg Fortress. May not be reproduced further without
permission of Augsburg Fortress.
-- for 65, reprinted from *Monday's Ministries* by Melvin Vos,
copyright © 1979 Fortress Press. Used by Permission of Augsburg
Fortress.
-- for 52, 90, 96, reprinted from *Prayers for Public Worship* by
Carl T. Uehling, copyright © 1972 Fortress Press. Used by
permission of Augsburg Fortress. May not be reproduced further
without permission of Augsburg Fortress.
-- for 48, 49, 79, 92, 94, 107, 113, 118, 136, 144, reprinted from
Prayers for Today's Church by R.H.L. Williams, copyright © 1977
Augsburg Publishing House. Used by permission of Augsburg
Fortress. May not be reproduced further without permission of
Augsburg Fortress.

BREAD FOR THE WORLD -- for 62, 129, used by permission of Publications Division, Bread for the World, 1100 Wayne Avenue, Suite 1000, Silver Springs, MD 20910.

AVERY BROOKE -- for 100, 137, as published by *St. Luke's Quarterly Journal*, © 1963, St. Luke's Episcopal Church, Darien, CT. Used by permission of author.

CENTRAL BOARD OF FINANCE OF THE CHURCH OF ENGLAND -- for 16: the "Ten Commandments and Our Lord's Summary of the Law" which are reproduced in a slightly adapted form from the "Order for Holy Communion, Rite A" in *The Alternative Service Book 1980*, copyright © the Central Board of Finance of the Church of England. Used by its permission.

CHRISTIAN EDUCATION PRESS -- for 50, from *The Book of Prayers for Church and Home*, compiled by Howard Paine and Bard Thompson, 1962.

THE CHURCH HYMNAL CORPORATION -- for 54, 56, 73, from *Book of Occasional Services*, copyright © 1979 by the Church Pension Fund and used by its permission.

CHURCH OF THE PROVINCE OF SOUTHERN AFRICA -- for 6, 59, form *The South African Liturgy 1975*, Publications Dept., Box 31792, Braamfontein, Cape Province 2017.

CLARETIAN PUBLICATIONS -- for 61, 131, from *Prayers in Community* by T. Maertens and M. DeBilde, translated by J. Ducharme. Fides/Claretian, Inc., Notre Dame.
-- for 21, 58, 115, from *Pray Like This: Materials for the Practice of Dynamic Group Prayer* by W.G. Storey. Fides/Claretian, Inc., Notre Dame, Indiana. The 5 litanies above used by permission of Claretian Publications, Chicago, IL.

CONCORDIA PUBLISHING HOUSE -- for 24, from *Help it All Make Sense, Lord*, copyright © 1972 by Concordia Publishing House and used by its permission.
-- for 101, from *Time to Pray: Daily Prayers for Youth*, © 1960 by Concordia Publishing House and used by its permission.

CSS PUBLISHING COMPANY -- for 30, 87, from *Contemporary Altar Prayers (Volume 3)* by Larry Hard, 1973. Reprinted by permission from CSS Publishing Co., 517 S. Main St., PO Box 4503 Lima, Ohio 45802-4503.

J.M. DENT & SONS LTD. -- for 120, from *Devotional Services for Public Worship, 1903*. Used by permission of J.M. Dent & Sons Ltd., publishers.

EGGYS 1993: WORKING GROUP ON LITURGY AND BIBLE STUDIES -- for 77, c/o Ernesto Barros Cordoso, Ladeira de Gloria, 98 Gloria, Rio de Janeiro, RJ CEP 22211-120.

MARY FORD-GRABOWSKY -- for 99.

MOREHOUSE PUBLISHING -- for 36, 134, from *The Covenant of Peace: A Liberation Prayer Book*, edited by John P. Brown and Richard York, copyright 1971 by Morehouse-Barlow Co. Used by permission of Morehouse Publishing.

MOWBRAY CASSELL -- for 29, from *Intercessions at Holy Communion on Themes for the Church Year* by Raymond Hockley, copyright 1980 by A.R. Mowbray and Co. Ltd.

-- for 121, from *Prayers for Use at the Alternative Services*, compiled and adapted by David Silk, copyright 1980 by A.R. Mowbray and Co. Ltd. The two litanies above used by permission of Messrs. Mowbray Cassell, London.

THE REVEREND HENRY L.H. MYERS -- for 71. Used by permission of the author, retired Episcopal chaplain to Vanderbilt University.

NEW WIN PUBLISHING, INC. -- for 19, reprinted from *Treat Me Cool, Lord*, copyright © 1968 by Carl F. Burke. By permission of New Win Publishing, Inc.

OFFICE OF CREATIVE MINISTRIES -- for 145. Office of Creative Ministries, United Methodist Church, P.O. Box 733, Columbia, Missouri 65205.

OXFORD UNIVERSITY PRESS -- for 33, from the *Cuddesdon College Office Book*, Revised Edition, 1961.

-- for 74, 81, 84, from *The Kingdom, The Power, The Glory* (American edition of the *Grey Book*). Copyright © 1933.

-- for 97, from *Spilled Milk: Litanies for Living* by Kay Smallzried, 1964.

-- for 108, 142, from the *Grey Book*.

PUEBLO PUBLISHING COMPANY -- for 140, 141, from *Prayers of the Faithful: Cycles A, B, C*, copyright © 1977 by Pueblo Publishing Co., Inc., and used by its permission.

REED CONSUMER BOOKS (on behalf of Eyre & Spottiswoode) -- for 128, an extract from the Silver Jubilee Service (1977) of Queen Elizabeth II. Eyre & Spottiswoode is part of Reed Consumer Books, Rushden, Northants, England.

SCM PRESS LTD -- for 8, 83, from *Contemporary Prayers for Public Worship*, edited by Caryl Micklem, copyright 1967 by SCM Press, and used by its permission.

-- for 85, 119, from *Epilogues and Prayers* by William Barclay, copyright 1963 by SCM Press, and used by its permission.

CHARLES SCRIBNER'S SONS -- for 86, adapted and reprinted with the permission of Scribner, an imprint of Simon & Schuster, Inc. from *A Diary of Private Prayer* by John Baillie. Copyright 1949 Charles Scribner's Sons; copyright renewed © 1977 Ian Fowler Baillie.

SHEED & WARD, INC. -- for 138, from *Prayers from the Burned-Out City*, by Robert W. Castle, Jr., copyright 1968 by Sheed & Ward, Inc., and used by its permission. (138 combines portions of "Litany for the City" and "Litany for the Poor.")

SOJOURNERS MAGAZINE -- for 139, 148, from August 1981 issue, pp. 18-19. Reprinted with permission from *Sojourners*, 2401 15th Street NW, Washington, DC 20009.

SPCK -- for 72, from the *Daily Office Revised*, © The Joint Liturgical Group SPCK/1978.
-- for 76, from *Ember Prayers: A Collection of Prayers for the Ministry of the Church*, compiled by John Neale, SPCK/1965.
The 2 litanies above used by permission of SPCK (The Society for Promoting Christian Knowledge), London.

STANDARD BOOK OF COMMON PRAYER, Canon Charles M. Guilbert, Custodian -- for 114, from *Prayers, Thanksgivings and Litanies*, © 1973 by Canon Guilbert and used by his permission.

KEITH WATKINS -- for 149. By permission of author, Professor of Worship at Christian Theological Seminary, Indianapolis. 149 used in his sermon at Yale, 1983.

WESTMINSTER JOHN KNOX PRESS -- for 3, 12, 124, from THE WORSHIPBOOK -- Services and Hymns. Copyright 1970 and 1972, The Westminster Press. Used by permission of Westminster John Knox Press.

WORLD COUNCIL OF CHURCHES -- for 78, by Kathy Galloway for the Ecumenical Decade of the Churches in Solidarity with Women 1988-1998. Used by permission World Council of Churches, Decade Desk.

WORLD LIBRARY PUBLICATIONS, INC. -- for 9, 20, 22, 23, 25, 80, copyright 1976, 1981, Lucien Deiss from *Come, Lord Jesus*. Distributed by World Library Publications, a Division of J.S. Paluch Company Inc., Schiller Park, IL.
-- for 17, 32, 38, 64, 75, 106, 126, from following issues of *Models for Ministers I*, copyright J.S. Paluch Company Inc., Schiller Park, IL: 17 (7/21/74); 32 (6/2/74); 38 (10/27/74); 64 (10/13/74); 75 (10/6/74); 106 (9/1/73 & 7/21/74); 126 (6/29/75).
The 13 litanies above used by permission of World Library Publications, Inc.

WORLD PUBLISHING COMPANY -- for 41, 42, 43, 45, 46, 47, from *Worship Services for Special Occasions*, compiled and edited by Norman L. Hersey, copyright 1970.

Every attempt has been made to credit the sources of copyrighted material used in this book. If any such acknowledgment has been inadvertently omitted or miscredited, receipt of such information would be appreciated.

Notes

Whenever an asterisk (*) occurs at the end of any of the litanies in this book, further information about that litany is given below. The various litanies are designated by their respective numbers which appear to the left of the title. All of the hymn tunes suggested here may be found in the *Lutheran Book of Worship* (1978) and in the (Episcopal) *Hymnal 1982*.

1.   *The Great Litany,* skillfully adapted from traditional material, first appeared in 1544. It was the work of Thomas Cranmer, principal architect of the first *Book of Common Prayer* (1549). This litany was the first official service to be prepared in the English language and was meant to be sung in procession.

If sung in this way today, the ministers and choir or the whole congregation may participate in the procession. Section I is sung in place and then the procession circles the inside or the exterior of the church while Sections II-V are sung. The final Section (VI) follows when all have returned to their original places. Music for the Great Litany may be found among the service music (S67) at the front of the *Hymnal 1982*.

6.   *The South African Liturgy* 1975 contains four alternative forms of intercession. This particular litany was proposed for inclusion by the "Africanization Committee" of the Church of the Province of Southern Africa.

9.   Six of the litanies in this book are taken from *Come, Lord Jesus,* the English version of *Prières Bibliques* by Lucien Deiss. The English edition contains musical settings for the antiphons or congregational responses in the various litanies.

10.   Musical settings of this litany may be found among the service music (S63 and S64) at the front of the *Hymnal 1982*.

11.   This litany, also known as the *Benedicite,* may be sung to settings found at the front of the *Hymnal 1982* (S228, S229 and S230). The canticle draws on the *Song of the Three Young Men,* one of the books in the Apocrypha.

15.   John Wesley first used a *Service for Such as would Enter into or Renew their Covenant with God* in August 1755. He later published it as a pamphlet in 1780. The form given here is drawn from the *Methodist Book of Offices 1936* which was prepared for use by British Methodists. The three sets of hymn stanzas may be sung to the following tunes: *(1) Hanover; (2) St. Magnus;* and (3) *Azmon.*

16.   The *Alternative Service Book 1980* is in use in the Church of England in conjunction with the *Book of Common Prayer* (1662). Unlike previous liturgical practice, each of the Ten Commandments is here combined with a positive injunction from the New Testament.

17.   This litany, taken from the July 21, 1974 issue of *Models for Ministers I,* is a further wedding of the Ten Commandments with New Testament teachings.

18.   This litany was composed for a liturgical notebook submitted in conjunction with a course, The Roots of Liturgy, at Yale Divinity School.

21.   The Advent Antiphons were traditionally sung before and after the Magnificat at Vespers from December 17 to December 23 inclusive. Each of the Antiphons welcomes the coming Messiah under one of the many titles ascribed to him in Holy Scripture.

27.   This litany appeared in the March 1978 issue of *Modern Liturgy* (Vol. 5, No. 2, p. 30).

28.   *The Orationes Sollemnes (Solemn Prayers)* were almost certainly part of the Roman Mass by the middle of the 5th century, if not earlier. They were removed at the end of the 5th century by Pope Gelasius who substituted the litany which now bears his name. However, they were retained as part of the liturgy for Good Friday. The periods of silent prayer are an important reminder of the priestly responsibility of the whole People of God to make intercession for the Church and for the world.

29.   The use of several leaders placed in different sections of the congregation would increase the effectiveness of this litany and heighten the identification of the worshippers with those who had some part in Christ's Passion.

32.   *Models for Ministers I,* issue of June 2, 1974.

35.   The saints and holy men and women invoked in this litany are included for the most part in either the Roman Catholic *Litany of the Saints* or in the listing of lesser Festivals and Commemorations in the *Lutheran Book of Worship.* Some additional names have been added to make this a genuinely ecumenical litany.

36.   The Free Church of Berkeley, California, first used this litany on June 15, 1968, "in a solidarity event for the Berrigans." Clearly, additional saints may also be invoked to "stand here beside us."

38.   *Models for Ministers I,* issue of October 27, 1974.

48.   To underline the ecumenical character of this litany and also the context in which it is being used, it would be desirable to choose two representatives for different traditions to lead it.

50.   This litany is from the *Book of Prayers for Church and Home* (Christian Education Press, Philadelphia, 1962). It is taken from "An Act of Intercession for the Whole Church of Christ," included in *A Suggested Use for Pentecost, Christian Unity Sunday,* prepared by the North American Provisional Committee of the World Council of Churches, undated, but about 1945; the final prayer is from the Liturgy of St. Mark.

51.   The various thanksgivings could be spoken in each case by a representative of that particular branch of the Christian family.

57.   *The Renewal of Baptismal Vows* is especially appropriate on Easter Day (or during the Easter Vigil), the Day of Pentecost, All Saints' Day (or the first Sunday in November), and the Feast of the Baptism of our Lord (the First Sunday after the Epiphany).

59.   The prayer at the presentation of the money-offering comes from the *South African Liturgy 1975.* In the Roman Catholic celebration of the Mass this prayer is not used. In the Mass the prayers for the bread and wine are said quietly by the celebrant while an offertory song is being sung. The celebrant may say these prayers in an audible voice if there is no offertory song. In that case the people may respond to each prayer by saying: "Blessed be God for ever."

64.   *Models for Ministers I,* issue of October 13, 1974.

69.   These words have traditionally been sung to the tune *Veni, Creator Spiritus.*

72.   This cycle of intercessions would be especially effective if used on seven consecutive days; it could, however, be used on the same day of the week over a period of seven weeks. It is the work of the *Joint Liturgical Group,* a British ecumenical body bringing together representatives of the Anglican, Roman Catholic, Methodist, Baptist, and United Reformed (Congregationalist-Presbyterian) Churches, the Church of Scotland, and the Churches of Christ.

75.   *Models for Ministers I,* issue of October 6, 1974.

77.   This litany from Puerto Rico was used at EGGYS 1993 (Ecumenical Global Gathering on Youth and Students) held in Rio de Janeiro, Brazil. It was included in a booklet in four languages *(Poems, Prayers and Songs)* prepared by the Working Group on Liturgy and Bible Studies for use during this international gathering.

78.   This is part of a longer act of worship prepared by Kathy Galloway of the Iona Community in Scotland for use during the Ecumenical Decade of the Churches in Solidarity with Women (1988-1998). It is to be found in a booklet in four languages *(I will pour out my Spirit: Mid-decade Worship Resources)* published by Programme Unit III (Women's Section) of the World Council of Churches.

82.   This is adapted from a litany prepared for use at a Festival Eucharist held in the Hartford Civic Center at the conclusion of the twenty-month Bicentennial Celebration (1784-1984) of the Episcopal Diocese of Connecticut.

92.   This litany was first used at the Anglican Cathedral in Liverpool, England. The final blessing is taken from the *Book of Occasional Services* where it is used at the conclusion of a service to celebrate the anniversary of a marriage.

93.   Psalm 112 is an "alphabetical psalm"; in the Hebrew original each successive line begins with a different letter of the alphabet. This unusual characteristic is reproduced here in the English version which is taken from *Family Worship in the Parish* by Donald Orin Wiseman.

99.   This is adapted from a litany prepared during the World Conference on Religion and Peace which took place at Princeton Theological Seminary, New Jersey in July 1990. Religious leaders representing forty countries and a dozen faiths selected as their theme, "The World's Religions for the World's Children," and they meant this litany to be a call "to put an end to the cruelty that helpless children are suffering in every part of the world today."

105.   Richard Granville Jones' hymn, written in 1964, was first used at a meeting of the Methodist Synod in Sheffield, England; it may be sung to the tune *Dix.*

106.   This litany draws on material published in two issues of *Models for Ministers I* (September 1, 1973, and July 21, 1974).

112.   The hymn stanzas may be sung to *Monkland,* a tune to be found in the *Hymnal 1982,* or to Daniel Moe's contemporary tune *Williams Bay* in the *Lutheran Book of Worship.*

117.   This can be found in *Praying With HIV/AIDS: Collects, Prayers and Litanies in A Time of Crisis,* published by Forward Movement Publications. The author has served as HIV/AIDS Ministry Consultant at the Episcopal Church Center in New York.

118.   This litany was used at a service held at the Anglican Cathedral in Liverpool, England; the concluding collect is taken from the *Book of Common Prayer 1979.*

126.   *Models for Ministers I,* issue of June 29, 1975.

127.   *Liturgy,* issue of May 1976 (Vol. 15, No. 5). This journal is published quarterly by the Liturgical Conference, an ecumenical association dedicated to the renewal of the Church's life and worship.

128.   Queen Elizabeth II ascended the throne on February 6, 1952 and her Silver Jubilee was officially celebrated on June 7, 1977. This litany in its original form was used in the Service of Thanksgiving held that day in St. Paul's Cathedral, London.

130.   The author is a member of the (Episcopal) Church of Our Savior in Cincinnati, Ohio.

133.   The opening measures of *Veni Emmanuel* may be used if the response after each period of silence is sung.

135.   The words recited by the congregation in the course of this litany make up the *General Confession* which has been a part of Anglican liturgy since the second *Book of Common Prayer (1552).*

138.   This is a conflation of two litanies included in *Prayers from the Burned-Out City.* Both the *Litany for the City* and the *Litany for the Poor* are clearly inspired in their radical content by Jesus' parable of the sheep and the goats (Matthew 25:31-46). There the great judgment is dependent

on one thing and one thing only: "Truly, I say to you, as you did it (not) to one of the least of these my brethren, you did it (not) to me."

139. Together with Litany 148, this is based on material first used by the Sojourners Fellowship of Washington, D.C., a community dedicated to peace and reconciliation. The words used here are taken from the *New Abolitionist Covenant,* the text of which appeared in the August 1981 issue of *Sojourners* (Vol. 10, No. 8, pp.18-19). This journal, published by the Sojourners Fellowship, now appears ten times a year.

147. This litany was used at a Eucharistic Celebration honoring the twenty-five years of the priesthood of Peter Ratcliff Holroyd. The service took place on December 16, 1989, at St. John's Church in Waterbury, Connecticut.

148.   The title of this litany is taken from Eucharistic Prayer C in the *Book of Common Prayer 1979.* Like Litany 139, this is based on material first used by the Sojourners Fellowship of Washington, D.C.

149. This litany was used by the author when he preached at Yale Divinity School in the spring of 1983. For many years Professor Watkins taught liturgics at Christian Theological Seminary in Indianapolis, Indiana.

150. This is based on the concluding section of *An Outline of the Faith commonly called the Catechism* in the *Book of Common Prayer 1979.* The hymn stanzas may be sung to the tune *Melita.*

Bibliography

The litanies in this collection were compiled from.the following sources which are listed alphabetically in the form in which they appear at the end of each particular litany.

The Alternative Service Book 1980: Services authorized for use in the Church of England in conjunction with *The Book of Common Prayer* (1662). Cambridge University Press, William Clowes (Publishers) Ltd., and S.P.C.K., 1980.

John Baillie: *A Diary of Private Prayer.* Charles Scribner's Sons, New York, 1949.

William Barclay: *Epilogues and Prayers.* Abingdon Press, New York and Nashville, 1963.

William Barclay: *Prayers for Help and Healing.* Harper and Row, New York and Evanston, 1968.

The Book of Common Prayer (1979). The Church Hymnal Corporation and Seabury Press, New York.

The Book of Occasional Services. The Church Hymnal Corporation, New York, 1979.

The Book of Prayers for Church and Home, compiled by Howard Paine and Bard Thompson. The Christian Education Press, Philadelphia, 1962.

Walter Russell Bowie: *Lift Up Your Hearts,* Enlarged Edition. Abingdon Press, New York and Nashville, 1956.

Bread for the World, 32 Union Square East, New York, NY 10003.

Carl F. Burke: *Treat Me Cool, Lord.* Association Press, New York, 1968.

Robert W. Castle, Jr.: *Prayers for the Burned-Out City.* Sheed and Ward, New York, 1968.

Contemporary Prayers for Public Worship, edited by Caryl Micklem. S.C.M. Press, Ltd., London, 1967.

The Covenant of Peace - A Liberation Prayer Book, compiled by John P. Brown and Richard L. York. Morehouse-Barlow Co., New York, 1971.

The Cuddesdon College Office Book, Revised Edition. Oxford University Press, London, 1961.

The Daily Office Revised (with other prayers and services) edited by Ronald C. D. Jasper on behalf of the Joint Liturgical Group. S.P.C.K., London, 1978.

Lucien Deiss: *Come, Lord Jesus* (French original: *Prières Bibliques).* World Library Publications, Inc., 5040 North Ravenswood, Chicago, IL 60640, 1976, 1981.

Devotional Services for Public Worship, compiled by John Hunter. J.M. Dent, Ltd., London, 1903.

Ember Prayers: *A Collection of Prayers for the Ministry of the Church,* compiled by John Neale. S.P.C.K., London, 1965.

Harry Emerson Fosdick: *A Book of Public Prayers.* Harper and Bros., New York, 1959.

Randolph Lloyd Frew: *Praying with HIV/AIDS: Collects, Prayers and Litanies in a Time of Crisis.* Forward Movement Publications, Cincinnati, Ohio, 1990.

Larry Hard: *Contemporary Altar Prayers (Volume 3).* C.S.S. Publishing Co., Inc., Lima, Ohio, 1973.

Raymond Hockley: *Intercessions at Holy Communion on Themes for the Church's Year.* A.R. Mowbray and Co., Ltd., London and Oxford, 1980.

The Hymnal 1982 - according to the use of the Episcopal Church. The Church Hymnal Corporation, New York, 1985.

I will pour out my Spirit: Mid-decade Worship Resources. The World Council of Churches, Geneva, 1992.

The Kingdom, the Power and the Glory. Services of Praise and Prayer for Occasional Use in Churches (American Edition of *The Grey Book*). Oxford University Press, New York, 1933.

Kyrie Eleison: Two Hundred Litanies, complied by Benjamin F. Musser. The Newman Bookshop, Westminster, Maryland, 1945.

Liturgy, published by The Liturgical Conference, 810 Rhode Island Avenue, N.E., Washington, DC 20018.

The Lutheran Book of Worship. Augsburg Publishing House, Minneapolis, 1978.

The Methodist Service Book. The Methodist Publishing House, Wimbledon, London, 1936.

Models for Ministers I. World Library Publications, Inc., 5040 North Ravenswood, Chicago, IL 60640.

Modern Liturgy, published by Resource Publications, 7291 Coronado Drive, San Jose, CA 95129.

Monday's Ministries: The Ministry of the Laity, edited by Raymond Tiemeyer. Parish Life Press, Philadelphia, 1979.

The Office of Creative Ministries: Missouri Area, United Methodist Church, P.O. Box 733, Columbia, Missouri 65205.

Poems, Prayers and Songs. Working Group on Liturgy and Bible Studies, Ecumenical Global Gathering on Youth and Students, Rio de Janeiro, 1993.

Pray, Like This: Materials for the Practice of Dynamic Group Prayer, compiled by William G. Storey. Fides Publishers, Inc., Notre Dame, Indiana, 1973.

Prayers for Today's Church, edited by Dick Williams. Augsburg Publishing House, Minneapolis, 1977.

Prayers for Use at the Alternative Services, compiled and adapted by David Silk. A.R. Mowbray and Co, Ltd., London and Oxford, 1980.

Prayers in Community (Volume I of *Contemporary Prayer),* edited by Thierry Maertens and Marguerite DeBilde, translated by Jerome J. DuCharme. Fides Publishers, Inc., Notre Dame, Indiana, 1974.

Prayer of the Faithful (for Sundays and Solemnities of Cycles A, B and C). Pueblo Publishing Co., New York, 1977.

Prayers, Thanksgiving, Litanies: prepared by the Standing Liturgical Commission of the Episcopal Church *(Prayer Book Studies 25).* Church Hymnal Corporation, New York, 1973.

The Roman Missal, revised by decree of the Second Vatican Council and published by authority of Pope Paul VI; English translation prepared by the International Commission on English in the Liturgy. Catholic Book Publishing Co., New York, 1974.

Rural People at Worship, compiled by Edward K. Ziegler. Agricultural Missions, Inc., New York, 1943.

Scripture Services: 18 Bible Themes, edited for group use by John Gallen, S.J. The Liturgical Press, Collegeville, Minnesota, 1963.

Kay Smallzried: *Litanies for Living - Spilled Milk.* Oxford University Press, New York, 1964.

Sojourners, 2401 15th Street N.W., Washington, DC 20009.

The South African Liturgy 1975. Publications Office, Church of the Province of Southern Africa, Claremont, Cape Province, South Africa, 1975.

The Student Prayer Book, edited and written by a Haddam House committee under the chairmanship of John Oliver Nelson. Association Press, New York, 1953.

Carl T. Uehling: *Prayers for Public Worship.* Fortress Press, Philadelphia, 1972.

Elmer N. Witt: *Help It All Make Sense, Lord.* Concordia Publishing House, St. Louis and London, 1972.

Elmer N. Witt: *Time to Pray. Daily Prayers for Youth.* Concordia Publishing House, St. Louis, undated (preface dated St Luke's Day, 1959).

The Worshipbook. Westminster Press, Philadelphia, 1970.

Worship for Today.- Suggestions and Ideas, edited by Richard Jones. Epworth Press, London, 1968.

Worship Services for Special Occasions, compiled and edited by Norman L. Hersey. World Publishing Co., New York and Cleveland, 1970.